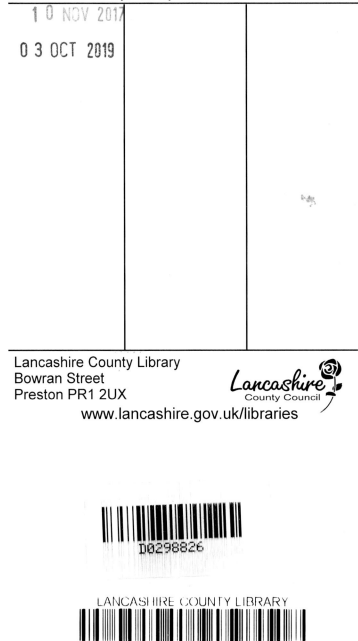

HEARTS AND MINDS

OLIVER LETWIN

HEARTS
AND
MINDS

THE BATTLE FOR THE CONSERVATIVE PARTY
FROM THATCHER TO THE PRESENT

Biteback Publishing

First published in Great Britain in 2017 by
Biteback Publishing Ltd
Westminster Tower
3 Albert Embankment
London SE1 7SP
Copyright © Oliver Letwin 2017

ISBN 978-1-78590-311-3

10 9 8 7 6 5 4 3 2 1

A CIP catalogue record for this book is available from the British Library.

Set in Minion Pro

Printed and bound in Great Britain by
CPI Group (UK) Ltd, Croydon CR0 4YY

CONTENTS

INTRODUCTION

This book is an attempt to explain how the central ideas and policies of the modern Conservative Party came into being, how they have played out over the period from Mrs Thatcher to Mrs May, and what needs to happen next.

It is emphatically not a work of historical scholarship. Instead of documenting events or concepts in a dispassionate, detailed and comprehensive manner, I have tried to enable the reader to see the main lines of the history through the eyes of an active participant.

There is little here to please those who see politics as a series of intrigues, manoeuvrings and theatrical gestures. Of course, politics does contain elements of theatre, and politicians do engage in intrigues and manoeuvres. But – however unfashionable it may seem to say so – I believe that most significant politicians are in fact, most of the time, concerned with the serious business of governing our country. So my focus is on how one set of politicians, over quite a long period of our recent past, have tried to lead the country in a particular direction as a result of holding a particular set of views about what will make the country a better place to live in.

I have steadfastly avoided any suggestion that Conservatives over this period have been following some perfect blueprint. On the contrary, I have tried to highlight the evolution of ideas and policies – as I and others gradually discerned things that were missing or defective. I hope that, by telling the story in this way, I may persuade the reader of another unfashionable proposition: that politicians are capable of recognising their mistakes and learning from them.

Above all, this is a story with a purpose – to show that social and economic liberalism, if correctly conceived, are capable of addressing the issues that confront us today; that they can answer to the needs of the least advantaged and of those who are 'just about managing'; that they can give a proper place to the environment and to the qualities (not just the quantities) of life in our society; that they can attract and inspire not only core Conservative voters but also the young metropolitan voters whom the Conservative Party now needs to attract and inspire; that, in short, they have a future and not just a past.

CHAPTER 1

AN ENDING

I am sitting in David Cameron's study at 10 Downing Street. It is early in the morning of Thursday 23 June 2016. We are discussing what to do if the country votes today for Brexit.

This is my chance, as Chancellor of the Duchy and one of David's closest colleagues, to persuade him that he can remain as Prime Minister. George Osborne – with whom I have discussed this in previous days – is in reflective mode, uncertain what to recommend. Ed Llewellyn (David's chief of staff) and Craig Oliver (the director of communications) are convinced that the only reasonable option for the PM is to resign if the vote is for Brexit. I am alone in arguing strongly the case for hanging on, regardless.

We have had many friendly, though often heated, debates about many things in this little room over the past six years. We have discussed how to manage policies, parliamentary battles, Cabinet committees, elections, coalitions, treaties, civil emergencies, political crises and administrative disasters. Most of us have been together through eleven years, two general elections, two governments and three referendums. Always, we have managed to pull off victory. Now, we are facing the real possibility of defeat.

My argument to David Cameron is simple. In the first place, staying in post is feasible even if the country votes for Brexit. A large proportion of the pro-Brexit Conservative MPs have signed a letter calling on him to stay regardless of the outcome of the referendum. Therefore, he can get enough votes to survive a leadership challenge. And secondly, he is the person best qualified to lead the country at a time when it will need the best possible leader. So he should remain in post.

Craig's argument is equally simple. He believes that if the country votes for Brexit and David seeks to remain as Prime Minister, there will be a wall of hostility from the media. Craig's professional judgement, as the PM's communications director, is that the intensity of this hostility will be irresistible. Others in the room add that, under these circumstances, the PM will be a hostage, effectively captured by the Brexiteers and unable to lead.

It is clear from an early stage in the conversation that I am losing the argument. Unsurprisingly, David has no personal enthusiasm for negotiating an exit from the EU, which he believes is the wrong course for the country and which involves tearing up the deal he has just negotiated with fellow EU heads of government. But even laying aside personal preference, he doesn't think he can credibly lead an exit after he has fought so hard to persuade the country to vote for remaining in the EU. He has nailed his colours to the mast, and if the ship goes down, he feels he must go down with it.

As usual, David lets the argument go on long enough for all the points on each side to be examined; but, as has also been his practice for eleven years in opposition and in government, he concludes with a clear decision. He will resign immediately if the result is for Brexit. In what will prove to be one of his last acts as Prime Minister, he sets in train the drafting of a resignation statement, for use if needed, and we move on to discussing the happier (though ultimately illusory) question of how to proceed if the final result favours remaining in the EU on the terms we have negotiated.

As I sit there, surrounded by the familiar ring of chairs – wing-backed armchairs for David and George, sofa and upright chairs for the rest of us – I am almost overcome by nostalgia. Is it really possible, after all we have been through together, after bringing the Conservative Party back into the centre ground of politics, after forging and maintaining a coalition everyone said would never last, after rescuing the country from bankruptcy, after instituting a radical programme of social, welfare and public service reform, after winning an outright victory at a general election for the first time in more than twenty years, that we are now on the brink of the PM's resignation and of a period of uncertainty for the country unprecedented in its recent peacetime history? Can this really be happening? Isn't it just a bad dream, from which we will wake up tomorrow?

And yet I know that this *is* what politics is really like. I know that I came into politics in order to participate in exactly the sort of discussions and debates that have taken place in this room. I have wanted, for almost all my adult life, to be at the centre of government – to play a part in taking the country in a certain direction. That dream has come true for six years. But now, as happens all too often in politics, the dream has been replaced by a nightmare, and the nightmare has come true too.

The meeting comes to a close, and I return to my office in 9 Downing Street. In only a few paces, out of the door of No. 10, down the street, past the little garden that my faithful civil servants and I have lovingly planted and tended these past years and through the back door of No. 9, I am in the cosy, panelled study which – together with a meeting room down the corridor looking onto No. 10 and the so-called private office where my private secretaries sit – has been for me the scene of such intense activity for so long. It was to this study that I returned only just over a year before, greeted with happy applause, after our general election victory. And now, all too conceivably, within twenty-four hours the country will change course and David Cameron will resign. How has it all gone so wrong?

The truth is that the spectre of the European Question has been hanging over our country and our party for three decades. I know this from personal experience, because I have been an active participant in Euroscepticism from 1987 onwards. In that year, my wife and I spent a summer holiday at Lake Annecy in the Alps. I took with me a pile of books about what were still at that time called the European Communities – the treaties themselves, the most important legal texts and textbooks about European law, and the best guides I could find to the operation of the EC institutions. As I read these volumes, sitting by the lakeside and occasionally looking up at the mountains, I experienced my own small secular Damascene revelation. It became clear to me that the Communities formed not just the free trade bloc that I had thought they did. Certainly, the establishment of the single market was underway and was a genuine attempt at creating the most complete system of free trade ever constructed between sovereign nations. But alongside, and indeed from the earliest days of the European Coal and Steel Community, there had been a parallel activity: an effort to forge a single European nation, a 'United States of Europe', with one currency, one citizenship, one set of laws, one army and one foreign policy.

The result of this awakening was that later in the year I wrote a pamphlet, entitled *Drift to Union*, in which I argued that – if we didn't watch out – we would be sucked into an emerging United States of Europe without our fellow citizens fully realising what was happening. I also argued that, while this might suit some other European countries and therefore could not be stopped from happening, it would never suit us in the UK; and that we should therefore pursue a long-term strategy of fostering instead a Europe of concentric circles, with the emerging United States of Europe at the centre, and independent countries such as ourselves in a free trade, single market circle around it.

When I sent this pamphlet to be published, by the Thatcherite Centre for Policy Studies, in late 1987, Hugh Thomas, then the chairman of the Centre, objected to the entire thesis of the pamphlet and clearly wanted to bin it as fast as possible. In the ensuing row, it became clear that there were fault lines in the tectonic plates of Thatcherism. As this was more than a year before Margaret Thatcher's famous speech at Bruges, the Lady herself had not yet spoken publicly about her own increasing Euroscepticism – and there was accordingly room for doubt about her position. Hugh and some others held that full-throated Europhilia was a required belief. Others at the centre were significantly more sceptical.

These early and largely invisible premonitions of disagreement about the UK's future role in Europe had no counterpart in the wider Conservative Party at that stage. Following the publication of my pamphlet, a few think tanks interested themselves in the subject and I found myself on various platforms disagreeing with various former diplomats about the future direction of the European Communities. But even after Mrs Thatcher's Bruges speech, the constitutional issues (as opposed to the ostensibly purely economic question of Britain's participation in the European Exchange Rate Mechanism) were pretty low on everyone's agenda. I marched up and down the country addressing small gatherings of Conservatives – to very little effect. The details of my travels are a merciful blur, but the degree of interest evoked by my arguments about the teleological nature of the European Court of Justice's jurisprudence is captured in my memory by the image of one elderly lady in the front row of a hall in north London, deeply asleep, subsiding gradually but inevitably into her neighbour's lap.

The Maastricht Treaty changed all that. Before the 1992 general election, when I was the Conservative candidate in Hampstead & Highgate, I (together with a group of other candidates) had signed a letter expressing alarm about the draft treaty and its proposals to expand the scope of action of the European Communities. I was soundly rapped over the knuckles by the party's high command. After my defeat in that election, I wrote a long series of articles in the *Daily Telegraph*, drawing out the many different ways in which I believed that Maastricht would drag Britain further and further towards becoming a province of an emerging United States of Europe, exactly as I had prophesied in my pamphlet, *Drift to Union*. The repeated indications of disfavour from Conservative Central Office that these articles evoked were of course nothing compared to the pressure that was being brought to bear by the whips on those opponents of Maastricht who had been lucky (or unlucky) enough to get elected as MPs in the 1992–97 parliament. As is now well documented, the Conservative Party was, by 1997, well and truly tearing itself apart on the question of European integration. What had been an obscure row within the Thatcherite stronghold of the Centre for Policy Studies in 1987 had ten years later become the centrepiece of Conservative politics.

Now, on referendum polling day, looking back at this history and recalling the multitudinous discussions of the European Question over the succeeding years in opposition and government, I am hard-pressed to identify where along the road so many of my colleagues and so many millions of my fellow citizens overtook me in the zeal of their antagonism to what has become the European Union. All through these years, I have thought of myself as a determined Eurosceptic (though never an outright Europhobe). I have argued passionately for keeping the pound rather than joining the euro. I opposed not only the Maastricht Treaty but also the Amsterdam, Nice and Lisbon treaties that succeeded it. I have sat with David Cameron and William Hague and George Osborne in discussion after discussion about how to arrest the tide of EU encroachments on our freedom of manoeuvre. I have worked with Conservative Cabinet colleagues, and have negotiated for hundreds of hours with Liberal Democrat Cabinet colleagues, to promote Theresa May's successful opt-out for Britain from many dozens of European directives governing justice and home affairs. I have pressed for and played a small part in obtaining renegotiation of the terms of our EU membership – to give us lasting protection against absorption into the euro, to constrain the ability of the European Court of Justice (ECJ) to expand the scope of EU law, and to write into the EU treaties the recognition that the EU is a multi-currency area within which some member states, including the UK, do not aim at an ever closer union.

From my point of view, that agreement has given us the opportunity to achieve what I have for so long desired – the creation of a Europe of concentric circles with an emerging federal state at the centre and a free trade single market around it, so that Britain can remain in the single market without being dragged into the federal state. So I have voted, on balance, but with conviction, to remain on the new terms.

But the ambitions that I set out in my pamphlet have somehow along the way become de-radicalised. To my surprise, having myself stayed in the same position from 1988 to 2016, I have been overtaken by the revolution. Views that once caused me to be classified as a dangerous Eurosceptic now cause me to be classified as an establishmentarian. And the British people – or at any rate something very much like a majority of them – have become so disenchanted with the European establishment that they are prepared if necessary to ditch the whole lot (free trade single market included) for the sake of getting out from under the yoke of European law.

For me, this is a double blow. Not only has the country chosen by far the riskier course, when there was at last the option to retain the gains of the single market without being dragged further into federalism, but we have also lost in the process a Prime Minister particularly well suited to the job, who was wholly committed to the modern, liberal, socially and environmentally progressive Conservatism in which I strongly believe.

Why has this happened?

No doubt the psephologists will be writing books for years about just what has persuaded so very many of our fellow citizens to regard our membership of the EU as an evil rather than a good. Is it really the feeling that somebody else is making our laws – that we have lost too much democracy? Or that we are sending vast amounts of money to Brussels that we could be using ourselves for some much better purpose? Or that immigration is out of control, and that we can't regain control of it without leaving the EU? Or is it a more general disenchantment with the establishment and the metropolitan elite which has translated itself into opposition to the EU on the grounds that the establishment and the metropolitan elite is pro-EU?

An amalgam of all these feelings has been on display in the referendum campaign itself and in the years leading up to it. As well as the polling evidence, there is the evidence of my own ears: I have heard people say each of these things, in one way or another, at meetings and on the streets both during the campaign and in preceding general elections and by-elections. But such feelings don't come to dominate the political landscape by accident. They are reinforced and spread by the media and by politicians operating through the media.

The rise of UKIP under the brilliantly relaxed demagoguery of Nigel Farage has certainly played its part. In my own constituency, UKIP has remained a fringe whose activists (though not its candidates) generally conform with David Cameron's memorable description of them as 'fruitcakes and closet racists mainly'. But, during the by-elections in Rochester and Clacton, I tramped the streets and came across UKIP activists of two very different kinds: on the one hand serious, decent and intelligent people whose aim is genuinely to regain control for our parliamentary democracy, and who regard this as worth doing at almost any price; and on the other, matching almost one for one, out-and-out ex-BNP hoodlums whose racism and xenophobia is well out of the closet. The remarkable thing is that Farage has brought these widely divergent types into an alliance that has broken through and become so much a part of British politics that even the BBC, for all its evident aversion, has had to treat it as a party with a place on more or less every platform. One tabloid newspaper, the *Daily Express*, has become a mouthpiece for UKIP. Other newspapers, with far wider circulations, have avoided supporting UKIP itself but have become powerful advocates of the 'better off out' school of thought so far as the EU is concerned. The Labour Party (which in principle remains massively Europhile) has lost much of its grip on many of its traditional core supporters, and has acquired a leader who pretty clearly wants to leave the EU without ever quite wanting to admit it. The Liberal Democrats (who used to be the torch-bearers' torch-bearers) have become demoralised and discredited.

No doubt one of the reasons that Farage's campaign has been so effective is that almost all of us on the liberal side of the immigration debate – both Conservative and Labour – have failed over many years to make the argument for immigration. Of course, we all recognise that there are limits to the speed with which the infrastructure and services of the country can absorb the pressures generated by increases in population – and indeed that there are limits to the speed with which new housing can be built in a small and relatively crowded island. But our concern to show that we recognise these facts has led us into a rhetoric that concedes too much to the 'Little Englanders'. It has come for many years to seem as if both the Labour and the Conservative parties regard migration only as a 'problem' and would really like to end it altogether, if only they had the power to achieve this goal. The positive arguments for steady migration – the skills and energy and cultural exuberance that it can bring to Britain – have been largely absent from the debate, ritually mentioned in speeches but little reported. It is no surprise that, in this intellectual climate, UKIP and its allies in the media and elsewhere have been able to base their arguments on the premise that immigration is, in itself, a bad thing for the country; and they have then been able to argue convincingly, because it is true, that if you want the UK to be able to block migration altogether, the only way of achieving this is to leave the EU.

All of this has undoubtedly contributed to the decisive shift in opinion against continued EU membership, much of it based on antagonism to migration. But I doubt that the shift would have been so great as it has been, were it not for the full-blooded leadership given to the Leave campaign by my Conservative colleagues. The really interesting and important development is that so many Conservative MPs – some of whom used to be less Eurosceptic than me – have now bypassed me and have become positive Brexiteers. They don't just want to be in an outer, single market circle; they want to be out altogether.

What journey have they been on?

In some cases, the evolution of ideas is pretty clear. My colleague Bill Cash provides a good example of a consistent (some might say repetitive) line of thought. I was not aware of Bill having made any particular contribution to thinking about the European Communities when I was writing my pamphlet in 1987; but by 1988 he had clearly come to much the same conclusions as I had about the danger of what he then described to Mrs Thatcher as 'creeping federalism' and, from the time when the Maastricht Treaty hove onto the horizon, his Euroscepticism was very much in evidence. As well as playing a significant part in the rebellions of Conservative backbenchers against the Maastricht legislation, he established a new European Foundation, to promote Eurosceptic arguments about the EU's direction of travel, and he became ferociously and loquaciously expert on the constitutional significance of EU law. This continued during the 1997–2001 parliament, when he was one of the senior backbenchers strongly supporting our opposition to the UK joining the euro, and his devotion to the cause never wavered through the years when he and I found ourselves together in Iain Duncan Smith's shadow Cabinet or in the succeeding years of opposition and government. During all those years one could not only be certain of hearing from him in the chamber of the House of Commons whenever a topic remotely (sometimes, very remotely) related to the EU was being debated, but also be pretty confident that not a week would pass without him buttonholing one in the lobbies in order to explain the significance of some chain of Euro-logic that might otherwise have escaped one's attention – often beginning with the query 'have you read my speech on…?'

The gradual development of Bill's views on our relationship to the EU provides a fascinating glimpse of what was later to take place in the minds of many other colleagues on the Conservative benches in Parliament. In 1986 – though already conscious of the risks of federalism – Bill was still a full-blooded (albeit not unreserved) supporter of the free trade aspects of the European Communities. In an article for *The Times* on 23 June of that year, he argued that 'the Internal market, free trade, competition, [and] deregulation … must be pursued vigorously' while adding that 'the creation of a single market will stimulate prosperity for the people of Europe unless it creates a political and institutional remoteness and complexity which is counter-productive'.

In 1988, the year of Mrs Thatcher's Bruges speech, Bill was still a supporter of the single market, writing (again in *The Times*) on 25 October that 'the EEC in principle has just about the right framework now. It will develop and must be reformed. The advantages it offers will help us to compete successfully with other continental giants.' Even at this stage, he had not quite reached the conclusion (which I had by then drawn in my pamphlet) that the creation of an emerging United States of Europe was inevitable, and that we should therefore seek to negotiate some means of staying in the single market while remaining outside the emerging federal structure. Instead, he regarded the 'creeping federalism' as something that could be defeated: 'Political union on the same scale is unnecessary and could provoke unwelcome hostility … It is those who demand European government who are damaging the chance of success.' Even as late as 2004, Bill was assuming that we should remain members of the EU, and was proposing domestic measures to curb Brussels through new legislation at Westminster that 'would … require British judges to give effect to British laws, passed by the voters' elected representatives, even if they were inconsistent or conflicted with European laws and treaties and the rulings of the Court of Justice' (*The Times*, 25 August 2004).

It was not until sometime between 2004 and 2009 (I suspect towards the end of that period, following signature of the Lisbon Treaty) that Bill eventually came to the conclusion that the UK should seek a kind of associate membership instead of participating in the EU itself, saying in a press release on 25 August 2009: 'It is a time for a new deal, beginning with the withdrawal of the instruments of ratification of the Lisbon Treaty, and ending with a Europe consisting of a democratic association of nation states, far removed from our existing binds within the European superstate.'

Where Bill Cash led, others of my colleagues followed. By 2011,

Bernard Jenkin (who had ironically been a Eurosceptic since reading my pamphlet in 1988, and who had fought the good fight against the Maastricht Treaty in the 1992–97 parliament) was writing: 'What Britain needs is … to seek a fundamental change in our relationship with our EU partners … in which Parliament, and not the institutions of the EU, determines the nature and extent of the UK's legal and political integration into the EU' (*Daily Telegraph*, 23 October 2011). Although there is an element of code here, with the clarity of hindsight I think one can read Bernard's sentence as a clear expression of support (indeed, as a demand) for exit from the EU, including from its single market, and the establishment for the UK of an 'associate membership' or participation in a new 'Democratic Association of Member States' of the sort envisaged by Bill Cash in 2009.

Again in retrospect, it seems clear that John Redwood, another passionate, principled and long-term Eurosceptic, had moved from a position of intense concern about encroaching federalism (which he had held consistently from the mid-1990s) to one of favouring outright Brexit. I cannot place exactly when this transition occurred; but anyone listening now, in the light of subsequent events, to the powerful speech he gave in the Commons in January 2013, where he talked of the need to 'regain the veto' and to forge 'a new relationship', would conclude that he had certainly reached this position by the middle of the 2010–15 parliament.

It is also now clear that some senior colleagues who, unlike Bill, Bernard, John or me, had not been seriously Eurosceptic in the late 1980s, and who had not fought against Maastricht, had come by the 2010s to favour Brexit. David Davis, the arch-Machiavelli of our generation of Conservative politicians, is the most striking exemplar. So far from objecting to Maastricht, he had worked as a whip to help the government get the Maastricht Treaty through the House of Commons, had then taken over from David Heathcoat-Amory as Europe Minister in July 1994, and had conducted his side of the leadership campaign against David Cameron in 2005 without any suggestion of favouring Brexit. But by 2012 he was in much the same place as Bill Cash, Bernard Jenkin and John Redwood. In a speech that year, entitled 'Europe: It's Time to Decide', he advocated a 'mandate referendum' in which the British people would be invited to vote in favour of 'taking back our justice and home affairs powers … immigration status powers … social and employment legislation … health and safety legislation', with a clear understanding that if these things could not be achieved within the EU's single market, then Britain should exit the EU and choose amongst 'a range of options, from EEA and EFTA membership like Norway … to a WTO-based minimalist relationship'.

As a former Europe Minister, and as a highly intelligent long-term observer of the European scene, David Davis will have been acutely conscious that, although we were able to (and indeed did) opt out of the great bulk of EU justice and home affairs legislation, no British government was going to be able to repatriate the whole of immigration powers, social and employment legislation and health and safety legislation while remaining a full participant in the EU single market. Moreover, he will have understood more than enough about the terms of Norway's membership of the EEA and EFTA to see that any meaningful repatriation of these powers would in fact also be incompatible with participation in those organisations. So what his speech, decoded, actually meant was that we should exit the EU and seek a different relationship with its member states.

In these years of the 2010–15 parliament, when the mood amongst many of the Eurosceptics on the Conservative benches was subtly shifting from acceptance of the single market aspect of the EU to what was (in effect, if not always yet explicitly) a belief in exiting the EU altogether, UKIP was making further headway. At the Conservative Party conference in the autumn of 2014, we watched helplessly as defections to UKIP were either rumoured or announced – and we went through the dark days of the Clacton and Rochester by-elections later that year, in which Douglas Carswell and Mark Reckless resigned both from the Conservative Party and from Parliament in order to fight (and win) their old seats as UKIP candidates. But there were no further defections after these two, and the great bulk of the parliamentary party had joined us on the endless train journeys to Clacton and Rochester, apparently more than happy to keep the Conservative flag flying. It was all too easy to interpret this as a sign that the centre of gravity amongst the great majority of the Eurosceptically inclined Conservative MPs remained in the position that I occupied, and had occupied since 1988 – against Britain being dragged into 'creeping federalism' but wanting to stay within the EU's single market.

It was against this background that I argued strongly for including in our 2015 manifesto a policy of renegotiation followed by referendum – with the clear assumption that we would leave if we did not get a good enough deal. There were three reasons for this. The first was a matter of principle. It seemed to me that the UK had been drawn by slow degrees into an EU that was unrecognisably different from the proposition that had been put to the people in the original referendum on remaining in the EU – without, at any point, being offered the opportunity to decide whether this was what they wanted. I had argued passionately for referendums on Maastricht, Amsterdam and Lisbon; but none had been forthcoming. We had legislated in the coalition years for a referendum to be held about any new treaty that transferred powers (thereby creating the so-called referendum lock); but there had been no new treaty proposed since that legislation had come onto the statute book. So the British people had been, so far, denied any opportunity to express a clear view on whether they were or were not content with the direction in which the EU was travelling. I believed that they had a right to express such a view, and for that view to determine our country's future.

The second reason for holding a referendum was a matter of reality. As I saw it, the choice that presented itself as we approached the 2015 election was not really a choice at all. Millions of people across the country had become totally disenchanted with the EU, and wanted a chance to express that view in a referendum. If we failed to guarantee a referendum, we were more than likely to lose enough seats to UKIP to deprive us of an overall majority – in which case, we would end up depending on UKIP support in Parliament, the condition of which would of course (ironically) be the holding of a referendum. And even if we actually managed to win a narrow overall majority, we would still find ourselves under irresistible pressure from the most Brexit-inclined of our own backbenchers to hold a referendum straight after the election. So I reasoned that, under most scenarios, if we were in government at all we would actually have to hold a referendum – in which case, why not guarantee in our manifesto that we would do so?

But in addition to the fact that a referendum seemed to me both right in principle and inevitable in practice, it also seemed to me to be a very useful device to maximise the chances of getting what I wanted us to get from the EU. I thought that, if the leaders of other EU member states saw that we were heading towards an 'in/out' referendum in the UK, they would be more likely to give us protection against absorption into the euro, real constraints on the ability of the ECJ to expand the scope of EU law, and a new recognition in a new treaty that the EU would permanently remain a multi-currency area within which some member states, including the UK, were specifically *not* aiming at establishing an ever closer union. I believed that obtaining these fundamental changes would gradually lead not only to a better position for Britain but also progressively to a different kind of EU, in which some member states within the Eurozone would make sense of the otherwise unsustainable common currency by becoming effectively a United States of Europe with federally controlled monetary, fiscal and other policies, while another set of member states would gradually join the UK in an outer circle of nations that were part of the single market, but did not participate in the euro, did not have their monetary and fiscal policies controlled by the EU, and were permanently and definitely not part of the United States of Europe.

For me, these were not new thoughts. Together with Steve Hilton (then David Cameron's strategy director), I had argued that we should offer a referendum in our manifesto before the 2010 general election. At that time, the argument against doing so was that an incoming administration in 2010 simply wouldn't have had the bandwidth to negotiate a new settlement with the other EU member states at a time when it was also trying to take Britain back into the black. That argument, put forcefully by William Hague and George Osborne, had won the day – and very possibly it was right. But the irony was that, by the time we had decided to have (and indeed really had no option but to have) a renegotiation and a referendum, the mood had turned strongly against the EU – and parliamentary colleagues who in 2010 or 2011 might have accepted the settlement negotiated in 2015 and 2016 were no longer willing to do so.

In any case, history could not be rewritten. The promise to have a renegotiation and referendum was made in 2015, not in 2010. And the renegotiation was therefore conducted against a much more ambitious set of demands from swathes of parliamentary colleagues who had moved well beyond accepting any terms that fell short of exiting the EU as a whole. My elation at the outcome of the negotiations in February 2016 was accordingly short-lived.

From my point of view, David Cameron had achieved everything that was needed: a special (and specially protected) status for the UK as a country permanently outside the Eurozone; a clear recognition – to be built into treaty – that the UK was not seeking 'ever closer union'; and an agreement that the European Court could not use ever closer union as a basis for expansionist interpretations of European law. It seemed clear to me that if the UK voted to continue membership on this basis, other EU countries outside the Eurozone would follow us with similar settlements that kept them permanently out of the euro, while those member states that remained in the Eurozone would turn themselves gradually into a much more fiscally integrated United States of Europe centred on Germany. In short, we would gradually move into the position I had wanted since 1988 – of being a member of the outer-circle, free trade single market, without being dragged into an emerging federal state.

This was indeed the view I expressed at the Cabinet meeting that took place just before the referendum campaign began. It was clear, listening to those around the table who were declaring for Brexit, that they didn't share my view of what had been achieved. Or, at any rate, they didn't think that achieving this much was nearly enough. They had reached the belief that Bill Cash, John Redwood, Bernard Jenkin, David Davis and others had reached: that the only way out from the grip of European law was to leave the EU altogether, including the single market.

Before that critical Cabinet meeting, there were two colleagues with whom I had discussed this central issue of the primacy of European law in some detail. The first of these was Michael Gove, who had been agitated about European jurisdictional creep throughout our six years together in government and had fully engaged in fighting this trend with his unusual combination of politesse and ferocity. Like me, he had evidently been shocked by the steady flow of new EU directives that greeted us when we first came to office in 2010. I used to go home each night, in those early days, with piles of these things in various stages of drafting (and equal piles of draft UK statutory instruments seeking to implement the directives). It was a heroic struggle to get to grips with them sufficiently to spot the bits that mattered before someone in some ministry signed up to things we didn't want to sign up to. And then, once the lawyers were gathered around the table, we'd discover that the ECJ had laid a daisy chain of judgments that made it quite impossible to do things that no treaty had ever intended to prohibit, or absolutely necessary to do things that no treaty had ever intended to mandate. It was the stuff of nightmares, and Michael was as determined as I was to do as much as we could to put a spanner in the wheels of the EU's legislative juggernaut. So, with frequent help from Steve Hilton, we made common cause in Cabinet committees and in meetings with Liberal Democrat colleagues. Our styles were somewhat different: Steve's explosions contrasted with the elegant but totally uncompromising virtuoso rhetoric from Michael and with my more plodding and technocratic efforts to find some common ground on which we and other ministerial colleagues could agree. But the motives were the same.

Michael and I had also cooperated closely on the separate but related development of a British Bill of Rights, for which he had become responsible once he took over from Chris Grayling as Justice Secretary. Of course, the European Convention on Human Rights is not in itself anything to do with the EU, as it emanates from the Council of Europe, which is an entirely separate body with a much larger membership than the EU. By the same token, the European Court of Human Rights (ECtHR) in Strasbourg is a completely different body from the European Court of Justice, which sits in Luxembourg. But the absorption of the Convention on Human Rights and of much of the Strasbourg jurisprudence into EU law by the EU's Charter of Fundamental Rights and by the ECJ has created a strong practical link between the two entities. And there is also a strong connection of ideas – because the Strasbourg court is given supremacy over our domestic UK courts by our Human Rights Act, in a way that is at least strikingly similar to the way in which the European Communities Act gives supremacy over our domestic UK courts to the ECJ. So Michael and I both wanted to strengthen our sovereignty in a new British Bill of Rights that would enable the UK Supreme Court to interpret the European Convention on Human Rights for itself without being bound by the sometimes bizarre jurisprudence of the ECtHR. In addition to the constitutional significance of this move, we hoped that it would have the practical effect of letting our Supreme Court's good sense correct some of the more tendentious judgments of the ECtHR – such as the decision that it was against human rights for the UK to ban prisoners from voting.

As we came to the EU referendum, the question was whether Michael would go beyond our joint efforts to shore up our domestic courts against the ECJ and the ECtHR and seek instead to get out of the grip of European law altogether. When I had caused a slight stir by saying before the 2015 election that we couldn't rule out leaving the EU if it proved impossible to negotiate a sufficiently strong new settlement with the other member states, Michael had strongly supported me. So I was very much aware that he was putting a lot of weight on exactly what the negotiations produced. As soon as the negotiations in Brussels were complete, I gathered from both David Cameron and George Osborne that Michael was weighing up which side to come down on. So, when I rang him to talk through my own view about what the negotiations had achieved, I was disheartened to hear the murmurs that greeted each phase of my argument. These might have been mistaken for assent by a less accustomed ear. But I knew from long experience how to interpret such susurrations from Michael: punctiliously polite but wholly non-committal responses of this sort indicated that he by no means agreed with my reading of the situation. I think he had hoped that the settlement would enable our judges to overrule or at least hugely restrain the ECJ even in relation to the interpretation of genuine single market legislation, but he had concluded that this 'get-out-of-jail-free card' (as he put it) wasn't in fact going to be legally feasible under the terms of the International Law Decision that had been negotiated. And (like many of our other parliamentary colleagues) he didn't share my belief that the negotiated settlement would lead gradually to an acceptable EU with an outer ring for the UK and an inner core for an emerging United States of Europe. Instead, he had been persuaded somewhere along the way that even the legal ties of the single market were too constricting and that nothing short of removing ourselves from the EU altogether would sufficiently protect us from the incursions into our law of the ECJ.

This particular question – how far we could put the interpretation of European law by our own judges above, or at least on an equal footing with, the judgments of the ECJ – had been very much at the front of my mind when I was having this discussion with Michael, because I had simultaneously (at David Cameron's request) been having a discussion about precisely this question with Boris Johnson. Boris was not, at this point, in the Cabinet itself; but, as the most popular and (apart from the PM) the best-known Conservative politician, he was clearly going to be a key figure in the forthcoming referendum. Unlike with Michael, I had not worked hand in glove with Boris for the previous eleven years; so I didn't have anything like as clear a sense of his views about the EU as I did in the case of Michael. But I had, on and off, talked to him about related matters. I remembered, for example, the occasion in

2001 when I had bumped into Boris late one night behind the Speaker's chair just outside the chamber of the Commons and had tried to persuade him that the election of Ken Clarke as Conservative leader in that year would cause significant difficulties for the party because of Ken's Europhile tendencies. The result was a Boris 'harrumph'. So I had always put him into the category of the only mildly Eurosceptical. Clearly, during the 2001–05 and 2005–10 parliaments, his Euroscepticism (like David Davis's) had hardened. On 4 December 2012, he had given a major speech advocating a completely changed relationship between the UK and the EU. But even at this stage, his views seemed much more in line with my own than with those of the Eurosceptics who had become Brexiteers: 'boil it down to the single market', he had said; and had gone on to say that 'we could construct a relationship with the EU that more closely resembled that of Norway or Switzerland – except that we would be inside the single market council, and able to shape legislation'.

In the days after we had completed the negotiations with the EU, when I began to discuss with Boris the possibility of strengthening the settlement by giving UK judges more power in UK law to resist the ECJ, it became clear to me that he had moved on again. These discussions were very informal affairs. Either Boris would come over to 9 Downing Street in the late-ish evening, bearing his monumentally large rucksack, or we would talk on the phone after an exchange of emails. Between one discussion and the next, I would be consulting a range of lawyers to see how we could use different kinds of domestic legislation to reinforce the legal effect of the International Law Decision that David Cameron had negotiated with the other EU member states. Looking back at this somewhat bizarre sequence of exchanges from the perspective of subsequent events, the precise details of the proposals no longer seem of much concern. But I recall certain tell-tale moments. There is Boris, sitting somewhat dishevelled on the chair in my little panelled study, running his hands through his hair and asking rhetorically whether, if the nation didn't vote to leave, we would wake up the morning after and feel that we had missed a great opportunity. There is Boris wondering aloud whether Michael Gove would favour Brexit and (correctly) surmising that he would. There is Boris expressing the conviction (one wondered at the time whether it was almost half the hope) that the Brexit side would lose the referendum. There is Boris explicitly expressing the hope that a majority in favour of Brexit might precipitate a renegotiation and a further referendum. But finally, there is the phone call to Boris at his home, during the course of which I become aware that I am talking not just to Boris himself but to a dinner party at which Michael Gove is also present. It is at this moment that it becomes clear to me that Boris is going to be a Brexiteer.

So the Brexit side of the referendum campaign acquired what it most needed to have, and what we, on the other side of the argument, most needed it *not* to have – two politicians capable of mobilising the people that Nigel Farage couldn't reach: the sensible, middle-of-the-road voters for whom the whole question was one of balance rather than a foregone conclusion. The point about Boris wasn't just that he was Boris. It was also what he wasn't: he wasn't a mad ideologue; he wasn't fixated on the EU; he wasn't a crusty old reactionary xenophobe. You just couldn't put him into any of the categories that turned off the sensible, middle-of-the-road people. And he was manifestly patriotic – so if he thought, on balance, we could do OK outside the EU single market, well, that became a plausible proposition. And the point about Michael was that he was organised and intellectually rigorous and manifestly principled. So he made the Brexit campaign seem something that serious people could back without feeling worried that they were in the hands of demagogues. I rank my failure to persuade either of them to join the Remain camp as one of the biggest failures of my political life.

The damage this did to the Remain campaign was beyond doubt. The only question was whether it would be enough to tilt the balance in favour of a Brexit majority. As we came to the end of the referendum period, it looked very much as though the answer to this question was, mercifully, no. On the evening of polling day when the last polls came in they looked very good for Remain. I chatted happily to George Osborne on the phone; had an illusorily jolly supper with my family; stayed up for the early part of the results; went to sleep somewhat concerned at the Sunderland result; turned on the TV again in the early hours, realising with a terrible sinking certainty that it was going to be a Brexit majority; and headed into Downing Street.

As I trudge along Albert Embankment, over Lambeth Bridge, and past the towers and spires of Parliament, clearer now in the very early summer morning after the torrential rain of polling day, Nadezhda Krupskaya's description of the beauty of the torch-lit processions of the Russian Revolution comes strangely into my mind. Or perhaps not so strangely. These are, in their own way, revolutionary circumstances. The electorate have removed an incumbent establishment, and not just in Downing Street. People and Parliament have regained power at the expense of courts, commissions and councils. We are in a new era, with new risks and new opportunities. Everything has changed.

Friday is a sequence of surreal flashes: David's resignation statement; the meetings in No. 10; the astonishing calm and dignity with which the PM accepts what, to those of us close to him, seems in personal and emotional terms a nearly unbearable situation. We are losing a leader who is as capable of engaging with the electorate and with Parliament as he is of managing a government; a leader whose open, modern, liberal, progressive version of Conservative politics has the capacity to attract sections of the population far beyond the Conservative core vote. And we are launching into a sea of uncertainty with no means of telling whether the new captain of the ship, whoever that may be, will have anything like these capacities and advantages.

But there is a country to run and, for the moment at least, it is still we who are meant to be running it. Clearly, the ordinary processes of Whitehall will continue while a change of Prime Minister is brought about. But I am acutely conscious that the election of the new leader will take several months. Jeremy Heywood (the Cabinet Secretary) and I agree that something is going to have to be done in the meantime to ensure that we can provide whoever is the incoming PM with the best possible preparation for negotiating Brexit. After a little initial hesitation, David Cameron also agrees – and asks me to work with Jeremy to put the preparatory work in hand. So we enter the next and, as it turns out, the last phase of my activities in Downing Street.

The first step is to find the right civil servant to head up the task. Jeremy has the inspired idea of appointing Oliver Robbins. Over the past six years, I have seen and worked with innumerable civil servants of all ranks from all round Whitehall – probably more than any other minister. Some have been obtuse or ill-informed or merchants of ghastly jargon; many have been extraordinarily able, dedicated and effective. But amongst the most senior officials two, in my time, have stood out above all the rest. Jeremy Heywood himself (with whom I have worked on a daily basis) has given me a masterclass in getting action out of vast bureaucracies. The other is Olly Robbins, whose crystalline presentations to the National Security Council have brought light and clarity to parts of the international scene that are shrouded in mist. If ever there were an area of our national life requiring Olly's ability to combine subtlety of perception with clarity and simplicity of presentation, the Brexit negotiation is it. So Olly is the right person.

There is, however, a problem. Olly has gone, relatively recently, to work at the Home Office for the Home Secretary, Theresa May, as her Second Permanent Secretary. It is by no means clear that Theresa will be willing to let him come over to the Cabinet Office to set up the preparations for Brexit. Nor is it clear that David Cameron has the moral authority to force this to happen, now that he has announced his resignation – especially given that Theresa is a very serious candidate for the leadership. I am mulling this over at home on the Sunday, when my mobile rings and the screen shows the name Theresa May. She is clearly canvassing for support. I explain to her that I have promised David that I will take no sides in the leadership contest and will instead try to ensure that we prepare as well as we can for whoever takes over to be able to conduct the Brexit negotiations after 9 September. This she describes as 'very sensible'. So far, so good. Then I add that we want to bring Olly Robbins over to the Cabinet Office to do the job. There is one of Theresa's famous pauses, followed by the observation that this would not be constructive from the point of view of the Home Office. Long experience of negotiating with Theresa persuades me that the best course of action is to let her ponder, rather than pressing the point. I reason that, if she thinks she may be the next PM, she will probably come soon enough to accept that the next PM needs to have the ground for the Brexit negotiations prepared by Olly Robbins rather than by anyone else.

As we enter Cabinet early in the next week, Theresa's mood has indeed softened. She refers jovially to the need to 'clone' Olly Robbins, and I have the distinct sense that we are moving towards a solution. About twenty-four hours later, it is confirmed. Theresa has worked out that both the national interest and her own interest as a potential PM are best served by having the right person in the right job.

The next step is to find out what the various runners and riders in the leadership election actually want to have prepared for them. I start with Michael Gove. My first question is whether he is acting for himself or for a combination of Boris and himself. He asks for a short time to finalise his arrangements – and then calls me to let me know that he himself is 'definitely, definitely' not standing for the leadership and that he is instead working with Boris as part of a double act. I receive this information gratefully, as it means I can deal just with Michael and can get two views about the necessary preparation for the price of one. I also mention to Boris that I am listening to Michael's requests on the basis that Michael is speaking for both of them – and receive what appears to be approval from him for this modus operandi. So Michael and I sit down in my office to discuss the substance. As one would have expected, Michael has a clear conception of what is wanted: he asks for a set of papers that will enable the incoming administration to negotiate as complete a system of free trade with the EU as is compatible with (a) the UK exercising control over migration, and (b) the UK being in total control of its own legal system so that the ECJ has no jurisdiction in this country.

Next, I pay a call on Theresa. Interestingly, she is much busier, and asks to see me in her room at the Commons late at night. I get the impression that her campaign for the leadership is a great deal more relentless than whatever Michael and Boris have managed to put together. But, on the substance of what needs to be prepared, there is little difference. She, too, wants us to ensure that the briefing for the incoming administration focuses on the critical issue of reconciling control over migration and over our own law with the greatest possible degree of free trade with the EU.

Thinking that I have now talked to the front runners, I decelerate the efforts to contact leadership candidates and wait instead to see how things shake down. There is no point, after all, in speaking in detail to people who fall out at an early stage. I turn, instead, to working with Jeremy and Olly to put together the first stages of an institutional structure and the beginnings of an analytical approach.

There is, in my experience, no substitute for reading the primary sources. So I start by sitting down and doing what, in all the years from 1987 onwards, I have never done: I read the free trade texts. I read the EFTA agreements, the EEA agreements, the Canada–EU free trade agreement, the GATT... My study begins to resemble the habitation of a free trade obsessive, with document after document digested and marked up. I also meet the succession of my own parliamentary colleagues and others who want to make sure that their views about the negotiations are fed into the initial stages of the discussion. John Redwood, Bernard Jenkin, Bill Cash, Iain Duncan Smith, Owen Paterson and many other Conservative MPs have well-formed, and in some cases highly coordinated, plans on the process and on particular aspects of the negotiations. But there are plenty of others who also want to discuss this: I appear before select committees in both the Lords and the Commons; I meet a delegation from the non-Corbynite elements of the Labour Party; I meet the Mayor of London. My meeting room, down the corridor from my study, begins to resemble Clapham Junction.

What emerges from all of this is actually – as is often the case – conceptually simple but mind-bogglingly difficult in political and diplomatic terms. There are basically two options. The new Prime Minister can start with the EEA agreement, which guarantees full access to all aspects of the single market, and then try to work out how to persuade the other EU member states to let us remove the free movement of labour that is an integral part of the EEA arrangements as well as the de facto jurisdiction of the ECJ over the interpretation of single market legislation. Or the new PM can start with the GATT (General Agreement on Tariffs and Trade, often described as the WTO rules), which guarantees almost nothing by way of free trade in services, and then work out how to negotiate line by line not only for tariffs a good deal lower than in the WTO arrangements (a relatively easy task) but also (with much, much greater difficulty) a set of agreements that allow us to sell professional and financial services into the EU market from outside the EU. Given that none of the EEA countries have achieved anything like what the first approach would demand, and that none of the parties to free trade agreements with the EU have achieved anything like what the second approach would demand, the job isn't easy – to put it mildly. But at least it is clear that one or the other of these approaches will have to be tried; and that is enough to get the official machine rolling forward on more detailed analysis of both options.

The other question is what to do about the legal situation. How should we deal with the triggering of Article 50, which sets in train the formal process for leaving the EU? How should we deal with the disentangling and/or re-establishment of the many forms of cooperation that we have with other EU member states? And how should we ensure that there is a continuity of law between the day before we leave the EU and the day after we have left? At first, these look like difficult questions, and there is certainly a welter of detail to be sorted out. But it becomes clear, even after a few days, that there is a distinct path through this particular forest: Article 50 doesn't actually need to be triggered until we want to trigger it; we can discuss the arrangements for post-Brexit cooperation informally with the other member states for however long it takes before we set the clock ticking for the formal negotiations; and we can establish legal continuity by using the repeal of the European Communities Act at the moment of Brexit to bring into UK law as much as we want of current European law – with plenty of scope for our own Parliament to amend or remove whatever elements of this we want, on our own timetable, post-Brexit.

So the big issue isn't any of this immensely fiddly detail: the fundamental political and diplomatic question remains how to reconcile retaining access to trade in services with grabbing back control over the legal system including immigration law. Undoubtedly, this is doable – but at a price. Even the very preliminary work that I have been able to do has made me absolutely clear that the preservation of these rights to sell retail services (like insurance or stocks and bonds) to people across Europe is critical to the prosperity of the City of London – which remains a huge part of our economy. And it's also clear that we are going to have to find something quite big to trade for a guarantee from the EU that we will retain these rights, since it isn't in the interests of Frankfurt or Paris (or even Zurich) that London should continue to sell such services into the EU and the EEA: on the contrary, the gnomes of all these three other financial centres would dearly love to see London lose its pre-eminence. I can't personally see how anything other than a continuing, large financial contribution from the UK to the EU is likely to overcome those interests and buy the UK the access to EU markets that we will need.

While all of this technocratic work is underway in and around 9 Downing Street, politics is not standing still. The Conservative parliamentary party is going through the process, round by round, of choosing its new leader, getting down to two candidates who will be presented as the shortlist to the wider Conservative membership. On the morning of Thursday 30 June, just a week after referendum polling day, I find myself sitting once again with David Cameron and George Osborne in David's study at No. 10. Boris Johnson is due to launch his leadership bid. There has been a surprise this morning: Michael Gove has at the last moment peeled off from Boris and has announced that he is running independently. This is particularly surprising to me given that Michael told me a few days previously that he would 'definitely, definitely' not be running. So Boris is coming to his launch under rather different circumstances than we had imagined. Needless to say, he is late. Nothing surprising in this: if heaven exists, Boris will be late presenting himself to St Peter. But, when he eventually appears on the big TV screen in the middle of David's office, he too has a further surprise for us. The speech is not developing as we would have expected. And it ends by Boris explaining to the supporters gathered eagerly before him that he will not in fact be running. The camera pans to the supporters, who look somewhat shell-shocked. I can't say the same for those present in David's room. There is a degree of what the Germans call schadenfreude.

It isn't until after the last round of the parliamentary process five days later that we finally discover that it won't be either Boris or Michael who will be facing Theresa in the next two months of campaigning across the country, but rather the relatively unknown Andrea Leadsom. Clearly, we must now check that the direction of our preparations will provide her with what she will want if she becomes the next PM. I have some difficulty tracking her down, but eventually reach her on Friday 8 July while she is en route from one engagement to another in her car. I am somewhat disconcerted to find that, unlike Michael and Theresa, she is focusing on the issue of tariffs. This seems to me to be a far less difficult issue than how we enable UK retailers of financial and professional services to continue to sell those services into the EU.

This is, however, just one of the things that is now worrying me about a potential Andrea Leadsom victory. I really doubt whether, at this juncture in our national affairs, the country can afford to have a Prime Minister with so little experience of frontline politics or of the centre of government. The more I think about it, the more concerned I become that the party members may choose Andrea on the grounds that she has been a Brexiteer and that she is a fresh face, with an attractive bounciness – when what the country clearly needs to meet the enormous challenge is the massive competence and experience that Theresa will bring to the job. Now, I am not prone to sleepless nights. I have been through many personal and collective political crises during more than thirty years in British public life. But I have never been as worried about a political outcome as I am about this. And it is as if I am imprisoned in my own body, unable to speak – because I have promised David Cameron, and David Cameron has promised Parliament, that I will play no part in the leadership election. Every fibre of my being is telling me to get out there and campaign tirelessly up and down the country for Theresa May; but I can't do it; I can't even so much as tell a newspaper what I think. It is the ultimate purdah.

And then, on Monday 11 July, less than seventy-two hours after I have spoken to her, Andrea withdraws from the race. Theresa will become PM. Whether she will prove to be as effective a political communicator as David Cameron, and whether she will be able to articulate a version of Conservatism as open and liberal as his, are questions that remain to be answered. But at least the country is back in safe, experienced hands. I have seldom experienced so strong a sense of relief.

And there is another, smaller reason for relief. Theresa has announced that her Brexit plans will be taken forward by Brexiteer ministers – so, instead of having to labour through the summer months until 9 September, I can down tools and hand this fascinating but utterly daunting task to someone else. Instead of the three days of holiday that I have planned, I can now have a proper summer break.

The only remaining question is whether I will have a permanent holiday from ministerial office or whether Theresa will want me to do some other job. It will take just a couple of days to find out.

CHAPTER 2

A CALL FROM
DOWNING STREET

I am walking past the Guards' Chapel on Birdcage Walk when the call comes from the Downing Street switchboard.

I make my way back to the House of Commons. The fact that I have been asked to go to the Prime Minister's room in the Commons, rather than to No. 10, tells me all I need to know. When a reshuffle is underway or a new government is being formed, the appointments take place at No. 10 so that the new ministers can be photographed by the waiting press photographers as they go in; the sackings, by contrast, occur in the privacy of the PM's office in the Palace of Westminster, where the press cannot penetrate. So, after eighteen years on the front bench, I am being sacked.

There is, of course, nothing surprising about this. Theresa May basically has two choices: she can go for maximal continuity with the Cameron regime; or she can go for a clean break in order to establish a new tone. The fact that she has already sacked George Osborne strongly suggests a clean-break strategy – and that must clearly involve getting rid of me, as one of the members of David Cameron's inner circle. I cannot blame Theresa for this. In her position, I think I would take the same view: it is much easier to run things your own way if you aren't surrounded by people who used to be running things their way; and she can maintain continuity of policy in many areas more easily if she isn't saddled with the accusation of just being 'Cameron-lite'. In addition, she needs to make room around the Cabinet table for the Brexiteers. All in all, getting rid of Osborne, Letwin and a dozen or so others seems to be a low price to pay for a decisive fresh start.

When I enter the office, she is graciousness itself, commending both the work I have done for David in government and the role I have played (often alongside her) in the years of opposition. But, without shilly-shallying (as is her style), she informs me that she is facing a considerable challenge following the Brexit vote and that the Cabinet she is forming does not have a place for me. I promise loyalty from the back benches – which I have every intention of displaying – and wish her luck, which she will need in abundance.

It is, as has often been remarked by others, a startlingly quick pro- cess. One minute, you are a Cabinet minister with tasks and worries and meetings and civil servants and a direct role in governing the country. The next minute, these things have all disappeared. Though still a legislator, you are no longer a part of the government machine; your diary is empty; your responsibilities have vanished and so have your civil servants. With great solicitude, sensitivity and efficiency, they take back your passes and your keys, and arrange for your books and personal effects to be delivered over from the centre of govern- ment to your office in the Mother of Parliaments.

As the kindly emails and text messages pour into my phone, I recall the time almost exactly thirty years ago when I first took my leave of Downing Street. On that occasion, it was of my own volition. Then, too, I went to the Prime Minister's room in the House of Commons – but the shoe was on the other foot. I was letting Mrs Thatcher know that I was leaving her Policy Unit in order to become a parliamentary candidate.

Mrs Thatcher put up a considerable show, tottering to the drinks cabinet and reaching for what I deeply suspected was in fact a glass of water. Kind words, fond farewells and memories of battles were shared. And then that was that. I remember wondering whether the best years of my life were behind me. I made a mental resolution to return to Parliament and to Downing Street as a legislator in my own right rather than as a staffer.

Those first Downing Street years had begun around my parents' dinner table in the elegant dwelling they ruinously leased from the Crown Estate. As often, one of the dinner guests was my parents' friend Keith Joseph, then the Education Secretary. But Keith was much more than just the Education Secretary. Together with Geoffrey Howe, he had been the originator of the break from Butskellism, blazing the trail for the route march to the market economy that Margaret Thatcher was now leading. Regarded by her as her mentor, he was now one of the most influential members of the Cabinet, occupying the unofficial position of chief ideologist.

My circumstances at the time were unusual and rather unsatisfactory. I was in the middle of a research fellowship at Princeton and was about to become a very junior and very unpaid fellow of Darwin College, Cambridge. Keith Joseph wanted to know if I knew of any young Cambridge dons who might be willing to spend a year working with him in the Department of Education and Science (DES). I said that I would myself be more than willing to do so. That was how I made my first, tentative entry into British politics.

The scene that greeted me when I arrived at the department – then resident in one of the ugliest 1960s skyscrapers in London – was bizarre in the extreme. There sat Keith, at the middle of a long, long table in a room high up in the sky, staring out mournfully at a desolate landscape of other high-rise buildings and railway tracks. From time to time, groups of officials would gather around him at this table. Ostensibly, the purpose of this running seminar was to bring in a voucher scheme for British schools that would enable parents to take the taxpayer's money to the school of their choice. I was meant to be helping him achieve this ambition. There was just one problem: the massed ranks of officials didn't want him to achieve it (he didn't), and he wanted to let them persuade him that he couldn't (they did).

True, we did get some things of real value done. With great help from Pauline Perry (then a chief inspector of schools and later a distinguished academic administrator and policy-maker), teacher training was reformed to make it a matter more of guided practice in the classroom, and less of empty theorising. The long, slow march towards equipping maintained schools with the apparatus required for them to operate independently from local education authorities was begun. And some of the good remaining grammar schools were saved, mainly through the energy of Stuart Sexton – a cheery, kind-hearted and bustling figure who was installed as special adviser before I came onto the scene, and who welcomed me into the fold with amazingly good grace.

But none of these modest achievements in any way compensated for the fact that, in the months I worked at the DES, we made what can only accurately be described as no progress at all towards the establishment of the voucher scheme to which Keith Joseph was, as he frequently stated, so 'intellectually attracted'. I watched with fascination how the officials – in particular, the Deputy Secretary for Schools (a man of formidable intellect and not inconsiderable charm) – used the indecision of their secretary of state to ensure that the nation was defended against the effects of what they regarded as one of Keith's more eccentric ideas. I came to the conclusion at that time, which I have never since had reason to revise, that officials will generally do what their political 'masters' ask if these political masters are sufficiently masterly, and not otherwise.

Long after my time at the DES, when I was travelling the world advising governments on privatisation, I witnessed countless examples of the same phenomenon – persuading me that this tendency is by no means peculiar to the UK. A prime example was the Military Secretary in Islamabad, who confidentially informed me that his job was to keep the Prime Minister (then the luckless Benazir Bhutto) 'very busy going from parade to parade'; in another, an appropriately Byzantine Turkish official kept us waiting in the outer office for a meeting that would have given the minister information for which he had asked, and then informed us casually that he had unfortunately had to arrange for the minister to leave via a different door to visit an earthquake zone; a third was the assistant to Fidel Castro who completed every last detail of the privatisation of the phone system of Cuba before mentioning to the minister for communications where our negotiating teams were located. All of these were sterling examples of what is, in my experience, the invariable rule that ministers get what they want only if they know what they want and are prepared to stick to it when the official machine produces difficulties or has other ideas.

In Keith Joseph, officials quickly identified that they had a politician on their hands who knew what he wanted, but was positively willing someone to explain to him why he couldn't have it. The look of pained triumph that crossed his handsome features each time a problem was identified by the Deputy Secretary was enough to prove to anyone with any emotional intelligence – and the Deputy Secretary was a man of very great emotional intelligence – that there was a constant demand for more problems. And, hey presto, no matter how many solutions Stuart Sexton and I produced, more problems emerged. Indeed, even when Mrs Thatcher became so impatient for a voucher scheme that she insisted on having Keith's meetings attended by the distinguished figure of Ferdy Mount (then the admirable head of the Downing Street Policy Unit) and the fiercely intelligent Robin Harris (another political appointee), the obstacles continued to be produced by the Deputy Secretary and accepted by Keith at a faster rate than we apparatchiks could produce means of surmounting them.

Nevertheless, there were some significant compensations for participating in this frustratingly inevitable failure. The first was getting to know Keith himself. I have so many fond memories: Keith, with the courage of a lion, facing down Mrs Thatcher when he wanted to merge O-levels and CSEs into the modern GCSE, and she most emphatically did not; Keith, with the fastidiousness of a seamstress, delicately wiping away the spit that had descended upon his suit from Arthur Scargill's thugs at a demonstration outside a party conference; Keith, with the modesty of a country vicar, introducing himself in the third person as 'the holder of my office' (now, who could that possibly be?). So it rolls on: memory after memory of a man whose seriousness of purpose never wavered, and who understood politics not as a game of thrones but as a search for truth.

Of course, even Keith, certainly the least worldly politician I have known, recognised that if you don't win the game sufficiently to be the government you can't make happen what you think ought to happen. And I'm sure – though I never once heard him speak about it in private or in public – that he harboured (or at least had harboured) personal ambitions. But one could see, working with him day by day, that he was genuinely actuated not by the desire to grab a headline or trump an opponent or overtake a rival, but by a desire to improve the lot of his fellow citizens. Perhaps to some readers who didn't know him, and who have acquired from the media a warped impression of politicians, this will seem a pious and implausible assertion. It is, however, an unvarnished account of what I found as I sat there in that dreadful building with this remarkable, anxious, courteous, curious, subtle, eccentric, honourable man.

Keith's seriousness of purpose did sometimes lead him astray. I recall an occasion on which I had to drive him to speak at Stowe School. The details of the journey are mercifully blurred in my memory; but the essential facts are that he was map-reading, we got hopelessly lost and we were very late – so late that we missed the dinner and kept the audience waiting for an hour or so in the auditorium before we arrived. Against this unpropitious background, Keith launched into a lecture about the origins of prosperity. His aim was to explain what economists call the 'lump of labour fallacy', and his method was to point out the fact that as human populations have grown over the ages work has been found for all: one person's job does not deprive another person of their job – because, as he put it, 'all producers are consumers and all consumers are producers'. To say that the boys of Stowe School were unenthusiastic about this late-night lecture is, I fear, an understatement. But it was part of Keith's ineffable charm that he recognised absolutely that he had failed when he had failed. My efforts in the car on the way back to comfort him with the thought that I, at least, had found the lecture interesting were met with a firm refusal: 'Don't even try,' he said, as he described to me his own experiences of working for a politician who had been an 'outstanding speaker ... outstandingly bad'.

And yet, as one looks back on it forty years on, I think one can confidently say that Keith, as a politician who occupied the connecting ground between theory and practice, did more to change the direction of British politics than most of those who were far more distinguished theoreticians and most of those who were far more accomplished practitioners. Certainly, he could not have achieved very much if Mrs Thatcher hadn't provided both the game-winning capacities and the administrative drive needed to implement the fundamental changes in the relationship between the state and society for which he argued. But, without his articulation of the argument, I am by no means sure that she would ever have succeeded.

What is most interesting, and what has been most misunderstood, about Keith as a pundit is the nature of the argument that he was making in the late 1970s and 1980s. It is popularly supposed that he was simply interested in rolling back the frontiers of the state. Nothing could be further from the truth. In reality, Keith's arguments for the 'common ground' and the 'social market' were aimed at establishing the contention that free markets, properly harnessed, are the most powerful engine yet invented by humanity for elevating the condition of the poor and the disadvantaged. In a way that presaged the later work of Iain Duncan Smith and David Cameron, he sought to persuade a sceptical intelligentsia that state monopoly was a recipe not only for economic inefficiency but also for the protection of vested interest at the expense of the most disadvantaged. His ambition was to find the means of offering those without wealth the same opportunities to make choices and to improve their lot as were taken for granted by those coming from more favoured backgrounds – hence his focus on what he termed the 'cycle of deprivation' and the need to overcome that cycle, not least by enabling parents with low incomes to liberate their children from poor schools and with taxpayers' money get them into better ones.

So, even though Keith didn't have the temperament to drive through the voucher scheme, he was making the arguments that needed to be made, back then in the 1980s – and by doing so, he was helping to shape the future course of British politics, not only in the Conservative Party itself but also in what emerged out of the Labour Party in the 1990s. It wouldn't be wholly unfair to say that Tony Blair, as much as David Cameron and now Theresa May, was an inheritor of Keith's fundamental proposition that the social market, rather than 1940s Clause IV state-monopoly socialism, is the best route to elevating the condition of the least well-off and of the most downtrodden.

When I look back at the lessons I learned from that period working for Keith, I am surprised to find that they included most of the most fundamental tenets of what later became my own political life. I learned that the disagreements between the participants in democratic politics are usually about means and not ends; that it is therefore both possible and appropriate to conduct political debate in a liberal democracy on the basis of rational argument rather than tribal loyalties; and that political arguments have real staying power when they connect the goals we mainly have in common with measures that genuinely tend towards the achievement of those goals, however controversial the measures may at the time appear. And, beyond all of these invaluable lessons about the conduct of political life (which have come, over the succeeding thirty-five years, to seem to me increasingly true and important), I think – in retrospect – that the seeds may also have been sown in my mind of the significance of the 'social market' and of social justice, which was fundamental to Keith's thought. I emphatically do not mean that I understood this at the time; indeed, Keith's deep perception of the cycle of deprivation, of the extent to which some of our fellow citizens are imprisoned in circumstances that destroy or substantially impair their own life chances and those of their children, was largely and shamefully absent from my own thinking at that time. Nevertheless, in much later years, as the focus on these issues gradually came to form the core of my own view of what the Conservative Party needed to espouse and project and implement, I came progressively to understand the profundity of Keith's point and to see that the free market economy is not sufficient, sustainable or defensible unless it also becomes a *social* market economy in which the prosperity engendered by free enterprise is harnessed in the service of promoting the life chances of the least advantaged.

In the spring of 1983, however, my life changed abruptly when Mrs Thatcher called a general election. As politically appointed special advisers automatically lose their jobs once an election is called, I was transferred out of the DES and went over to my other London 'home', the Conservative Research Department (which had in fact been paying my salary as Keith's supernumerary part-time special adviser for the previous year or so).

The move to 32 Smith Square was no hardship, because the Research Department at that time was a highly attractive place to be. It was headed by Peter Cropper, an oracular and congenial man whose opening shot when, at Keith Joseph's instigation, I first entered his payroll was: 'I hope you won't make the mistake of supposing that the Conservative Research Department does any research.' And of course he was quite right: the point of the outfit was not to delve into deep mysteries in pursuit of original discoveries but rather to organise and produce the facts and figures that would enable the party to fight elections in an informed and effective way. The department's most notable product was the then-fabled *Campaign Guide*, edited for many years by my old and dear friend Alistair Cooke (who now goes under the alias of Lord Lexden).

Like me, Alistair had been a student at Cambridge of the legendary Maurice Cowling – a fellow of Peterhouse and the high priest of High Toryism, who had spent a lifetime writing and teaching about the connections between high politics, religion and political theory. Unlike me, however, Alistair had gone on to have a serious career as an academic historian and had eventually arrived at the Research Department as a guru on Northern Ireland. It was this interest in Northern Ireland that had, I think, brought him into contact with the fiercely unionist and at that time hugely influential journalist T. E. 'Peter' Utley, who was a consultant director of the department and ran a regular seminar for the 'desk officers' (as we were somewhat oddly described). Between them, Cropper, Cooke and Utley had managed to create an atmosphere that somehow held in balance elements of the academic with elements of the practical. In this, they were much aided by the presence of the deputy director, Tony Greenland – a man of quiet charm whose prose style was almost as perfectly formed as Alistair's and who had found the secret of contentment at an early age; he told me once, over a drink around the corner from Smith Square, that he had originally intended to stay only a few months at the Research Department but had found it so congenial that he had simply remained for the rest of his working life. To these core figures were added an array of highly talented and, in one way or another, unusual characters including another old and dear friend, the brilliantly incisive and articulate Katherine Ramsey.

It was in this pleasing environment that I helped Alistair before the election to prepare the great *Campaign Guide*. (I recall, in particular, the trouble we took to make the section on the Common Agricultural Policy – then a nightmare of quotas and milk lakes and butter mountains and sheep premiums – comprehensible to Conservative candidates at the election; whether anyone actually ever read it, I shall never know.) And then, during the election itself, I helped Tony to produce the Daily Notes – a compilation of items that were relevant to the particular day of the campaign and that were produced overnight so as to be available to our candidates when they read the newspapers over breakfast before going out on the campaign trail.

I should at this point correct one tiny part of the Conservative Party's history which may otherwise remain for ever uncorrected. The production of the Daily Notes was so intense a process that it required either Tony or me to be present in the office for something like eighteen hours a day. As a result, we divided tasks and also divided the periods of the day when one or other of us would be present. This made the whole arrangement entirely civilised. But it also had the effect that particular notes would be produced either by Tony or by me, as the case might be, frequently with little or no involvement of the other. This was especially true of one note which was probably to have a profound impact on my future life.

The note in question was on education vouchers, the very policy on which I had, with such spectacular lack of success, laboured so hard with Keith Joseph at the Department of Education and Science. For some reason, this policy had become a live issue on a particular day during the 1983 election – and it was Tony who happened to be in the office late in the day when the request came through for a note to be furnished immediately. What I knew, but Tony did not, was that the policy had been to all intents and purposes dropped as a result of the fact that Keith had not managed to get it into a shape (had, indeed, triumphantly persuaded himself that it could not be got into a shape) that would satisfy him. Not knowing the inwardness of all this, Tony wrote a note strongly suggesting that vouchers were on the cards for the next parliament if the government was re-elected.

The next morning, all hell broke loose. The daily papers were full of the note. Vouchers, it seemed, were back on!

Enter Lord Beloff – otherwise known as the academic Max Beloff. I can't, at this distance of time, quite remember exactly what official position in the Conservative Party, if any, Max at that stage held. But he was certainly present in Conservative Central Office, and he was a power in the land. And he did *not* approve of education vouchers. And he did *not* approve of Keith Joseph. And he immediately (and very understandably) concluded that the note in question had been written by none other than the young deputy editor of the Daily Notes and Keith Joseph's special adviser – viz. me.

A huge row accordingly erupted in the office, directed at me. And I really didn't have the heart to point out that the note in question was, as a matter of plain fact, nothing whatsoever to do with me.

As it turned out, this was just as well – because, when the whole episode was brought to Mrs Thatcher's attention at her morning meeting a couple of floors lower down the building, she (I was told) surprised everyone by failing to react as expected, and indeed waxed lyrical about the hard work that I and others had done to try to produce a workable education voucher scheme. I very much suspect that it was this episode during the election that was responsible for fixing the fact of my existence in her mind and hence for her reaction to Ferdy Mount's proposal that I should be brought into her Policy Unit in Downing Street straight after the election.

At any rate, the next thing I knew, the election was over, Mrs Thatcher was back in Downing Street, and I was sitting with her and Ferdy in her study having what had been described to me as a job interview. I have had some excruciating job interviews. One was for a fellowship at an Oxford college: I entered the room; the fellowship was ranged around three sides of the room; in the middle of the fourth side, a small coffee table was stationed next to an upright chair; on the coffee table were exam papers; I was asked whether I could teach the subjects they covered; the answers to the first four were 'no', 'no', 'no' and 'no'; I was not selected. Another was for a parliamentary seat: I had what can only be described as a row with one of the questioners; I was not selected; and that was just one of several constituencies in which it was clear from a very early stage that my services were not going to be required. But in the case of Mrs T. and the Policy Unit it was apparent from the start that all was going to be well, since the first thing she said when

I entered the room was 'welcome on board'. The rest of the time was spent discussing the need to bring the Department of Education and Science under control – a subject about which she had strong views, derived from her own tenure as Education Secretary and her sense that 'dear Keith' was allowing himself to be directed by his officials rather than the other way around. All seemed set fair for a stimulating job in No. 10.

Or at least, so it seemed for the first few weeks. But then there was the speech to the scientists. This was one of the worst experiences of my life.

The basic position was entirely benign and unexceptional. Mrs Thatcher was giving a speech to a large and distinguished body of scientists. The government's chief scientific adviser, Robin Nicholson, and I were meant to write it. This was all fine and dandy, because Robin was a charming and knowledgeable man, and he and I were both interested in the question of the relationship between government, applied science and pure science. We wrote what I thought was rather a useful exposition of the main issues, though a bit flat; Ferdy Mount (who was and is a wordsmith of astonishing virtuosity) then turned the first part of it into something almost poetic. All in all, I despatched it to the Prime Minister on the Friday evening with rather a song in my heart. Alas, I didn't know anything at that stage about her methods for making speeches.

At the weekend, I was summoned to Chequers. This was my first-ever visit there. All very exciting for a young person. I beetled down there in our little red Volkswagen.

The choice of car was my first error. When I arrived at the gravel outside the main door, Mrs T. was there to greet me; she surveyed the car with supreme disdain. 'That', she accurately remarked, 'is a German car.' (Actually, it sounded more like 'Churmaan car'.) 'Yes, Prime

Minister,' I replied cheerily, 'and it works.' 'Churmaan!' she repeated, and turned swiftly into the house.

This was not the worst of it. After putting my bags into my bedroom, I came downstairs to find her in the front drawing room – the room in which, at a much later stage in this story, I chatted with Samantha Cameron during the 2015 general election. Mrs T. was standing in front of the fireplace, next to Robin Nicholson. She was saying (and I'm pretty sure that the timing of it was deliberate), 'Yes, and that speech, just like this one, was a dead loss.' From that point onwards, things degenerated. We had an enormous argument about what the speech should say. I could hardly believe that this was all happening – but she wouldn't let up, and I was absolutely convinced, with the certainty of youth, that she was wrong. So we went at it, hammer and tongs. Battle raged through drinks, and then through dinner, despite the very welcome but wholly futile efforts of Denis Thatcher to protect me from her wrath.

As I set off the next morning, I had a conversation with Robin and expressed the view to him that I would probably not be working with him much longer. 'Oh no,' he said, 'you don't understand; she likes a good argument.' He was right. She never subsequently alluded to the event. But she gave the speech, more or less as written. And she seemed perfectly happy to go on having me around.

In time, I came to see that this was entirely consistent with her whole approach to those who worked for her. She wanted to know whether you knew what you were talking about, and whether you could defend it effectively against a barrage of objections. To test this, she was quite prepared to act as the howitzer that chucked the barrage of objections at you. If you quailed, she would dismiss you as 'weak' or 'feeble' (words that were pretty low down on her list of desirable qualities). She was also completely capable of talking straight over you, apparently failing to register the point you were making. But all of this was, from her point of view, nothing more than a dialectical method aimed at finding out whether you could stand your ground or whether the ground would give way under your argument if she chucked enough at you and it. The proof of this lay in the fact that things you had said, and that you thought she hadn't even heard, much less taken in while she was talking over you, would reappear a couple of days later as obvious truths retold by her – without, it has to be said, any attribution whatsoever.

I have often reflected on why this unusual conversational method caused such extraordinary offence to some of her most senior and distinguished colleagues – and why some of them never seemed to understand that this was simply her method for getting to what she would have described as 'the point'. I think the real answer is that, though she certainly had more than her fair share of vanity (as almost all elected politicians do), she had absolutely no pomposity. She didn't think for a moment: 'I'm the PM; this person is an important minister of the Crown; I must behave with due decorum.' She just thought: 'I'm the PM; this chap is meant to be running X; I need to know whether he knows what he's doing' – and away she went.

This (actually endearing) lack of sense of her own and other people's standing could have disastrous consequences. On one occasion she was presented at a Cabinet committee meeting with a slightly convoluted (but not wholly meretricious) argument by a particular secretary of state who was very clearly drawing the argument in question from the brief provided by his departmental officials. Instead of taking the argument head-on, which could well have resulted in her getting lost in some intelligently constructed weeds, Mrs T. employed a series of debating techniques of ascending irrelevance, culminating in a repeated demand to know whether the secretary of state in question had the least idea how much a certain category of person received in social security benefits of a certain kind at a certain date long gone. Needless to say, she – whose memory for fact was genuinely astonishing – did remember this irrelevant detail. Equally inevitably, the secretary of state did not. I sat there thinking, 'Why doesn't he say "Prime Minister, I have absolutely no idea what the answer to that question is, but the question itself is wholly irrelevant to the argument and I really think you need to look at the merits of the argument rather than at these extraneous facts"?' But of course he was much too grand, much too decorous and much too cross to do any such thing. And so you could see her classifying him as 'feeble'. And you could see him notching up another reason for regarding her as impossible.

Nor was it only her senior colleagues with whom she lacked all sense of personal position and pomposity. The same was true when she dealt with far less exalted interlocutors. Like many MPs, she tried to keep Fridays for her constituency work; and so it came to pass that, on a certain Friday, I was asked to accompany her to Finchley in case tricky questions of education policy arose when she met local representatives of the National Union of Teachers at her constituency surgery. We duly arrived at the rather run-down offices of Finchley Conservative Association. After establishing herself at a slightly rickety table with me sitting next to her, Mrs T. indicated that she was ready to see the NUT representatives. In came two young women who, to judge by their body language, were very definitely not admirers. She treated them exactly as she treated her Cabinet colleagues. 'Well,' she said, 'what have you come to say?' – or words to that effect. The two young women, faced with the hated totem right opposite them across the Formica-topped table, lost courage completely; they dried up; their mouths opened slightly, but no sound emerged. She gave them no quarter. After a prolonged pause, she enquired again what they had to say. They had, unfortunately, nothing to say, or were at any rate wholly unable to summon up the many things they had no doubt intended or hoped to say. They got up and left. You could see her thinking 'feeble'.

These, then, were the terms of trade with Mrs T. As a junior member of her Policy Unit, you could say what you liked to her, but whatever you said had to be something you were prepared to defend in the face of heavy fire, and the defence had to be based on first-hand knowledge and clear argument. If you could manage such unforgiving engagement, you had the precious opportunity to talk on more or less equal terms with one of the great global leaders and you had a real chance of gaining her confidence sufficiently in a particular domain to influence her decisions. It was immensely exhilarating.

But there was more to it than just this sense of being 'on the inside'. There was also the sense that she personally cared about you – however amazing this might seem given the disparity of age and position. On the morning after the Brighton bomb, following that ghastly night of death and injury, during which I had left my windowless bedroom and climbed down the fire escape of the Grand Hotel behind Keith Joseph (dressed in a red silk dressing gown and carrying his red box), I came into the auditorium where the party conference was proceeding. Someone rushed up to me to say that the PM had asked for me; when I reached her it became clear that her only purpose was to ascertain that I was in one piece. She had done the same, I think, for the other members of her staff who had been with her in the Grand Hotel. That she should have taken such trouble over us when she needed to give the speech of her life, and after a night in which she had almost lost her life, was infinitely flattering and touching. It was indeed the speech of her life, expressing all the indomitable courage and resolute determination that made her what she was. As I stood listening to her in the hall, Keith came up beside me. I looked over at him, and saw the tears rolling down his face.

And of course it wasn't just the level of engagement or the flattering sense that she cared. It was also the sense of being part of a mission that made those three years in Downing Street so enthralling. Looking back on it now, one can ask what that mission was. We certainly thought we were doing something, making progress, changing things. But what were we – what was she – really doing? In what direction were we progressing? What kind of change were we bringing about?

Accounts of the Thatcher mission have varied widely. Some have suggested that she was a free marketeer, seeking to roll back the frontiers of the state in order to increase personal independence; others have said that she was really trying to centralise power, crush the unions and weaken intermediate institutions such as local government; on yet another account – provided, as it happens, by my mother – Mrs T.'s mission was essentially a moral or psychological one, to restore in Britain the vigorous virtues that had been sapped away by decades of beer, sandwiches and Butskellism. In Charles Moore's authoritative biography, one can find elements of all of these themes. No doubt the debate about what was really, in retrospect, the core of her ambition and of her achievement will continue for many years to come. But, as I recollect what it felt like from the inside of her policy machine, my sense is that any account of the positive result she was trying to achieve is bound to miss the essential point.

To me, at least, she seemed then – and she still seems to me now – to have been principally interested in solving problems. The list of problems wasn't invented by her; it was commonly recognised even by many people who were very far from being naturally sympathetic towards her. There were the trade union barons, who were capable of holding the country to ransom either in the interests of their members or in the interests of an ideological crusade, with devastating effects on our economy. There were nationalised industries that lost huge amounts of money and produced cars or aircraft or ships or services that no one wanted to buy. There were local authorities, some of which were aiming at something close to revolution and others of which were either wildly extravagant or were running services (including housing and schools) that were seriously substandard. All of these bread-and-butter problems had the cumulative effect of costing UK taxpayers an enormous amount, causing deficits and public borrowing, and making the country pretty much a laughing stock across the globe.

The overwhelming impression I had, working for Mrs T. day by day, was that if you wanted to get her attention and persuade her to take a certain approach you needed to identify a real-life problem like one of these and then suggest a way of dealing with it. Practical solutions to real and commonly acknowledged problems were at a premium. Dreams of how to make something that was already OK even better were at a discount. And ideological imperatives were just about absent. I think this is a great part of why she was able to win elections: she wasn't asking people to sign up for some theoretical analysis invented by Keith Joseph; instead, she was asking people to decide who was most likely to solve problems that she, and they, thought were crying out for a solution; and that was a kind of question that the British electorate were prepared to answer – and they answered in her favour on every occasion she put it to them.

This, I think, explains why commentators frequently complain about the inconsistencies in her approach. When it came to the unions or the local authorities, she was happy to centralise power. When it came to housing or schools, she was happy to hand power over to families and individuals. When it came to nationalised industries, she aimed at privatisation and rolling back the frontiers of the state. But when it came to defence, she was dead set on increasing the role and power of the state. If you'd asked her why and how she could think all of these things at once, she would have looked at you with blank incredulity: in each case, she was simply doing what she thought would best solve the particular practical problem in hand. She was clear that you couldn't fight the Russians with education vouchers, and you couldn't tame Derek Hatton or Arthur Scargill just by giving homeowners the right to buy or union members the right to ballot. This willingness to adopt different means to reach different ends was a great part of what made working for her exhilarating. This is why we had the sense that we were helping to solve real problems, that we were making progress – that we were really getting somewhere.

Does this mean that there was no underlying philosophy, that Keith Joseph's great endeavour to promote the social market was an irrelevance, that Mrs T. was just a 'whatever works on the day' politician?

I don't think so. Because, while there was no theoretical goal and a great willingness to adopt solutions appropriate to the solving of particular problems, there were some trademark approaches. She left us in no doubt of her belief that, by and large, markets, free enterprise and individual endeavour were the great engines of prosperity; that socialism and command economies and welfare dependencies were enemies of prosperity; and that the problems of the UK originated in attitudes and institutions that acted to entrench socialism and dependency rather than fostering free enterprise and individual endeavour. And she was very definitely a fiscal conservative. She had thoroughly absorbed – indeed, I think she believed with her whole soul – the idea that you couldn't spend money you hadn't got, and that this applied ultimately as much to states as it did to households.

How do I know these things about her approach? Is it because, Keith Joseph-style, she suggested reading matter for us to absorb? Is it because she gave us, orally or in her written responses to our notes, perfectly formed lectures about the theory of the thing? Most certainly not. But somehow, amidst the remorseless pressure of events and of practical problem-solving, her basic attitudes did very forcefully transmit themselves in what she said and wrote and in what she left unsaid and unwritten. I very well knew that, to persuade her of a particular course of action, I needed to be sure not only how and why it would solve a particular practical problem but also how and why it was the sort of action that would tend over time to advance free enterprise and individual endeavour. You simply would not have dreamed of sending her a note which advocated a solution that was based on any other approach.

This was the background against which I found myself working on local government finance. I can't at this distance in time remember how or why I came to be allocated that task. But it was certainly something that needed attention from the Policy Unit.

The system was a total mess. The grants from central government to local government had been designed in a way that encouraged additional expenditure by local government, because local government got a percentage of each additional pound it spent from central government. Many local government leaders concluded, reasonably enough, that they might as well spend more of other people's money on their own populations. This had led to an enormous money-go-round. Worse still, successive governments (from the time when Tony Crosland said 'the party's over' onwards) had tried to constrain the expenditure by adding complicated new features to the grant system such as 'negative marginal rates of grant' for councils that spent above certain thresholds. But the question then arose: what is a reasonable threshold for council X or council Y? And this in turn had led to a system of criteria for grants so complicated that no minister could conceivably be expected to understand or predict what the computer would spew up if you made a particular change in a particular year.

It was the complexity and irrationality of the grant system, together with the tendency of far-left councils to take huge amounts of money from local businesses until they had virtually squeezed them out from their areas, that led to the feeling on my part that we really needed a complete change in the method of financing local government. And Mrs T. agreed. If ever there was a problem that needed sorting out, then this was one – and sort it out she would. Charles Moore has charted the sequel in his biography of Mrs Thatcher much more accurately than I could hope to do myself after all of these years. He brings out the fact that, contrary to popular suspicion, neither John Redwood (then the head of the Policy Unit) nor I were as keen as some others on the poll tax as part of the change in the local government finance system; though I certainly cannot claim to have had the foresight that led Nigel Lawson (then Chancellor of the Exchequer) and David Wolfson (then Mrs T.'s chief of staff) to predict that the tax itself would prove to be a disaster. I was happy to support the replacement of domestic rates by the new tax as a part of an overall reform that radically simplified the grant system and removed the intrinsic incentives for councils to overspend other people's money, so long as the number of losers and the severity of their losses could be constrained.

It was, as we now know, a total failure – which the Major administration was quite right to undo. And it undoubtedly contributed in a significant way to the destruction of Mrs T. What we shall never know is whether it would have been anything like as much of a problem if it had been introduced gradually as originally intended. Two big issues would have remained: the fact that it was, for all but the poorest, a flat tax which cost the same for millionaires as for middle-income owners; and the fact that it bore heavily on the large number of middle-income families with adult children living at home. Whether a tax with these two characteristics would ever have been regarded as fair,

I now doubt. But the thing that really turned it into a disaster was the decision – made long after my time, following an over-enthusiastic reception of the policy at a Conservative Party conference – to introduce it in one fell swoop, thereby imposing impossible strains on family budgets for those families who were significant losers. That made the abstract question of unfairness poignant and real and immediate, and ultimately intolerable.

Looking back on this episode, which has been more or less hung round my neck for the rest of my time in politics, I have learned two very important lessons from it. The first is that the demand for fairness doesn't just apply to systems as a whole (e.g. the tax system as a whole) but also to each particular part of a system. Electorates in a democracy just won't accept (and they are probably right not to accept) any one item that goes beyond the limits of the fair, regardless of how far other features of the whole system compensate for the unfairness of that one item. And the second thing I learned from what happened after I had left is that, even if you might be able to get people to accept certain changes over time, if you introduce a sudden change that falsifies expectations you are very likely to generate an unsustainable amount of opposition. Perhaps, in the end, these two points meld into one another, because a sudden change that falsifies expectations is in itself a kind of unfairness; people feel that it isn't fair if they've built their lives on one set of expectations and some government comes along and disrupts that.

But of course, at the time, these rather belated recognitions didn't trouble me. Indeed, nothing much troubled me other than the thought that, sooner or later, I'd have to give up this charmed existence in Mrs T.'s Policy Unit.

What was it, I wonder, that made it so rewarding to be a member of this team? In part, of course, it was the proximity to power – the sense that, if you could get traction with the boss, you could help to change the world. Peter Hennessy, some years later, produced a book called *The Hidden Wiring* about the way that government works; on its cover is a photo of one of Mrs T.'s meetings in the Cabinet Room; and there, sitting on a chair at the back of the room is a rather youthful me; it was intoxicating at such a young age to be that close to the scene of the action. But at least as important was the milieu in which I found myself in the Policy Unit.

The unit was by no means the exclusive source of direct policy advice to the Prime Minister. Within No. 10, she had not only her private office, staffed by the highest-flying civil servants (two of whom were later to become heads of the civil service), but also her advisers on foreign policy, who were distinguished diplomats – and of course her economic adviser, Alan Walters, who taught me an enormous amount about economic forecasting and macroeconomic relationships. During almost all the time I was in the building, Alan was locked in dispute with the Treasury (a condition of affairs that had preceded my arrival and continued, indeed intensified, after I left). In my time, the essence of the dispute seemed to be that the Treasury believed its models, whereas Alan believed that models produced whatever results the equations in them told them to produce, and that the equations were written by people who had certain theories; so the models were really just telling you what these particular theories were predicting. His tests for things like whether the economy was really heating up or cooling down were much more anecdotal. For example, he had worked out that, in an age before Uber, the use of taxis was the ultimate discretionary expenditure: when people are feeling hard up, they can easily walk, take a bus or train, or drive themselves to where they need to go; but when people are feeling well-off there isn't, or at least wasn't then, an alternative nearly so convenient as a taxi. So he regularly took taxis and asked taxi-drivers how business was doing. If their business was booming he concluded that the economy in the relevant city was hot, and if the taxi-drivers were glum he concluded that the economy was cool, regardless of what the Treasury model was saying. I imagine that it was exactly this sort of sophisticated simplicity that made Mrs T. so inclined to trust Alan and her foreign policy advisers and her first-rate private secretaries like Charles Powell, Robin Butler, Michael Scholar and Andrew Turnbull, all people who wore a lot of learning lightly.

These senior and distinguished Downing Street advisers were complemented by other 'irregulars' who had one kind of access or another to her – sometimes performing immensely important tasks, like the first-hand information that David Hart gave her about the pitched battles of the miners' strike. But the Policy Unit – while essentially precluded from giving advice on foreign policy and macroeconomics, and while consisting of people far less experienced and younger than some of these other advisers – nevertheless did, at least in my time, play a serious role. We sat in rooms on the second floor towards the front of the house, occupying much the same terrain that unit was to occupy during the Cameron years. I myself shared an office with the remarkable Christopher Monckton – a man who had previously been editor of the Catholic journal *The Universe* and whose interests were indeed catholic to the point of being universal. Christopher obtained the most lovely pictures from the Government Art Collection, and we sat surrounded by them in this beautifully furnished eighteenth-century room with its tall windows looking onto Downing Street, directly above the Patronage Secretary, who was responsible for advising on ecclesiastical and academic appointments. While the Patronage Secretary received a seemingly unending stream of interesting-looking ecclesiastical visitors, Christopher waged war on various parts of Whitehall. His scope was vast, taking on projects as widely dispersed as privatising the water boards and replacing long thin ships with short fat ships (about which almost the entire naval establishment disagreed with him, and about which he turned out to be right).

Down the corridor, also at the front of the building, lay what was (when I first arrived) Ferdy Mount's office. Ferdy was not only my direct boss as head of the Policy Unit but was also a friend of my parents, and hence in some sense or other of a different generation. However, he is the least pompous of people – perhaps that was part of the secret of the success of his relationship with Mrs T. – and, from the start, he treated all of us as colleagues rather than subordinates. As well as his miraculous facility with the English language, Ferdy established an at-mosphere of civilisation and calm. He was to be found at his desk after lunch, reading state papers while smoking a cigar and chuckling gently over the latest 'Rolls-Royce minute' that had come purring over from the Cabinet Secretary, Robert Armstrong. He guided the unit with quiet delicacy, and somehow found over and over again the words in which Mrs T. could adequately express her problem-cracking mission.

Ferdy's deputy, Nick Owen, rapidly became and has since remained a lifelong friend. He had been Keith Joseph's chief economist when Keith was Secretary of State for Industry, and had (I imagine) come to the Policy Unit with Keith's endorsement. He was and is a micro-economist of considerable distinction, whose notes on infrastructure, trade, agriculture, industry and procurement (including defence pro-curement) were models of concision and clarity. His wry humour and gentle goodwill complemented Ferdy's and added to the urbanity and charm of the unit.

In time, Ferdy brought into the unit the formidable figure of John Redwood, who then (upon Ferdy's move back into journalism and the literary world) became its head. The world now knows John as an MP of long standing, a former Cabinet and shadow Cabinet minister, a contender for the leadership of the Conservative Party, a leading and highly articulate Brexiteer, an important investment banker, industrialist and academic. What the world, or at least much of it, does not know is the warmth, humour and generosity of this much misunderstood colleague and friend. Having worked closely with him, not only during these years in the Policy Unit but also at Rothschild when we were beginning the international privatisations that swept the world in the late 1980s and 1990s, I can testify to the presence of these qualities – and also to the huge intellectual and practical energy that he brought to the unit, leading us onward, involving us in a continuing discussion of every important domestic issue that came across his desk, pushing forward the programme of trade union reform, privatisation, popular capitalism and public expenditure control that was so much a hallmark of those years.

And this was not all. A series of other remarkable figures passed through the unit or came to remain during my time there – John Wybrew from Shell, David Pascall from BP, Bob Young from manufacturing industry, Peter Shipley and Hartley Booth specialising in social policy. Two in particular stand out in my memory – perhaps because they too have become lifelong friends.

The first of these, David 'Two Brains' Willetts, who was already a friend from university days and who was to become in due course a close colleague in opposition and in government, arrived as a secondee from the Treasury. He quickly established himself as the resident guru on health and social security, producing analyses of exceptional clarity. Together with John Redwood and Nick Owen, he contributed an academic precision and detachment to the proceedings of the unit. This was a splendid counterpoise to the robust industrial logic and huge emotional energy applied by Peter Warry, the second figure. Of all the remarkable people in the unit, Peter was perhaps the most unusual.

With degrees in engineering, economics and law (not to mention a sideline in ancient ceramics), he used his wide experience in different industrial sectors to take on a series of battles with bureaucrats who were trying to sustain what he regarded as entirely unsustainable subsidies to nationalised industries, and did so with a mixture of charm and pugnacity that I have never seen equalled in any administrative encounter anywhere in the world.

Working day by day amongst these subtle and serious but also engaging, lively-minded and generous-spirited people as we drove forward the agenda – liberating enterprise, opening up the economy, pruning away layers of bureaucracy, and pressing forward reform of the public services and the welfare system – I felt that I was doing my bit to help Mrs T. slay the dragons she was determined to slay. There was a sense of making history, and doing so in the best of company.

There was also the endless fascination of dealing with the bureaucracy. One of the great challenges facing any serious politician is how to engage effectively with officialdom, as a representative, as a legislator, as a special adviser or as a minister. This requires emotional insight as much as (in some cases, more than) intellectual grasp. The person facing you frequently has what you, as a politician, do not have – the immediate power to make something happen, or indeed to prevent it happening through inaction. The ability of the machine to absorb political prodding, and to react by doing... nothing, is almost infinite. So you have to feel what is going on in the bureaucratic mind: this person opposite is an equivalent centre of self, with their own preoccupations, not necessarily directly related to the ostensible subject of the conversation. To succeed, you have to know when to talk and when to listen.

In the spring of 1984, I was sitting next to my old friend Richard Ehrman at a large table in an anonymous office high up in Tothill Street, near St James's Park. Richard was then the special adviser to the Employment Secretary, Tom King. We were trying to produce a White Paper on employment, later to be entitled *Training for Jobs.* The situation out there in the real world was dire. Unemployment – and, in particular, long-term youth unemployment – was appallingly high and appallingly persistent. The labour market was just not providing enough jobs to employ all those who wanted work – despite the fact that the price of labour should theoretically have adjusted to the point where supply and demand for it equalled one another. Something was getting in the way.

I had been sitting in meeting after meeting to discuss why this was happening. One of the reasons was clearly that we were failing to train young people to do the jobs that would make it worthwhile for employers in viable industries to take them on. This was something that the Prime Minister wanted changed – and changed fast. So my remit was to pull, push, persuade and cajole the Department of Employment into producing radical change. Tom King agreed wholeheartedly with the Prime Minister's aim. So Richard's remit was broadly the same. But he had another task – which was to prevent me from alienating the officials of the department, on whose goodwill he and Tom depended.

Richard and I produced one draft of a White Paper. It is safe to say that the Department of Employment officials were not keen on our draft. They thought it was far too political a document – not suitable, they said, for publication as a government paper. They had produced their own. The difference, in truth, is not that one was less political than the other. It is that ours was radical, but amateur, whereas theirs was professional, but unadventurous. We had a meeting with Tom to discuss the conflicting drafts. The Permanent Secretary of the department, the majestic Michael Quinlan, produced an irenic solution drawn, classically, from the cricketing world: 'Mr Letwin and Mr Ehrman', he told Tom, 'have produced a Botham draft; officials have produced a Boycott draft; what we need is a Gower draft, combining the best of each.' Tom (more apt to use naval metaphors) had most willingly accepted this method of steering through what he was fond of calling 'troubled waters'. So here we were, the officials and Richard and me, trying to put together a draft that combined the best of each.

I was very conscious of the danger that our radicalism would in fact be watered down so far as to make the 'Gower draft' indistinguishable from the previous official 'Boycott draft'. The officials were equally concerned that the new draft should avoid what they saw as the naïvety of our original. So we were at it, hammer and tongs. Of course, the discussion maintained every conceivable courtesy, but the argument was vigorous. At a certain point, Richard smuggled me a hand-written note. When I glanced down at it, I observed that it contained the words 'do not tax these good people too far'. Clearly, Richard was concerned that I was about to provoke a reaction which he would not be able to contain. So I moderated the pace and strength of my attack bowling. The result was unlikely to be fully satisfactory to the PM – but there would always be another day, because she would have to approve it before it was published and I would be able to send her a covering note when it was submitted to her. So discretion at this point was probably the better part of valour. As I left the department and walked back to Downing Street, I reflected – not for the first time, and most definitely not for the last – that the art of dealing with civil servants (whose company I almost always enjoy) is to find a way of sharing their civilised mode of conversation while maintaining scepticism about the establishment defeatism to which their life inside the machine constantly threatens to make them prone.

Of course, it wasn't all plain sailing. It's possible now, knowing how it all turned out, to fall into the error of supposing that it was an easy ride. It was nothing of the kind. I remember vividly the weekend when

I was sent home to read all the books I could find on the General Strike – because we thought that the following week would see the docks and the railways coming out in support of Arthur Scargill and his striking coal-miners. There seemed every chance that, despite all the stocking of coal and the careful management of the electricity supply industry to keep the lights on throughout the coal strike, we would be defeated (as Edward Heath's government had been defeated) by the sheer level of industrial disruption. In the event, the dock strike collapsed. But it was a close shave. At another stage, there was something alarmingly close to a revolution in Derek Hatton's Liverpool – with Hatton himself, as I saw at first hand, surrounded by a group of heavies who were clearly more Bolshevik than Menshevik. There was also, throughout my time in the Policy Unit, ghastly, persistent, entrenched unemployment. I sat for hour after hour in committees attempting to understand why the labour market wasn't providing enough jobs; and I travelled across large parts of the country, investigating Youth Training Schemes, Community Programmes and any other projects I could find that offered even the slightest hope that we might be able to get people back to work. It really wasn't an easy time at all. But I think what made it so satisfying was that we all in the Policy Unit believed – and certainly I believed – that the direction was right. We really felt that we were making progress.

And yet, when I reflect now on those years and on the problems we helped Mrs T. to address, I am struck by the shaming sense that, at the strategic level, we did little or nothing to fill what I now see as the vital gap in her understanding and in her programme. We grasped her agenda, and we assisted her in driving it forward, to what I believe was the great advantage of the country. But we did not confront her with the condition of those right at the bottom of the heap, the families in entrenched poverty, unemployment, poor schooling, addiction, debt spirals, family breakdown.

How did this happen? How did it come about that Margaret Thatcher herself and those of us working in those crucial years in the mid-1980s so spectacularly failed to see the elephant in the room?

I spoke with her on many occasions about those who had been failed by the education system, and she made it abundantly clear at any opportunity that she was determined to Do Something about it. She fully recognised that some people were left wrecked on the shoals of inadequate public services and a wrongly designed welfare system and she was more than willing to take administrative steps that would begin to improve the welfare system and the public services – whether by sponsoring the efforts of Norman Fowler and David Willetts to remove marginal rates of benefit withdrawal over 100 per cent, or by introducing Family Credit (the first-ever in-work benefit) to help cure the 'unemployment trap', or by introducing the Youth Training Scheme for young unemployed people, or by leading older people back into work through the Community Programme. I spent a considerable part of my time in the Policy Unit occupied with each of these items, often working with David. I always had the strong sense that we would receive all the backing we needed from Mrs T. to make these things happen. And Ferdy Mount (who had by far the greatest emotional intelligence about Mrs T.'s deepest instincts) must have shared that perception, because he enthusiastically backed Richard Ehrman and me to write the first draft of the employment White Paper that, alongside Richard, I had debated with officials at the Department of Employment; indeed, Ferdy had contributed to that draft his usual dose of poetry ('unemployment is man-made').

There was also one preoccupation of Mrs Thatcher's at that time which definitely echoes Iain Duncan Smith's 'Breakdown Britain' analysis, or the emphasis that David Cameron and Theresa May have placed on the 'life chances' agenda. This was her repeated attempt to inject energy into what was called 'family policy'. She absolutely recognised that the conditions of life in which the child grows up will almost always have a huge influence on the character and prospects of the adult. From this, at least in part, sprang her deep and oft-expressed belief in marriage. No doubt, there was a religious and socially conservative element to this belief; but it was clear from much that she said in discussing family policy that she saw the family as a great engine for social progress or (in the case of dysfunctional families) for social regress. In that sense, at least, she certainly recognised that children are formed by their family background.

However, as I look back on that period, I am ashamed for her, and ashamed of myself, that, unlike Keith Joseph, I don't believe she ever really took on board the extent to which some people are victims of the society in which they grow up and subsist, and I don't believe that at that time I did either. She was so keen to re-emphasise personal responsibility and the 'vigorous virtues' that she, and we who were infused with her spirit, missed the other side of the equation – that some people in some conditions of life just aren't able, without a massive amount of external help of the most intrusive and paternalistic and sympathetic kind, to escape from those conditions of life.

I think, reviewing the whole history of the Conservative Party from 1979 to 2016, that this failure to recognise the imprisonment of some souls by their social circumstances was one of the two most important causes of the political malaise from which we Conservatives suffered in the years after 1997 and which was not finally cured until David Cameron arrived on the scene in the years after 2005. And I think it was also this failure of imagination that made the (technically inaccurate) accusation that Mrs T. thought there was 'no such thing as society' so damaging. In my experience, it's often this way with inaccurate accusations: they really stick when, under the superficial inaccuracy, there lurks some deeper truth. I believe that Jim Callaghan, in relation to the strikes during the 'winter of discontent' that led to the end of his premiership, never quite said the now famous words 'Crisis, what crisis?'; but the inaccurate attribution stuck because underneath the inaccuracy lay the truth that, after undermining Barbara Castle's *In Place of Strife* White Paper, he failed over several years to produce any answer to the industrial unrest that proved his undoing. In a similar way, I'm pretty sure that the pundits somehow intuited that, whatever Mrs T.'s words were and whatever the context actually made them mean, she and we did in some deep sense underestimate the power of social forces. And they were right. And I'm afraid that, at that time, I was unwittingly part of the problem – though I'm happy to say that, at a later stage in this story, I think I did some things to help others forge a solution.

What makes this profound gap in Mrs T.'s understanding of our society so strange is that there were actually two sets of very senior ministers in her government who did, I think, understand the extent of the cycle of deprivation and the extent to which some of our fellow citizens are trapped in that cycle. The first such 'set' consisted of one member, namely Keith Joseph. And the second set consisted of the so-called 'wets' – of whom we might take Ian Gilmour as a distinguished example. Why didn't the shared perception of these two, Keith and Ian, coming as they did from very different angles, have any real impact on Mrs T.'s consciousness at that time? I think the answer is different in each case. So far as Keith was concerned, she treasured his championship of the free market but it was all too easy to dismiss his preoccupation with the cycle of deprivation as just an eccentricity. Meanwhile, she was inclined to ignore the valid social message promulgated by Ian and the other distinguished 'wets' on the grounds that they had failed to re-alise how far Britain needed to be rescued and could be rescued by free markets and sound money and sound public finances; they were, in her view, 'wet' – and therefore 'wrong'; it simply didn't occur to her that they might be 'wet' and 'wrong' about economic policy while being civilised, compassionate and right about social policy.

But it is not enough of an explanation to say that Keith Joseph's preoccupation with the conditions of life of the 'underclass' could be dismissed as one of 'dear Keith's eccentricities' or that the Gilmourites, with their concern for those in our society who were imprisoned by circumstance, could be dismissed as 'wet'. The question remains: why was there an inclination to dismiss these preoccupations and concerns? Why didn't Mrs T., why didn't we in the Policy Unit, enthusiastically take up where Keith had left off? Why didn't we see the question of life chances as an issue every bit as important as the rescuing of the British economy, the liberating of enterprise, the improvement of public services and the control of public expenditure?

To answer these questions, one has to look at the origins of the ideas that animated Thatcherism.

CHAPTER 3

THE INTELLECTUAL ORIGINS OF THATCHERISM

It's a slightly uncanny feeling for me to write about the intellectual origins of Thatcherism because they are, to a very considerable extent, my own intellectual origins. This strange coincidence comes about because although I grew up in the company of my parents as most people do, the friends gathered around my parents' table were as close as you can get to the people who gave Thatcherism its intellectual foundations.

Both of my parents (Bill and Shirley Letwin) were academics. They met at the University of Chicago as very young students in the late 1930s, under a programme designed to take bright youngsters out of bad schools at an early age. They both came from Ukrainian Jewish families who had emigrated to the US in the aftermath of the Russian Revolution.

The University of Chicago in the 1930s and early 1940s was in an extraordinary state. Under the inspiration of Robert Hutchins, a radical president, and his coadjutor Mortimer Adler, it had developed an approach to liberal learning which was, so far as I am aware, unique. For undergraduates, this was centred on the 'great books programme' which Adler had brought over from Columbia University, in which students (regardless of the disciplines in which they were majoring) were led to read a large collection of the philosophical and other works thought to have formed the intellectual background to Western civilisation. I still possess the series of the great books in fine hardback editions. But this, though unusual at the time, has been copied by a number of other universities in North America. The really exceptional feature of Chicago was the fact that graduate students in the humanities and social sciences (which both of my parents became before reaching the age of twenty) were able to participate in what was known as the Committee on Social Thought.

The characters who inhabited and flowed through the committee in those years were truly an astonishing assembly. I'm sure that someone either has written or will write a full and detailed account; but I can give a flavour for what was going on if I list just some of the figures involved. There was John Nef, the economic historian who changed the understanding of the Industrial Revolution; there was Stanley Bennett, the historian from Cambridge who can lay claim with a few Cambridge contemporaries to having invented social history; there was T. S. Eliot and Saul Bellow; there was the literary critic Joan Bennett; there was the classicist, horseman and farmer David Grene and the sociologist Ed Banfield. After the war, in 1950, they were joined by the economist and political theorist F. A. Hayek. This was an atmosphere rich in every form of intellectual oxygen.

Perhaps even more remarkably, the committee and the faculties of the University of Chicago subsisted in an open network. And so too did my parents. Edward Levi (later himself president of the university and Attorney General of the United States) gave my father his first academic job at the Law Faculty, but he was part of a continuing conversation with the members of the committee and their graduate students; so was Milton Friedman, then and subsequently teaching in the Economics Faculty, who taught my father economics and became a close friend of both of my parents; and, from 1949 onwards, there was the brooding figure of Leo Strauss, who held a chair outside the committee and never had any significant influence on the development of liberal free market politics, but whose anti-liberal, Platonist theorising provided a useful counterpoint. Of all these noteworthy characters, it is I think Friedman, Hayek and Banfield who give the University of Chicago its claim to be one of the three institutions that provided Thatcherism with its intellectual foundations.

After the war in the Pacific, during which my father worked in airborne intelligence and my mother for the State Department and various universities, they both returned to Chicago and the committee – but then both came to the London School of Economics to continue their doctoral work. Later, both taught at the LSE during various periods when they were living in the UK.

It is often supposed that the LSE is an institution of the left. And indeed there is some basis for this view since its originators in the 1890s, the Webbs and George Bernard Shaw, were the original Fabians; moreover, its students (and even some of its staff) played a significant role in the crypto-revolutionary era of the late 1960s, again in a distinctively leftist direction. But the LSE has also been the scene of thinking of a very different kind. When my parents arrived, they came to an institution containing three giants of the intellectual right. Hayek was still in residence, at the Economics Faculty (not yet having travelled in the opposite direction across the Atlantic to the Committee on Social Thought in Chicago). So too was the philosopher of science and political theorist Karl Popper, in the Philosophy Faculty. And, in the Government Department, there was Michael Oakeshott. It was these three characters who gave the LSE its claim to be the second of the three institutions that helped to form the intellectual foundations of Thatcherism.

There is, however, one other institution that has to be included in any attribution of the intellectual origins of Thatcherism – and that is the Institute of Economic Affairs (IEA). Founded in 1952 by the businessman Antony Fisher, its mission from an early stage was to promulgate the kind of free market economics being propounded by Hayek and Friedman. It had the great good luck to be led in this by three friends of my parents – Ralph Harris, Arthur Seldon and John Wood.

Because my parents were intimately connected and remained connected throughout their lives with all three of these institutions (Chicago, the LSE and the IEA), they formed – whether intentionally or otherwise – a kind of intersection set in the Venn diagram. As I grew up, my parents' various homes were filled with all of these people – and with an array of many other academics, journalists and politicians. Their hospitality became a sort of salon for the thinkers of the free market right, though always with the spice of some participants whose views were of a different hue. From a ridiculously early age, I was allowed (perhaps even encouraged) to participate in the lively discussions that characterised their dinner table. It was a sort of university of free market thought, right there on your plate.

But what was it that I learned in this 'university'? What was the essence of the thinking that characterised Hayek, Friedman, Banfield, Popper, Oakeshott, Harris, Seldon and Wood? There were, of course, enormous differences between them. No serious scholar would allow the suggestion that they were saying the same thing as one another, or even that they were thinking about quite the same topics as one another. But I think that some important common themes do emerge.

To begin with, there is the focus on freedom. I think it is fair to say that, for all of these thinkers in their various ways, the concept of freedom is fundamental. To grasp the significance, the emotional impact of this concept at that time to these people, one has to remember that the formative political experiences of their adult lives were Hitler and Stalin. For them, fascism and communism were not abstractions or items of merely historical interest. Rather, these were the enemies under whose shadows they had lived. Starting their careers in the 1930s, 1940s and 1950s, recent and current exhibitions of totalitarian tyranny were vividly before their eyes. The assumption we now (falsely) make that our own freedom can be taken for granted was not something for which they were remotely tempted to fall. They had seen the bombs descending, heard the gunshot, witnessed the concentration camps, the Gulag Archipelago and the Great Leap Forward, and known the fear of all-out nuclear exchange. So, in inter-related ways, they carved out theories of freedom.

Hayek's theory of freedom is perhaps the best known. In two great works, *The Constitution of Liberty* and *The Road to Serfdom*, he made two fundamental arguments about the connection between freedom and economic activity. The first argument, contained in *The Constitution of Liberty*, was that economic prosperity ultimately depends on free markets, which are themselves the product of a liberal society governed by the rule of law which makes it possible for individuals to engage in the orderly transactions of a market economy. The second argument, contained in *The Road to Serfdom*, was that the social freedom of the individual (freedom of expression, freedom of choice of lifestyle, freedom from arbitrary actions of the state) is intimately linked to economic freedom – because economic activity is inextricably intertwined with all other forms of activity, and a state that controls all forms of economic activity will therefore inevitably acquire power over every other aspect of a citizen's life.

It was as a schoolboy, long before I actually read either of these books, that I absorbed from Hayek's talk at my parents' table these two basic ideas. Something about this tall, somewhat austere figure seemed to me at that young age to hint at romance – perhaps because I heard that he had been trained in the Austrian cavalry, or perhaps because I was told he might get (as he did indeed eventually get) a Nobel Prize for his technical work in economics; I can't be sure, at this remove, what it was that gave him his allure, but allure he certainly had, and this somehow made the ideas stick in my youthful mind. I got the gist: that social freedom depends on economic freedom, and that economic prosperity depends on social freedom under the rule of law; economic freedom and social freedom are ultimately two sides of the same coin, and the coin is prosperity.

This was different from, but closely allied to, Milton Friedman's argument about the relationship between free markets and freedom of choice. I recall, as a child, being taken by this diminutive and infinitely sweet-natured Nobel laureate and his wife Rose, also a distinguished economist, from their house in rural Vermont (where Ed and Laura Banfield also lived) into town to be bought a splendid American Indian headdress. As this magnificent item was being purchased, Milton gave me an explanation of the method by which price information is transferred in a free market which many years later appeared in a slightly different form in his book *Free to Choose*. 'If you buy enough of these feathers,' he explained,

> someone somewhere will run out of feathers and the price will go up, so someone else somewhere else who wouldn't previously have bothered to collect feathers will start to do so – and all of this will happen without anyone anywhere deciding just how many feathers are needed or how many people should spend how much time collecting them.

About fifteen years on, when I was an undergraduate, I reminded Milton of this episode; he told me that he had recently returned from China, where the Minister of Supply had asked him who controlled supply in America – and, after some thought, he had replied: 'The Chicago Commodity Exchange.' The point, here, is that a free market economy allows people to make choices about what they do because, instead of central planning being required to run their lives for them, the free choices of individuals and the effects of these choices on prices create the basis for an efficient matching of production to demand. As for Hayek, Friedman saw economic freedom and social freedom as two sides of the coin of prosperity.

It is a matter of huge significance for the development of Thatcherism that these political theories of freedom were developed by two immensely distinguished economists. It is also of huge significance that it was the social and political theories of these economists, Hayek and Friedman, that most influenced Antony Fisher when he set up the IEA around the corner from Parliament in 1955 – and which thereafter guided the thinking of Ralph Harris, Arthur Seldon and John Wood at the institute. Indeed, it is significant that the institute itself was conceived and described as being something that would deal with 'Economic Affairs'. Yes, the theories were essentially social and political, but they were inextricably bound up with economics: hence, almost unconsciously, they were theories about the freedom of economic actors. And as for the non-economic actors, the people locked out of economic activity by conditions of life that rendered them unemployable – what about their freedom? The answer implied, even if never given, was: 'Not a problem we can solve.'

But it wasn't just the economists whose conceptions of freedom left out the victims of social breakdown. Neither Popper nor Oakeshott nor Banfield was an economist; but all three contributed, in their own ways to a conception of social freedom that had no real place for these people.

Like Hayek, Karl Popper emerged from Austria in the late 1930s. Unlike Hayek, he was a Jew (though by race rather than religion) and was therefore lucky to leave when he did – rather strangely coming to the LSE via an academic job in New Zealand. A philosopher of great range, his most important work was probably in the philosophy of science; but he turned his attention also to political theory – and was, alongside Hayek and Friedman, one of the founders of the free market Mont Pelerin Society, with which my parents were also associated, and of which Mrs Thatcher later became a somewhat distant admirer. Popper's great defence of freedom is contained in his book *The Open Society and Its Enemies*. It will probably sound absurd, but it is nevertheless true that I felt physically sick with excitement when I first read *The Open Society* – a literary experience that I have had on only three other occasions, when reading Ryle's *Concept of Mind*, Jolliffe's *Angevin Kingship* and Tolstoy's *Anna Karenina*, all (sadly) before the age of twenty-one; I doubt I am any longer capable of such excitement.

Popper's book is basically directed against theoreticians like Plato, Hegel and Marx, who believe that history is unfolding inevitably towards a desirable end. Popper argues that this unfounded 'historicism' leads such theoreticians to favour a state-sponsored 'official' version of the truth which will supposedly enable society to move smoothly towards the desirable end. And he argues that they are in fact the enemies of progress because real progress can come about only when human beings are able to contest all accounts of truth in a liberal democracy that permits freedom of thought and expression.

In other words, for Popper, the point of freedom is not so much that it delivers economic advantage or personal satisfaction, but rather that it is a precondition for scientific and intellectual progress. This is a powerful and interesting thesis. But of course it is also a thesis that derives from a concern with high culture rather than from a concern with the fate of the most disadvantaged in society. If you were Marx (at least on a good day), you might well reply: 'OK, so you say my view of the state doesn't lead to truth; but truth is less important to the least advantaged than opportunity for self-advancement.' The problem with Popper is not what his thesis tells us about the value of freedom but what it doesn't tell us about the other things we value.

In a different way, the same can be said about Michael Oakeshott's political philosophy. Oakeshott was neither Austrian nor American. He was as English as English could be. For many years a fellow of Caius College, Cambridge, he came as the professor of government to the LSE after a period of semi-covert activity on the Continent during the war in the marvellously named Phantom unit (of which the distinguished journalist Peregrine Worsthorne, another close friend of my parents, had also been a member). He was a pure philosopher in the English Hegelian tradition; he lived partly in a cottage at Langton Matravers in east Dorset and partly in a loft at Covent Garden round the corner from the LSE; he drove what Noël Coward would have described as a half-timbered Austin car, played mah-jong without use of the winds (which he regarded for some reason as 'improper') and wrote in a style of peculiar charm which was all of his own making.

Oakeshott's political theory was constructed around an unwavering scepticism about the capacity of the state to determine the correct course of action for its citizens to take. He argued that, to provide for stability and the rule of law, the state has to be something intrinsically different from any 'enterprise association' (group of people, business or other entity) which pursues a particular aim. The exercise of power by the state can be legitimate, in Oakeshott's view, only if the state itself eschews being such an 'enterprise association', and acts instead as a 'civil association' whose laws (or, in his terms, 'adverbial rules' of conduct) apply fairly and equally to all under all circumstances, regardless of the particular private aims they may have. So, for example, the state may have a law against murder, which benefits all of its citizens, and which applies regardless of whether they are engaged in banking or sailing or running a church; but it cannot legitimately have a law that forces its citizens to engage in banking or sailing or running a church, because this would constitute the state using the power of law to promote a cause desired by only some of its citizens at the expense of others and would therefore be unfair and repressive.

Though cast in very different terms, there is a remarkable similarity between this highly philosophical analysis of Oakeshott and the much more econocentric theories of freedom propounded by Hayek and Friedman. In the end, what all three of these thinkers were arguing – albeit in very different styles and from somewhat different points of view – is that individuals in a society need to be governed by the rule of law, but that the laws should govern the limits within which these individuals go about whatever they choose to be their business rather than attempting to force them to make it their business to do one thing rather than another. Individual choice in; planned economies and planned societies out – just as, for Popper, it was a case of open society in, closed societies out.

And the consequence is that Oakeshott, like Hayek, Friedman and Popper, had absolutely no account of how the state should deal with the problem of those whose conditions of life have locked them out of formulating or implementing enterprises – those who are alienated from the mainstream as a result of being the victims of social break-down. Indeed, Oakeshott implies that it would be positively wrong for the state to take on the project of attempting to rescue these victims from the broken-down conditions in which they are condemned to live, because doing so would turn the state into an 'enterprise association' devoted to pursuing this particular end rather than restricting itself to setting the 'adverbial' rules within which private citizens or voluntary bodies would need to operate if they chose to undertake such an enterprise.

This highly abstract theory was mirrored (I believe, wholly unconsciously) in a much more practical way by Ed Banfield in his famous sociological work, *The Unheavenly City*. By the time I was conscious of my parents' friends, Ed and his wife Laura had moved from the Committee on Social Thought in Chicago to Harvard – and (as well as having a holiday home in Vermont, near the Friedmans) they were living near my parents in Cambridge, Massachusetts during the years when my father was teaching at MIT and my mother at Harvard. Ed was a truly inspiring human being. Tall, stooped, sardonic and kindly, he had as a young man been entirely paralysed by polio; but, starting (I believe) with his eyebrows, he had gradually recovered by sheer willpower the use of his muscles and was when I knew him reasonably mobile.

At Harvard, Ed was surrounded by sociologists, economists and political theorists of one leftist shade or another – including some of my parents' closest friends, such as Krister Stendhal (dean of the Divinity School, later Bishop of Stockholm) and Dan Bell (whose books *The Coming of Post-Industrial Society, The End of Ideology* and *The Cultural Contradictions of Capitalism* were probably the most influential sociological works in twentieth-century America). But Ed was indomitable, and indomitably a man of the right. The argument he made in *The Unheavenly City* was that programmes of social welfare in fact diminished the life chances of the recipients. This, as one might imagine, set the cat squarely amongst the pigeons at a time when Lyndon Johnson's 'Great Society' was engaging in the first large-scale American attempt to match some aspects of Britain's welfare state. But Ed didn't care about cats and pigeons. He cared about evidence, and he had amassed considerable evidence for the proposition that social welfare programmes in American cities had been counter-productive. What didn't occur to him – it is now easy to see in retrospect – was that this may have been caused by the particular *structure* of the welfare programmes in question rather than by welfare programmes as such. But, be that as it may, the movement of ideas from Hayek, via Friedman, Popper and Oakeshott, to Banfield is clear:

- First, freedom is defined in terms of the freedom of economic actors, thereby implicitly ignoring the freedom of those excluded from economic activity by social breakdown.
- Then the efficient functioning of the free market is held to be dependent on the state refraining from interference in the free choices of individuals, thereby ignoring those who are in no position to make such choices because of the conditions of their lives.
- Next, freedom is to be defended as the essential precondition for intellectual progress, thereby ignoring those who are interested in escaping from conditions of misery rather than in making new discoveries.
- Then justice, fairness and social stability are held to depend upon the state refraining from adopting specific enterprises, implicitly even from the enterprise of rescuing individuals from conditions of social breakdown.
- Finally it is argued that programmes of social welfare aimed at such individuals are in any case counter-productive for those individuals.

And all of this, in one form or another, through the nexus of Chicago, the LSE, the Mont Pelerin Society and innumerable other informal networks, including my parents' salons, became the basic framework of thought within which the Institute of Economic Affairs operated in the 1960s and 1970s. And it is out of this basic framework of thought, promulgated most notably by the IEA, that not only Margaret Thatcher's own attitudes, but also the attitudes of those of us who were around her in the 1980s, were formed.

If this is an accurate account, it is little wonder that neither she nor we properly attended to the issues of life chances and social breakdown that so rightly but ineffectually preoccupied both Keith Joseph and the Gilmourite 'wets'. But can the story really have been as simple as this? Are ideas and theories really as powerful as this when it comes to practical politics?

I certainly wouldn't want to claim that practical politics always derives from theory, or even that the attitudes of practical politicians are always affected significantly by a particular group of theorists. I can think of some examples in my political lifetime of significant politicians who have been wholly innocent of any theorising whatsoever. In the time that I watched Willie Whitelaw at work in Whitehall during the 1980s, I never had the slightest sense that he had an interest in political or economic theories; he never referred to them; he never said anything that suggested he was aware of them; and I very strongly suspect that, if anyone had been foolish enough to ask him what he thought about them, the person in question would have been told rapidly enough that 'theory is all very well, but what about the practice?'

But the fact remains that even those in politics who least attend to theories are in fact affected by the nature of the theoretical debate that is going on around them. In the Britain of the 1980s, politicians were talking in terms that would have been wholly unfamiliar to those in the contemporary Kremlin, just as they would have been to the Britain of the Middle Ages. The concepts and the language that are used in practical political discussion do always derive, at least to some extent, from the theoretical discourse of the age and place – and the practical discussion is therefore bound to be affected by the ideological or theological or technical concepts embedded in that theoretical discussion.

What is more, Mrs T. and Keith Joseph and the people around them all the way from the late 1970s onwards did specifically attend to the theoreticians. The IEA (and, once Mrs T. and Keith had set it up, the Centre for Policy Studies, as well as the Conservative Philosophy Group, which gathered in Jonathan Aitken's house) was a meeting point where practical politicians and theoreticians very consciously came together – with an intensity of engagement between the practical and the theoretical that has not really occurred in British Conservative politics since those days. And, in discussion of practical issues with Mrs T. or with Keith, I very frequently found them referring (as if by second nature) to political and economic thinkers. This wasn't restricted to those of whom they approved. On one occasion, I was standing in the private office downstairs in No. 10 rather late in the evening when Mrs T. came down the stairs, plonked a book on the desk of one of the private secretaries and said, 'I have been reading this. It is absolute NONSENSE.' The book turned out to be Schumacher's *Small Is Beautiful* – a collection of essays on ecology and economics that had been published about ten years earlier and which has recently been made fashionable by the somewhat unlikely combination of Steve Hilton and Satish Kumar. When a highly active Prime Minister is spending her time reading theoretical works by economists and is coming to strong views on the validity or invalidity of their theorising then you know that, if ever there was a time when theory directly affected practice, this was it.

It was, indeed, this unusually high level of interaction between theoreticians and practitioners that brought the free market liberal thinkers into the mainstream. In the 1950s and 1960s, Hayek, Friedman, Banfield, Popper, Oakeshott and the IEA were virtually unknown to all but technical economists (and even then it was only Hayek and Friedman who would have been recognised). By the late 1970s, the mediation of their ideas by the politicians – above all, Keith Joseph, Geoffrey Howe and Margaret Thatcher – had brought them into the mainstream in the UK, while a similar transformation would be accomplished a few years later in the USA by Ronald Reagan. By the 1980s, it was not just the professors, nor even just the professors and the politicians, but also the journalists who had become familiar with all of this free market liberal academic literature, and had come to understand it as (and thereby to help to make it) a profound influence on public discourse and political debate.

There is, however, more to this failure to focus sufficiently on social justice than just the high degree of interaction between theory and practice during that phase of British politics. The fundamental reason that both the theoreticians and those of us engaged in practical politics in the 1980s paid much too little attention to life chances and the broken society was that we were all focused instead on the question that preoccupied Hayek, Friedman, Popper and Oakeshott – the question of the proper boundary between where the state ought to be strong and where it ought to leave well alone. And there were, in turn, reasons we were so focused on that question rather than any other.

These reasons fall into two separate but inter-related categories: those that had to do with the global scene, and those that had to do with domestic politics.

As at all other times in our democracy, domestic politics in the mid-1980s was defined not by what the participants agreed about so much as by what they disagreed about. Keith Joseph, in a way that I have come more and more to admire and which I later tried to emulate, was always seeking the 'common ground'. But the media aren't interested in the common ground; they are interested in the field of battle. And elections aren't won and lost on the common ground; to the extent that their outcomes are determined by ideas and policies rather than personalities and issues of competence, they are won or lost on the battlefield of those conflicting ideas and policies.

In the mid-1980s, *both* sides in British politics were fighting over the size of the state. The question was not how far the state could intervene to rescue the least advantaged from the conditions that destroyed their life chances. The question was, instead, how far the state should intervene to support (or, as those on our side of the argument insisted, to fail to support and to succeed only in constraining) the *majority* of the population. This comes back to me most powerfully in the eloquent speech given by Neil Kinnock towards the end of the 1983 general election. He said:

If Margaret Thatcher is re-elected as Prime Minister on Thursday, I warn you. I warn you that you will have pain – when healing and relief depend upon payment. I warn you that you will have ignorance – when talents are untended and wits are wasted, when learning is a privilege and not a right. I warn you that you will have poverty – when pensions slip and benefits are whittled away by a government that won't pay in an economy that can't pay. I warn you that you will be cold – when fuel charges are used as a tax system that the rich don't notice and the poor can't afford. I warn you that you must not expect work – when many cannot spend, more will not be able to earn. When they don't earn, they don't spend. When they don't spend, work dies. I warn you not to go into the streets alone after dark or into the streets in large crowds of protest in the light. I warn you that you will be quiet – when the curfew of fear and the gibbet of unemployment make you obedient. I warn you that you will have defence of a sort – with a risk and at a price that passes all understanding. I warn you that you will be homebound – when fares and transport bills kill leisure and lock you up. I warn you that you will borrow less – when credit, loans, mortgages and easy payments are refused to people on your melting income. If Margaret Thatcher wins on Thursday, I warn you not to be ordinary. I warn you not to be young. I warn you not to fall ill. And I warn you not to grow old.

If we look behind the power of the rhetoric to the substance of the argument, what do we find? Was this a speech in which Kinnock admitted the advantages arising for the vast majority of the population from a free market economy, but challenged Mrs T. on the fate of the people left behind? On the contrary, it was a speech in which Kinnock wanted his listeners to believe that with Mrs T's free market economy, there would be charges for the NHS ('when healing and relief depend upon payment'), educational opportunities restricted to the rich ('when learning is a privilege and not a right'), economic recession ('when many cannot spend, more will not be able to earn'), ruinous spending on strong defence and the nuclear deterrent ('defence of a sort – with a risk and at a price that passes all understanding'), and a visiting of all of these disastrous effects of free market economics on the 'young' and the 'old' alike. It is worth noting that none of the predictions made by Kinnock actually came true: because he trained his guns on the wrong target, he failed to observe the real problem, which was that the free market *can* sustain public services and *does* work for the majority, but doesn't work unaided for everyone.

Yes, there were contrarian voices – and some of them came from directions other than Keith Joseph and the Gilmourite 'wets'. There was Bishop Jenkins of Durham, who was already making the argument of his later book *Market Whys and Human Wherefores* – that trickle-down economics don't work, an argument which I have often found myself thinking about in following years. There was the Archbishop of Canterbury's report *Faith in the City*, which drew attention to the fate of the underclass. But even these warnings were all too easy to ignore because – as rereading *Faith in the City* or another book by Bishop Jenkins, *Dilemmas of Freedom*, today brings home very clearly – they came from people who (even more than the Gilmourites) were sceptical about the whole Thatcherite free market project, and attributed the problems they were witnessing not to the absence of an effective life chances strategy but, like Neil Kinnock, to what they regarded as the fundamental defects of a market (as opposed to what was then called a 'mixed') economy.

So there was a battleground. And you were basically on one side of it or the other. You were either for socialism and the planned economy, or you were for Mrs T. and the free market. Of course, there was Keith Joseph, passionately promoting the free market while muttering darkly about the 'social market' and the 'common ground' and the 'cycle of deprivation'; but that was just 'dear Keith'. For the rest of us, engaged in practical politics, there were just the two sides of the argument, and you had to choose your side. So we chose the side that was right about what would generate prosperity for the vast majority; we chose the side that Hayek and Friedman and Popper and Oakeshott had made intellectually respectable after decades in which socialism in its various forms had dominated the intellectual landscape; we chose sides, and we focused on the things that 'our side' needed to do to make a reality of our hopes for prosperity and progress.

But I think there was one further, more regrettable, feature of our politics in those days that reinforced our tendency to focus on the main battlefield of the free market versus the planned economy and led us to underestimate the effect that social breakdown was having on the life chances of some of our fellow citizens. This feature is captured in the phrase 'one of us'. I can't recall Mrs T. actually using this phrase in my presence on a specific occasion, but I wouldn't have been in the least surprised if she had done – because one certainly had the sense that there was a 'them' and there was an 'us'. In part, of course, this just reflected the fact that there was a battle on between the free marketeers and the planned economy brigade: 'we' were on one side; Neil Kinnock (who was the leader of the opposition during almost all of my time in Downing Street) was on the other side. But the problem was that 'us' came to mean something much narrower than just the Conservative Party or even the government. There was a slight whiff of revolutionary zeal in the air. You knew that you were likely to be classed either as part of the revolution or as part of the reaction – and the reaction consisted not only of those who were out-and-out 'socialists' (a term that Mrs T. used with considerable ferocity) but also of those who were 'weak' and 'feeble'. Of course, this didn't concern Keith, whose moral courage made him indifferent to classifications imposed on him by anyone, including Mrs T., and whose utter loyalty and impeccable free market credentials in any case made it impossible for her or anyone else to classify him as anything except 'one of us'. But, for the rest of 'us', I think there was an implicit sense that if you wanted to be part of the revolution you had to display sufficient revolutionary zeal to avoid being seen as 'weak' or 'feeble'. I don't want to overplay this: no one ever said anything to me that made this in any way explicit, and the atmosphere certainly wasn't anything like that created by genuine sectarians. But there was nevertheless a tinge of the sectarian and more than a tinge of the partisan.

I have come to think, subsequently, that even the slightest hint of the sectarian and even the mildest forms of partisanship are a very bad thing in democratic politics. They tend to make you miss the truth in what the other side are saying; they thereby make your own arguments less persuasive; and most of all – as in this case – they prevent you from seeing the elephant in the room because you are so determined to keep your head pointing in a different direction. I think if we had focused on the life chances of the least advantaged and if we had explored the impact of social breakdown on those life chances, we would have been at least suspected of some kind of weakening or of 'going native' or of 'becoming wet'; and I suspect that this was somehow apparent to us in some subtle way, and that it did prevent us from attending to the elephant in the room. Revolutionary zeal was required at that time in our nation's history to enable Margaret Thatcher to slay the dragons she was very rightly attempting to slay – but it had, as it always does, some undesirable side effects.

It would not, though, be fair to say that it was just the intensity of the domestic political battleground or the revolutionary zeal for the battle that led us to underplay the social justice agenda. The international scene also played its part.

The mid-1980s was a time when it still wasn't clear whether the Cold War was really and permanently over. It's a matter for the historians to decide what actually happened and in what sequence. But I can testify from personal experience that, to those of us sitting at the centre of the British governmental machine, it did not appear by any means obvious at that time that communism was dead or even dying. On the contrary, the fact that a couple of billion people in the world were still living in totalitarian societies with planned economies seemed very salient. So we weren't just fighting a battle about the future of Britain; this was part of a battle about the future of the whole world.

Nor was it just a question of the free world versus communism. Within the free world itself, a multitude of countries had been hit by the post-war tidal wave of nationalisation, centralised planning and controls on trade and exchange. As John Redwood (and later John Whittingdale) and I discovered when we went on from Downing Street to advise governments around the world on privatisation, the arguments which had raged in the UK in the late 1970s and 1980s were raging still in many other parts of the globe into the 1990s. In our current world – a world in which Eastern and central Europe have been liberated, Putin embraces capitalism, if not all the other features of civilised life, and the Chinese Communist Party presides over the world's most effervescent free market economy – it is difficult to remember that all of this was undreamt of by us (or, I think, by almost anyone else) in the heyday of Thatcherism. We were locked not only in a battle for freedom and free markets in Britain but in a global battle of ideas. And this, too, I feel sure on reflection, was part of what made us so keen to keep focused on that battle, in a way that had the destructive side effect of making us far less interested in life chances and social justice than we should have been, or than Keith Joseph would have liked us to be.

Since those years, I have often asked myself how far this was predetermined and how far it was just an accident of history. Is there, in other words, something about the intellectual foundations of Thatcherism – the free market theory from Chicago, the LSE and the IEA – that made it inevitable that a government armed with this theoretical weaponry and faced with epic battles both at home and abroad would be so consumed by revolutionary zeal that it would miss a crucial feature of the domestic scene?

The unmistakable conclusion I have reached is that, though it was explicable for this to happen, given the circumstances, it was by no means inevitable. Indeed, I think it would have been wholly avoidable if we had all paid more attention to Keith's idea of the social market. Since this wrong turning subsequently became one of the two fundamental problems of the Conservative Party, it is worth dwelling on the nature of the mistake and on why Mrs T. and those of us around her made it.

If the mood of revolutionary zeal (the fear of not appearing to be 'one of us') was the emotional basis for the error, the intellectual basis was our failure to understand one of the deepest truths about free societies and free markets. We failed to recognise what prevents an individual from making the choices that are the hallmark of these societies and markets.

Hayek, Friedman, Popper and Oakeshott share the same conception of the individual as a person who is capable of making rational choices, formulating projects and engaging in enterprises. This conception of the individual as an autonomous actor was naturally and unquestioningly shared by Mrs T. And of course there is an enormous amount that is right in it: most individuals are autonomous actors; they are capable of making rational choices, formulating projects and engaging in enterprises. It is indeed, as both Mrs T. instinctively and the theorists more consciously believed, both patronising and wrong to think of our fellow citizens in any other way. The history of the past hundred years has shown that a society in which the state enables individuals to make choices, challenge prevailing ideas and launch enterprises of their own is the type of society in which truth, prosperity and well-being are most likely to find a home. In all of this, Mrs T. and the theorists who helped her along were on the side of progress and enlightenment; she and they recognised that communism and socialism and fascism were likely to end by imprisoning the human spirit. Hence the huge efforts to roll back the frontiers of the state to the point where, instead of constraining individual enterprise, it could provide a framework for individual enterprise – Oakeshott's civil association in support of Popper's open society or the free market of Hayek or Friedman.

But what neither Mrs T. nor these theorists really grasped was that some people at some times in their lives are deprived by circumstance from exercising any effective choice – and therefore cannot participate properly as autonomous actors in a free society and a free market. This is what Iain Duncan Smith powerfully illustrated two decades later in his portrait of Breakdown Britain. He identified families caught in a ghastly nexus of unemployment, poor schooling, family breakdown, debt spiral and drug dependency. The point he recognised – and that we failed to recognise in the 1980s – is that, for families in this condition, there is no way out without help. Frameworks are not enough. The normal apparatus of the welfare state as it existed in the 1980s was not enough. The vicious circles are just too powerful: you can't get out of debt if you can't get into work; you can't get into work or pull the family together if you can't get out of drug dependency; you can't get out of drug dependency when you are crippled by the anxiety that goes with the breakdown of relationships and the terror of debt. For those of our fellow citizens caught in this nexus of chaos, the concept of an individual making autonomous choices in a free market just doesn't come near to applying. Yes, the people caught in this condition of life are surrounded by others who can perfectly well make free choices in a free market; but they themselves are not what Milton Friedman called 'free to choose'. And for many of those who are caught in this way, the cycle is inter-generational – it is genuinely what Keith Joseph called a 'cycle of deprivation'; the afflictions of the parents are visited upon the children.

There is nothing here that contradicts the fundamental arguments being made by Mrs T. and her theoreticians. The observation that special action needs to be taken to improve the life chances of those caught in the cycle of deprivation is completely compatible with the argument that free markets and free societies are the engines of prosperity and well-being for the overwhelming majority. Indeed, once one looks at things the right way round, it becomes clear that the need to address the cycle of deprivation is a positive implication of free market theory. If the state is meant to promote prosperity and well-being by providing a framework for autonomous choice, then it needs to ensure that all its citizens can participate in the free market by making autonomous choices rather than be excluded by the conditions of their lives. The only remaining question is how to ensure that the means used to lift some people out of the cycle of deprivation don't lead to the rest of the population being suffocated by socialism.

I wish I could say that, by the time I left Downing Street in 1986, all of this was clear to me. But it wasn't. I had grown up in an intoxicating atmosphere of open society theoreticians. I had joined Mrs T.'s staff at a time when she was fighting the fight against socialism and slaying the dragons of the day. It was an irresistible combination of theory and practice. I left on the day after I was selected as the prospective parliamentary candidate for Hackney North & Stoke Newington – and I departed with the sense that, whatever the future might hold, I had had the unbelievable good fortune to spend time at the centre of a great, reforming government that was setting the country in the right direction. Only later in this story did I come to realise what was missing – and how badly it was missing.

CHAPTER 4

DAYS OF OPPOSITION

After being roundly defeated at Hackney North in 1987 and at Hampstead & Highgate in 1992, I finally managed to get into the House of Commons in 1997 as the MP for West Dorset. I was overjoyed to have reached Westminster at last. But the Conservative Party in Parliament was in a state of shock. After winning four general elections in a row, it had experienced a crushing defeat. The general election of 1997 had swept Tony Blair's New Labour to power, removing swathes of long-standing Conservative members. We were outnumbered by more than two to one. Those of us who had been elected or re-elected seemed to fall into three categories. About a third of the Conservative members were former ministers, some of them very senior national figures (including the former Prime Minister, John Major); another third were long-time backbenchers; and the final third consisted of those of us who had just been elected for the first time. The former ministers were understandably affected by the experience of wholesale defeat after eighteen years of Conservative governments, and by the fact that the civil servants, red boxes and Whitehall offices had all gone mysteriously missing. The long-term backbenchers were occupied doing various things of varying degrees of importance in the House of Commons. And those of us who had been newly elected as MPs were… very new.

In the first few weeks, we didn't have any individual places to work and were assigned temporary desks in a committee room high up in the House of Commons. From this eyrie, I wrote by hand a large number of letters to people who had written to congratulate me on my election or who were seeking my support for one thing or another. Together with absorbing the atmosphere of the chamber, participating in the early stages of the election for the new leader of the Conservative Party, and beginning to work out how to get things done for constituents, this occupied enough time to give me some (rather illusory) sense of being usefully employed. However, once I had managed to secure a cubicle of my own in a corner of the Palace of Westminster and had made my (inevitably very bad) maiden speech, I sat down at my newly acquired desk in front of my newly acquired computer and tapped out the dreadful words 'What is the present purpose of the Conservative Party?' I remember staring at these words for hour after hour. All attempts to provide an answer to my very pertinent question proved fruitless. For light relief, I agreed to meet a party of constituents over a cup of tea in the House of Commons. They duly arrived; we sat down in the Pugin Room, with its views over the Thames and its majestic wallpapers; I rather thought I was putting on a good show. But my quiet sense of elation was quickly deflated when a young man who was one of their number asked what I was intending to do over the course of the parliament 'given that the electorate has so clearly said that they don't want to hear from you for the next five years'. I couldn't give any answer that convinced me, let alone any answer that convinced him.

It is in retrospect easy to see why we were in such a fix at that time. The origin of the problem lay in two words: Tony Blair. In 1997, Blair and the Labour government he was leading not only held a commanding position in Parliament and in the country at large but also appeared to be in favour of all the things we were in favour of. We believed in proper control of public expenditure; Blair and Gordon Brown were maintaining the eye-wateringly tough controls on expenditure that Ken Clarke had established at the tail end of the Conservative years – controls so tough that I doubt Ken would have maintained them in all their purity if he had remained Chancellor after 1997. We believed in free markets and private industry; Blair and his ministers were promoting competition and entrepreneurial activity, and were ruthlessly opposed to any renationalisation of businesses that had been privatised – they were even talking about further privatisations. We believed in the trade union reforms of the Thatcher years; Blair was committed to preserving them. We believed in strong defence and NATO; Blair was committed to maintaining them. In short, the Thatcher inheritance seemed safe in Blair's hands – and every time one thought he might veer away from it, he announced another Thatcherite policy.

Even worse from the Conservative Party's point of view – though certainly advantageous for the country – was the fact that Blair had spotted the defect in the purist version of Thatcherism that the Conservative Party had mistakenly believed itself to have inherited. Like Keith Joseph and the 'wets', he had sensed that, to make free market economics attractive and acceptable, they had to be balanced by a real focus on social justice. In Blair's hands, the free market of 1997 was to be a social market of the kind envisaged by Keith, with the welfare system redesigned by Frank Field to bring people into work, the school system redesigned by David Blunkett to restore standards in the fundamental skills for children whose parents couldn't afford to send them to independent schools, loans introduced to fund the universities for students from all backgrounds rather than handing out state subsidies to middle-class families, and so forth. During my time as our candidate in Hackney North, I had seen at first hand the crying need for such things to be done, and had understood for the first time the full force of what Keith and the 'wets' had been on about. My eyes had been opened to the missing element of the free market revolution; and now Blair's New Labour seemed to have grasped both parts of the point. It was offering the free market *and* the focus on social justice that was its necessary counterpart.

So there I was in my dark little cubicle, staring at the screen, wondering what the purpose of the Conservative Party was at a time when Blair's Labour government in its early years was carrying through both what our agenda had been and what it now ought to have been. No doubt, there were other Conservative MPs secretly facing much the same perplexity in those first months of the 1997–2001 parliament. But, as I look back at those early days of opposition now, I am amazed by the fact that we didn't really talk collectively about the problem. Perhaps we new MPs were afraid to admit to one another that the problem existed.

Perhaps, also, the availability of displacement activity enabled us to avoid broaching this thorny topic. There was certainly plenty to do. In the first place, we could oppose. We were told that someone (was it perhaps Randolph Churchill?) had once said that the first duty of Her Majesty's Opposition was to oppose. And oppose we did. We opposed the minimum wage (wrongly assuming that it would cause increased unemployment). We opposed the independence of the Bank of England (presumably because it was being proposed by a Labour government). And the momentum of opposition carried us, a few years later, into opposing student fees and student loans. At a later stage in this story, we had to reverse all of these positions, and I was myself instrumental in helping to do so. But even as a fledgling MP in the first months of that first parliament after 1997, I remember having a sneaking suspicion that opposing things which it seemed, on the face of it, perfectly sensible for the government to be doing must somehow be the wrong strategy for Her Majesty's Opposition.

The second displacement activity was to concern ourselves with defending unpopular causes. And so it was that, at midnight on 11 March 1998, I found myself in the chamber of the House of Commons about to speak on the Wireless Telegraphy Bill. Why? Certainly not out of any particular interest in this innocuous and highly technical piece of legislation. The Labour minister Barbara Roche (who seemed a decent cove) had brought this dull but worthy Bill through its various stages in good shape. Now we were at what is called the report stage, at which the details of the legislation are discussed on the floor of the House itself rather than upstairs in one of the committee rooms. Any member can speak. And I had been asked to speak for a very long time, alongside a trio of Conservative backbenchers. Our job was to keep the proceedings going until the early (or, preferably, the not so early) hours.

The point was to prolong the parliamentary day. Michael Foster, the sponsor of the Hunting Bill, had cunningly put down an amendment to his own Bill late in the evening, reducing it to just one clause, in the hope that this would prevent us from 'talking it out' by producing endless refinements. Therefore, our lawyers needed to draft up a huge series of additional amendments (in order to preserve the scope for endless debate), and these, too, needed to be put down before the close of that day's business. So I was despatched to speak on the Wireless Telegraphy Bill... and speak... and speak.

I had two problems, and two advantages. The problems were that I knew little about the Wireless Telegraphy Bill and had nothing constructive to say about it. The advantages were that I knew a great deal about wireless telegraphy (i.e. mobile communications) in general, and that the Speaker's chair in the chamber of the House was occupied by Mr Deputy Speaker Martin, whose sweetness of character was accompanied by a slightly fuzzy apprehension of the matters in hand. I imagined that he might be tempted to suppose that any remarks of mine about the past and future of mobile communications which referred from time to time to 'wireless telegraphy' were germane to the debate and were hence 'in order' from the point of view of the rules of the House.

My speculation about the wide limits of the Deputy Speaker's tolerance proved, in the event, correct. Together with my stalwart colleagues, Tim Boswell, Ian Bruce and Andrew Lansley (all of whom were operating on the same principles), we kept the ball tossing from one of us to another until around 3 a.m. – long enough to do the job, so far as the Foster Bill was concerned. It was my first, and thankfully my last, experience of providing what is called in the parliamentary jargon a 'filibuster'. It is a form of out-of-body experience. As the hours passed, I could hear my orotund absurdities roll forward; I observed myself responding with obsequious grace to colleagues who mercifully intervened – 'I am so grateful to my honourable friend…', 'my honourable friend's point is perspicuous…', 'I do not, of course, pretend to so detailed a grasp of the issues as my honourable friend…' On and on, with much rhyme and little reason. The puzzlement of the government officials in the box (wholly ignorant of the reasons for this ludicrous loquacity) and the mounting disbelief of the estimable Ms Roche (likewise ignorant of our motives) were a marvel to behold. The Deputy Speaker, if not actually asleep, was clearly having considerable difficulty keeping awake. Was this, I wondered, what I had actually come to Parliament to do? Was this how a rational legislature in a modern liberal democracy should really function? But of course I had to do my duty, on and on.

The third displacement activity was to focus on the constitution.

Tony Blair was busily engaged in devolving power to a new parliament in Scotland, a new assembly in Wales and a new mayor in London. He was also engaged in creating the Freedom of Information Act, the Human Rights Act and an array of other constitutional and quasi-constitutional adjustments – including a new system for UK parliamentary elections known as AV+, which had been proposed by the former Labour Home Secretary Roy Jenkins. There was a good deal wrong with a lot of this fast-moving constitutional change, and we alighted on the problems with joy. Here, we thought, were things we could *really* get our teeth into. I was much involved in this process, since my first job on the opposition front bench, after just a year in Parliament, was as a junior spokesman in the constitutional affairs team energetically led by Liam Fox. As well as touring the country with Liam and the other members of the team, speaking to vanishingly tiny audiences about the dangers of rushed constitutional change, my particular job was to prevent Lord Jenkins's AV+ electoral system from coming to fruition. It rapidly became clear to me that the secret of success was to assemble a sufficient number of Labour backbenchers and peers to oppose it. This was relatively easy to accomplish because AV+ was a hideously complicated electoral system, whose effects were highly unpredictable and by no means necessarily proportional. Once I had ascertained that the Labour backbenchers in the Commons were mobilising on their own, I turned my attention to the Labour Party in the Lords. This gave rise to a series of delightful and instructive conversations with Labour figures of yesteryear, including the former Labour Prime Minister Jim Callaghan. When I called on the great man in his office at the Lords, he immediately assured me that he did not favour a change in the electoral system for general elections. The merit, he assured me, of the existing first-past-the-post system was that it produced decisive shifts of government when that was what the people wanted: 'It got rid of me when people were fed up with Labour, and it got rid of you when people were fed up with the Conservatives.' As the most junior member of a heavily outgunned opposition front bench, it was fun to be conversing in this way with former Prime Ministers. Lord Jenkins's AV+ electoral system duly collapsed under the weight of opposition from within the Labour Party itself. All very satisfactory.

But I still had the suspicion that this focus on the constitution wasn't really answering the question on my computer screen. You couldn't sufficiently explain the need for the Conservative Party in terms of preventing Tony Blair from making certain constitutional changes. That would certainly have been a basis for founding a pressure group. But a whole political party – an entity seeking to form the next government – surely needed more than this as a programme to present to the electorate.

Apart from the availability of displacement activity, what else prevented us from sitting down together in order to think through the meaning and purpose of the Conservative Party at the end of the 1990s? Part of the problem, I think, was the nature of the election for a new party leader. John Major had resigned straight after the general election, and under the rules of the party at that time it fell to the 165 remaining Conservative MPs to choose his successor. This was an exciting thing to be doing. Much seemed to be at stake. We were all busily engaged in campaigning for one potential leader or another. But, in all of this happy frenzy, were we thinking seriously about the strategy and purpose of the party in Blair's Britain? I can find no evidence from my own experience or from what followed that we were doing any such thing. I myself was in John Redwood's camp – because he was a former boss and a friend whose acumen I admired (and still admire); moreover, he had already had the courage to run unsuccessfully for the leadership against John Major before the general election, at a time when the likelihood of defeat for the Major government at the hands of Tony Blair was apparent for all to see. But I cannot recall us using the leadership election to promote any profound analysis of the party's Blair-induced existential crisis. And I don't think anybody else's campaign was doing so either. It all basically seemed to come down to two things: the most suitable person to be leader, and the attitude of potential leaders to the EU. Broadly, Ken Clarke looked to most of the parliamentary party like the most suitable person to be leader; but he was 'unsound' on the EU. So it had to be William Hague, who looked like the next most suitable person to be leader, and who was 'sound' on the EU.

Rather than producing any proper debate about the direction and meaning of the party at that moment of crisis, the leadership election produced fragmentary utterances: Alan Clark (an old war-horse, returned to Parliament in 1997 after a period of absence) bizarrely calling William Hague 'a visceral left-winger'; the leader columns of the *Daily Telegraph* excoriating the last-minute Redwood–Clarke alliance; Mrs Thatcher calling (fruitlessly) to tell me that I had a duty to back William rather than Ken once John Redwood was out of the race; William Hague, once victorious, magnanimously inviting the whole parliamentary party (rather than just his own supporters) to his victory drinks; Cecil Parkinson at those drinks comparing William's age to the rather greater age of Tony Blair when Blair had become the leader of the Labour Party. But what Cecil should have said, or at least should have thought, was that there was another difference. Blair became leader with an absolutely clear view of what New Labour meant, how it related to the Thatcher revolution, and how it would win a general election, whereas when William (whose personal talents in many ways exceeded Blair's) became leader we had no equivalent clarity.

The nature of the leadership contest in 1997 mattered more than one might think, because leadership elections are periods during which parties have a sort of permission to stage an internal debate of a kind that is virtually precluded the rest of the time. While you are having a leadership contest, the media and the party membership accept that there will be a clash of programmes and strategies and personalities – which is then resolved by the election of a particular leader. During the contest itself, even the most lurid journalist can't really write a story suggesting that some figure in the party is being 'disloyal' if the figure in question is putting forward a view that is fundamentally different from those put forward by others in the party, because there is effectively no leader and hence no one to whom one can be disloyal. By contrast, as soon as a leader is in place, almost any attempt to put forward any new idea that is made by anyone other than the leader themselves or someone clearly authorised by the leader will quickly be seized upon by the media as a case of 'Tories at war' (or, as the case may be, 'Labour at war'); accusations of disloyalty ricochet; and the leader's office has to assert authority by shutting down the argument.

So the rushed leadership election of 1997, and the absence during that leadership election of any fundamental debate about the Conservative response to Blair, was an important contributor to the problem that we had in the ensuing years. But I think there was another, equally important, contributor. This was the idea of 'soundness'. There is, to my mind, hardly any concept that does more damage in politics or in public policy. The history of revolution is of course full of this concept. 'Soundness' is used by revolutionaries to justify successive phases of the revolution eating up the proponents of the previous phase – the Jacobins denouncing the Girondins as unsound, only to be followed by one Jacobin (Robespierre) denouncing another (Danton) as unsound; or the Bolsheviks denouncing the Mensheviks as unsound, only to be followed by one Bolshevik (Stalin) denouncing another (Trotsky) as unsound. The pattern is familiar. And so is the language. Those engaging in the denunciation claim to follow a 'pure' version of whatever is the prevailing ideology, and the 'unsound' person or group is accused of falling away from that purity. Now of course the consequences of being denounced as 'unsound' in the Conservative Party of the late 1990s were considerably less extreme than the consequences for Danton or Trotsky. But the basic idea was the same: someone or some small knot of people would claim or imply that he or she or they were the proud possessors of the true principles of Thatcherism and that some other person or persons had somehow fallen away from adherence to these principles. It was a matter of orthodoxy and heresy – and if you weren't orthodox, then you were heretical.

I'm afraid that one of the disadvantages of the Thatcher years was that this sort of talk had become to some degree institutionalised in the party. In the 1980s, you were either 'one of us' or you were not. And we suffered from this aspect of the legacy in the 1997–2001 parliament, because it made many of us unconsciously reluctant to think outside the boundaries of the familiar at a time when the new political dynamic created by Blair required exactly that sort of thinking. The simple certainties of the Thatcher years – the battle against socialism – had (at least for the time being) disappeared, and we needed a new strategy to take on Blair's New Labour. But we couldn't easily devise such a strategy while we were constrained by the fear of being branded as 'unsound' or 'wet' by those inside and outside Parliament who imagined themselves to be the guardians of the true flame.

This is just one small historical example of the much wider and deeper danger of the rhetoric of ideological purity and soundness. The essential problem is that paying attention to such ideological purity prevents attention being paid to the facts. Instead of asking whether something will work in practice, the ideological purist is determined to ask whether the thing in question conforms with whatever theory he or she is peddling. Of course, the effect of this focus on theory instead of practice is at its most damaging when the theory itself is crazy; we can see that all too clearly in the current spectacle of violent Islamist extremism. But even when the theory is at root sensible, the injunction to concentrate on supposed adherence to the purity of the ideology rather than on the practical results of differing strategies is a route at best to political failure and at worst to some very bad results for our fellow human beings.

This, then, was the condition of the Conservative parliamentary party when I joined it in 1997 – shocked by defeat, shackled by misplaced conceptions of ideological purity, rushed into a leadership election before it could collectively develop any clear sense of purpose relevant to Blair's Britain, and all too willing to be distracted into any activity that masked the fundamental problem of the missing strategy. How was this considerable challenge to be met? Following William Hague's election as leader, four people in that first parliament made sustained attempts to find a solution: William Hague himself, Michael Portillo (after his return in a 1999 by-election), Francis Maude and Ann Widdecombe.

William Hague has an enviable range of talents. If he had never so much as entered politics, much less been Leader of the Opposition and subsequently a magnificent Foreign Secretary, his biographies of Pitt and Wilberforce would have been regarded as a significant achievement. At the despatch box in the House of Commons, he had a command in debate matched in my time only by Tony Blair and David Cameron. His speeches, always good, have sometimes come near to greatness – combining the hilarious with the deadly serious to powerful effect. His combination of cleverness, competence, balanced judgement and charm has made him a formidable leader and statesman. As Blair himself acknowledged, William – as a tactician and as a debater – was every bit Blair's equal. This left the question of strategy and purpose.

William's attempt to answer this question came in four parts. There was a positive theme – that people who worked hard and saved hard should be rewarded; there was an administrative ambition – that public expenditure should be kept within strict limits; there was a constitutional aim – that Britain should keep the pound and should avoid being dragged into further European treaties without referendums ('in Europe but not run by Europe'); and there was a populist theme – that the immigration and asylum systems should be brought under control. Each of these strands had much to recommend it. Indeed, looking back from the vantage point of 2017, each can be seen to be prescient. But somehow they didn't amount to a convincing alternative to New Labour at the turn of the millennium.

The first thing missing was a sense of coherence. With New Labour, one knew that the party was firmly on the side of modern Britain – or, as the New Labour propagandists put it, 'Cool Britannia'. This Blairite attachment to modern Britain brought together an acceptance of the Thatcherite free market inheritance with the minimum wage, tax credits, a determination to root out racism and sexism, constitutional reform, the Millennium Dome, measures to improve work–life balance, an enthusiasm for digital technology and many other symbols of 'modernisation'. It had at least an appearance of being a coherent strategy: you could grasp (and indeed I think the electorate did at that time grasp) what Blair was 'on about'. By contrast, although the four strands of William's approach were entirely compatible with one another, and each was a sensible response to a real issue, together they left one wondering what the overall direction of the party really was.

This problem was accentuated by the fact that the other three big figures surrounding William in the later stages of the 1997–2001 parliament had two differing views about how the apparent incoherence should be resolved. Although both camps were happy enough to accept William's emphasis on the need to reward those who work hard, save hard and try hard to do the right thing, none of the rest of us spent much time developing this potentially powerful idea. Instead, Francis Maude and Michael Portillo took hold of two of William's themes and tried to fashion a Eurosceptic, fiscally prudent version of Blair's socially liberal modernisation programme; whereas Ann Widdecombe was steadfastly in favour of a far more socially conservative approach which highlighted the need for William's other theme – immigration control – and allied this to the promotion of 'traditional values', including tough action on crime. This tension between the Maude–Portillo strategy and the Widdecombe strategy became known in some quarters as a battle between 'mods and rockers'. With hindsight, one can see in that battle the origins of the debate between social liberals and social conservatives that continued within the Conservative Party in one form or another throughout the years that followed – with the social conservatives in the ascendant during the leaderships of Iain Duncan Smith and Michael Howard, but the social liberals gaining the upper hand under David Cameron (and actually still – though with a less emphatic rhetoric – under Theresa May).

Many years later, at the 2006 party conference, I witnessed an episode that illustrates the nature of the conflicting political cultures. Francis Maude was at that time party chairman, and I was chairman of the party's Policy Review. We had been together to a church near the conference venue, which we and a group of other MPs and conference delegates had been helping to renovate as part of a programme known as Conservative Social Action. We were both due to be appearing on the platform at the conference for a panel session with Ann Widdecombe (who had by that time left the front bench). Unfortunately, the minibus arranged to bring us back to the conference hall was slightly late. Francis solved this problem by appearing backstage ready to go onto the platform in his DIY gear, complete with large splashes of paint. To say that Ann was surprised by Francis's appearance would be something of an understatement. It is not literally true that her eyes popped out of her head. But she certainly gave a striking demonstration of the physical basis for the cliché. As she and I walked behind Francis onto the podium, she muttered audibly that the time had clearly come for her to leave politics.

But the tensions between Ann's social conservatism and the modernism espoused by Francis and Michael had already been exposed to a wider public in a much more vivid form as early as the party conference of October 2000. At that point, shortly before the 2001 general election, William was the leader of the opposition and the other three were firmly established in the most senior shadow Cabinet posts: Ann was shadow Home Secretary, Michael was shadow Chancellor and Francis was shadow Foreign Secretary. That pre-election conference should have been the launch pad for William's argument to the electorate. But it was not to be. During the conference itself, I joined Michael for a preparatory discussion with the other members of the shadow Treasury team (of which, as shadow Chief Secretary, I was then also a part). He was clearly disturbed by a policy on cannabis that Ann was about to announce. I didn't press him on this, as the details had not been disclosed to all of us in the shadow Cabinet and it was evidently a closely held secret to which only the most senior members were privy. It turned out, some hours later, that Ann's policy proposal was to institute a £100 fixed penalty for the possession of cannabis. No wonder Michael was concerned. Given that a high proportion of the young people in Britain had at some time possessed at least a small amount of cannabis, this was bound to be a highly controversial policy and, while not hugely important in itself, it vividly illustrated the divide between the tough, socially conservative approach that Ann favoured (making no concessions whatsoever to current trends) and the modernising, socially liberal approach being promoted by Michael and Francis.

In the aftermath, it was suggested by some commentators that the 'Portillistas' had somehow engineered a plot to undo this policy. If so, it must have been a very secret operation, because I never heard the slightest suggestion that any such thing was taking place. From my own point of view, the sequence of events was as follows. I was driving back to West Dorset from the conference. I had just entered the car park at West Bay near Bridport when I received a call from James Arbuthnot, then the Chief Whip, telling me that journalists were asking members of the shadow Cabinet whether they had ever smoked cannabis, and instructing me to tell the simple truth if I was asked this question. Not long after this call ended, I received a call from a journalist asking the very question about which I had been warned. As instructed, I duly told the journalist the truth – which happened to be that, though myself very prissy about any experimentation with drugs, some friends of mine at university had very aggravatingly put cannabis into my pipe and had later admitted this fact when they discovered that (possibly because I didn't fully inhale my pipe) the dope had had no discernible effect on me. The next morning, I woke up to find my house surrounded by journalists and TV cameras. It transpired that a considerable proportion of the shadow Cabinet had truthfully admitted to smoking cannabis in their youth, and that my story was one of the more newsworthy variants. The policy was quietly shelved.

It was against this background of differing views on the way forward that the shadow Treasury team began to develop a new fiscal and monetary policy. This was to form both the beginning of my serious involvement in formulating public policy as an elected politician and the basis for the first crisis of my political career.

My first job in the Treasury team came in 1999, two years after entering Parliament. Roy Jenkins's ill-fated AV+ electoral reform proposals had by that time died away, and I was moved from my constitutional affairs brief to be the shadow Financial Secretary to the Treasury under Francis Maude, who was then heading the team as shadow Chancellor. As well as his modernising zeal, Francis brought to this task the seriousness of purpose and incisive grasp of public administration that had made him a successful minister in the Thatcher and Major governments and that were later to make him a hugely important reforming force in the Cameron governments. He is a strategic thinker – but not in the sense of just aiming to win long-range political battles. As much as any politician that I have met here or elsewhere, he really cares about the degree to which the administrative system produces efficient outcomes for the citizen. The result was that he taught us in the shadow Treasury team to combine attention to administrative detail with an effort to discern which details would really matter in the long run. That in turn led him to focus on the question of the independence of the Bank of England – which we had recklessly opposed in the early months of our time in opposition, but which had by 1999 clearly been accepted both by the economists and by industry as the best way of controlling inflation. Clearly, any opposition that wanted to position itself as a serious alternative to the Blair government needed to find a way of reversing tack and accepting the independence of the Bank's Monetary Policy Committee as a permanent feature of the UK's framework for monetary control. I was therefore set to the task of organising a review by a group of serious figures including Peter Middleton (a former permanent secretary of the Treasury who was then chairman of one of the clearing banks) and David Lees (a member of the court of governors of the Bank of England and also the chief executive of a major industrial company) as well as some prominent economists. The review concluded, inevitably, that the independence of the Bank was a good thing – and thereby provided the basis for a change of the official Conservative policy, which has ever since been solidly in favour of the Monetary Policy Committee being independent of government, as it should have been all along.

Alongside monetary policy, I was responsible for the opposition's stance on the details of tax policy. Accordingly, at midday on Tuesday 20 June 2000, I was discussing the details of the Finance Bill in Standing Committee H. We had had more than twenty sittings of the committee, and we had now reached the infamous Schedule 30, dealing with double taxation relief. Dawn Primarolo, the Paymaster General, was responsible for defending the measures in this schedule. As shadow Financial Secretary, I had the task of unpicking the problems.

Over the preceding weeks, I had spent many hours penetrating the intricacies of the schedule with the help of armies of accountants and CBI (Confederation of British Industry) officials. It had become clear to me that, in a worthy effort to prevent leakage of tax revenues, the Inland Revenue had created a system which would prevent global companies from setting up their headquarters in the UK and would thereby do irreversible damage to the UK economy. This could not have been the intention of Treasury ministers; but I am pretty sure that no one had explained to Dawn Primarolo how the schedule worked in sufficient detail for her to see why this unintended effect would indeed be its consequence.

Now was my chance – through carefully non-partisan forensic analysis of the schedule – to persuade Dawn (and, even more importantly, to persuade the Treasury and Inland Revenue officials on the bench behind her) that there was a real problem here. I had all the time in the world. The Paymaster General and her civil servants were a captive audience; that is the great merit of the standing committee system, particularly as it applies to Finance Bills. As I progressed stage by stage through the argument, I was suffused with the sensation that this *was* why I had come to the House of Commons. Unlike spouting nonsense in a filibuster or scoring trivial partisan points, this was something really worth doing: it would affect the job prospects and hence the lives of countless numbers of my fellow citizens, and it was something that I could do only because I was a member of the legislature. Of course, no one outside a very restricted circle would ever know that I had done it; but I would know – if I succeeded in persuading Dawn and her officials to change the schedule.

As I looked at the officials, and then listened to Dawn, I had the strong sense that they had in fact taken the point. We seemed to be – and it later became definitely apparent that we were – on the way to a different draft with completely different effects.

But monetary policy and the details of tax policy were the easy bits. The really difficult challenge was public spending. I moved onto this terrain later in 2000 when I became shadow Chief Secretary to the Treasury and hence joined the shadow Cabinet for the first time. By that stage, Francis had moved across to being shadow Foreign Secretary and Michael Portillo had become shadow Chancellor. With what turned out to be less than a year to go before the general election of 2001, my task was to help William Hague and Michael construct a public expenditure programme for an incoming Conservative administration. We were not, of course, under the illusion that we were likely to win that election – Blair was still riding high and (quite apart from the unresolved issue about the direction of the Conservative Party) the public were showing no sign of thinking that it was time for a change; indeed, Michael epigrammatically and accurately described the traditional pre-election briefing session at which we as the shadow

Treasury team explained our programme to the permanent secretary of the Treasury as 'a pleasing fantasy'. Nevertheless, it was clearly important, if we were to make serious progress towards a reversal of the 1997 massacre and the possibility of a Conservative government at the next election, that we should construct and present a credible fiscal programme.

In the years between 1997 and 2001, Gordon Brown had kept a fairly tight lid on the Labour government's spending; so, as in most other areas of policy at that time, there wasn't too much for a fiscally conservative opposition to complain about so far as the fiscal accounts in that parliament were concerned. By 2001, public sector net debt stood at just under 35 per cent of GDP – a figure that Mrs Thatcher would have regarded as entirely respectable. We therefore turned our attention to the trends that had been established, rather than to the effects that had so far been generated. In particular, it was noticeable that Brown had begun to increase public spending at a rate faster than the rate of increase of the economy. In 2001, Brown was proposing to increase inflation-adjusted public spending by 3.7 per cent per year, or about 30 per cent faster than the 2.7 per cent growth rate of the economy in that year, and faster than the growth rate of any year of the 1997–2001 parliament. We speculated that expenditure growth of this order would substantially outpace economic growth in the period between 2002 and 2005, forcing a Labour government either to raise taxes or to raise borrowing. I therefore proposed (and Michael and William agreed) that we should establish the principle that, under a Conservative administration, the long-term rate of increase of public spending should not exceed the rate of growth of the economy; and we agreed also to present in our manifesto a near-term path for public expenditure that would see it growing by an inflation-adjusted 3.1 per cent per year in contrast to Brown's 3.7 per cent. (As a matter of historical record, our hypotheses proved correct, since the UK economy subsequently grew by less than 3 per cent in each of the years 2002–05 other than 2003, and the average annual compound growth rate of the economy in those years was almost exactly the 3.1 per cent that we had speculatively set as the rate of growth for public spending – so our near-term path would probably have enabled a Conservative government to fulfil its long-term principle for public spending.)

Within these aggregates, William, Michael and the shadow Cabinet as a whole had a strong desire to deliver tax cuts as a way of fulfilling William's commitment to reward those who worked hard, saved hard and tried to do the right thing. This meant reductions on fuel duty (which had become a hot topic during the course of the 1997–2001 parliament), on businesses, on savers, on pensioners and on married couples. There was also a demand (very sensibly) that we should find the money to increase spending on the NHS, increase the basic state pension, protect the savings and homes of elderly people in long-term care and endow the universities. I therefore set about finding a series of corresponding offsetting savings with colleagues holding the various portfolios in other areas of public spending. I am not sure, looking back, just how many of these would have proved feasible to implement in their entirety; some adjustments at the margins might well have been needed to stay within the totals to which we had committed. But that turned out not to be the big problem.

The big problem was the question of what this all amounted to. Were we, or were we not, proposing a fiscal policy substantially different from Labour? If you looked at the total public expenditure proposed by the two parties for the last forecast year of 2003/04 (three years into the new parliament), the gap was about £8 billion, or roughly 2 per cent of what was then total public expenditure. On the face of it, this didn't seem like much of a difference between us and Labour. And various commentators made it clear that they didn't think it amounted to a row of beans. We therefore had two choices: we could either stick rigidly to talking about the £8 billion and accept that the change we were proposing was fractional. Or we could point out that the long-term effect of Brown's intention to let public spending grow faster than the rate of economic growth would be very substantially different from the effect of Conservative governments capping the growth of public spending in line with the growth of the economy. Michael (who had, I think, correctly discerned that the electorate was in no mood for any radical departure from Labour's plans) was very happy to stick rigidly to the £8 billion savings in 2003/04 and accept that this was not much different from Labour's plan for the same period. But, as it happened, this question came up in a discussion with William, at which I pointed out the compounding effect of our policy compared with Labour's over a number of years, and showed that it would be considerable, reaching £20 billion (or some 5 per cent of total public expenditure) over two par-liaments. This, alas, was to prove my undoing. William, when pressed on the same point by journalists from the *Financial Times* at the start of the election campaign, referred them to me for an explanation of why our policy was more significant than one might at first think. I was duly called by the *FT*, ran through my compounding rigmarole showing the much greater long-term effects of different rates of growth in public spending, and thereby unwittingly generated the story that we were really intending to reduce public spending by £20 billion. Naturally, in the heat of the election campaign, all the fine distinctions between one period and another were lost; the media immediately assumed that this was some sort of 'secret plan'. Michael was quite understandably furious, because he had been carefully avoiding any suggestion that we were radically departing from Labour's spending plans, and had been seeking to maintain strict message discipline. Accordingly, instead of being allowed to appear at a press conference in order to explain in detail why what I had said was in fact entirely consistent with the announced policy, I was instructed to avoid the media. As I was fighting my own seat in West Dorset with a thin majority, this was no easy task – and it was made substantially more difficult by the brilliantly comic way in which Labour played up the episode, hiring a man in a Sherlock Holmes outfit with two bloodhounds to appear at all of William's press conferences, ostensibly attempting to sniff out my whereabouts. In retrospect, I am not sure it actually made much difference to the outcome of the general election; but it was a massive distraction of a sort that no opposition leader or shadow Chancellor would have wanted. I was pretty convinced that my political career had come to a full stop.

This somewhat surreal sequence also made me consider – I think for the first time since joining the front bench in 1998 – the underlying problem that we were facing. As I lurked in West Dorset avoiding the news-hounds and seeking much-needed additional votes from my bemused constituents, the early days of the 1997–2001 parliament and my computer screen with its unanswered question came back to me with renewed force. My constitutional and fiscal activities on the front bench had been sufficiently interesting and demanding to distract my attention from these more fundamental issues. But the belief that my time on the front bench was about to end gave me the jolt required to make me see that I couldn't yet answer the question on my computer screen. What *was* the purpose of the Conservative Party in Blair's Britain? It seemed to me that we hadn't resolved the socially liberal versus socially traditionalist tensions that had divided the Portillo–Maude camp from the Widdecombe camp. And, above all, we hadn't yet provided any convincing answer to the social crisis of alienation, exclusion from the mainstream and cycles of deprivation that I had uncomprehendingly seen in the northern cities in the 1980s and had at last come to understand as the most important problem facing our country when I was the candidate in Hackney North in the lead-up to the 1987 election.

There was no doubt that Blair himself, and those closest to him, had grasped the immensity of this problem of diminished life chances and exclusion from the mainstream. As well as his famous concentration on improving schools (represented by his typically memorable slogan 'education, education, education'), he had commissioned a series of attempts to bring those who were outside the mainstream back into it. But, worthy though these initiatives were, they showed every sign (like our own school reforms and family policies in the Thatcher/Major years) of being far too slight and superficial a set of changes. Blair was not making the huge strides required to create real life chances for those deprived of them. True, Frank Field in his all-too-brief tenure as minister for welfare reform had attempted a thorough-going reform of the welfare system; but this (though, unusually, supported by us under the inspired leadership of Iain Duncan Smith when he was shadow Secretary for Social Security) had been drastically curtailed by Frank's own colleagues Gordon Brown and Harriet Harman, to the point where the only serious reform that emerged was the replacement of Mrs Thatcher's system of Family Credit by a more comprehensive system of tax credits. This represented some progress; but the basic social injustice of people trapped by their circumstances in totally unsatisfactory conditions of life remained – and desperately needed to be addressed.

I asked myself in the wilderness days of the closing stages of the 2001 election campaign what our answer to this fundamental challenge really was. Where in the manifesto to which I had heavily contributed could one find this answer? There was one glimmer of hope in the section devoted to the creation of an Office of Civil Society (perhaps the seed of an idea which was later to flower), and I recalled with some satisfaction the support that I had given to this proposal. But one office does not make a programme. And, as I looked back on my time in that parliament, I was ashamed to discover that I could not credit myself with any other serious effort to restore social justice by resolving the crisis of social exclusion after the days, right at the beginning of the parliament, when – as an eager first-year backbencher – I had slightly helped Iain Duncan Smith in his efforts to back the largely failed Field agenda. I resolved that, if I was elected to serve in the succeeding parliament, whatever fate might befall me in that parliament, I would not let the same thing happen; I would use my place in it to push forward an agenda of social reform.

Little did I know how fate would conspire to make that possible.

The first surprise was the fact that, admittedly by a very slim majority, I did manage to hold onto my seat as the MP for West Dorset. I have always attributed this to the highly personalised campaign run against me by my Liberal Democrat opponent in that particular election. I guessed that people in West Dorset would not react well to the kind of campaign the Liberal Democrats were running (basically, pictures of Letwin with horns on), and my confidence in this prophecy increased when several avowed Liberal Democrat supporters told me on their doorsteps that they wouldn't normally have dreamed of voting for me but that they were so dismayed by my opponent's personal attacks that they were now intending to support me. Normally, of course, these things don't make any difference to the outcome one way or the other, but when the result is very close, they can tip the balance; and the balance was tipped in my favour – just.

The second surprise was on the day after the election. Instead of the dismissal I had expected, I received the news that William was stepping down as leader of the party and then, in quick succession, I had calls from Francis Maude (soliciting my vote for Michael Portillo) and from Iain Duncan Smith (soliciting my vote for himself). As Michael and Francis were the people most committed to the social liberalism and modernisation that I was convinced the party needed to espouse, and as Iain was by a considerable distance the person who most clearly grasped what I regarded as the urgent need for a new and serious Conservative approach to social justice and the life chances agenda, these two calls might have posed a serious dilemma. What swung it was my conviction that it was Michael who most had the stature and the public appeal to win a general election in 2005 or 2006.

I had known of Michael since his undergraduate days at Cambridge, where he had been taught by my mother. My mother's academic standards were high – but even judged by those high standards, Michael had passed with flying colours. Both she and the ineffable Maurice Cowling (later, my own supervisor in political thought at Cambridge) described him as one of the outstanding students of his generation. I had next come across Michael, and had been hugely impressed by him, when he had returned to Whitehall in 1983 as a special adviser after a spell in industry and had then entered Parliament in a 1984 by-election. Soon after becoming an MP, he had very kindly come to speak for me in Hackney; as he swept in, lifting the spirits of the audience with his confidence and then inspiring them with his rhetoric, I had very much the sense that we were in the presence of a future leader. His rapid rise in the years after 1984, ending with his time as Defence Secretary in the Major government, is well chronicled elsewhere – as is the extent to which his politics had been changed by the experience of losing his seat in 1997. By the time that I came to be a member of his shadow Treasury team, he had acquired an extraordinary presence which, underpinned by a piercing intelligence, made him a formidable operator both inside and outside the House of Commons. I had seen at close quarters both the force of his liberal instincts and the brilliance with which he despatched official business: crisp, elegant, incisive and decisive. I had worked with him in finally ditching our misconceived opposition to the minimum wage and in reaffirming Francis's support for the independence of the Bank of England. He seemed to me in every way suited to lead the party.

It is to Michael's credit that in the aftermath of the second general election defeat of 2001 he was determined to obtain not just the leadership itself but also a mandate for a fundamental shift in attitude. He didn't want to leave any room for the sorts of tension that had made it so difficult for us to promote a unified programme in the 1997–2001 parliament. As a result, although he emphasised his attachment to free market economics and to fundamental reform of bureaucracy in the public services, he was absolutely uncompromising about the need for the party to embrace Blair's modernisation. The ludicrous remaining Conservative hang-ups about gay relationships were to be ditched. This was to be a modern, inclusive, liberal party. I welcomed all of this enthusiastically. Many of our colleagues did not. And Michael took no prisoners. On one occasion during the leadership election, when Francis and I asked him how a meeting with a particular colleague had gone, Michael replied that it had been a terrific discussion, in which he had made it clear to the colleague in question that he totally disagreed with him about more or less everything. Not a conventional method of courting votes.

The upshot of this uncompromising campaign was that – despite more or less unanimous support for Michael from the shadow Cabinet and a sizeable early lead – the social conservatives in the parliamentary party in the end voted comprehensively for Iain Duncan Smith whereas the liberal-minded vote was split between Michael and Ken Clarke, and the Europhiles voted solidly for Ken. Once the parliamentary phase of the leadership election had reached the last three candidates, Michael was knocked out of the contest by a small margin and the voluntary party was then required to choose between Ken and Iain. At this stage, I concluded that if we couldn't have full-blooded liberal modernism, at least we could preserve our Euroscepticism and have a full-blooded approach to the fundamental problem of social justice. This meant supporting Iain, which I duly did in a series of open meetings around the country.

The eventual 60/40 vote of the voluntary party in favour of Iain led to what was, from my point of view, a wholly surprising result. I received, out of the blue, a call from him asking me to become his shadow Home Secretary. As I (gratefully) accepted, I was struck – not for the last time – by the extraordinary gyrations of democratic politics: far from being cast into outer darkness following my debacle in the 2001 general election, I was now, just three months later, being pushed into the limelight. Moreover, I was serendipitously positioned to promote exactly the agenda of social reform that I had promised myself I would in the 2001–05 parliament – at last making up for lost time by applying the lessons of Hackney.

Many commentators, looking back at Iain's time as Leader of the Opposition, focus on the problems he encountered. And there certainly were problems. It took far too long to get the leader's office into a fully functioning state. Relationships with the treasurers and donors went through a distinctly rocky patch. So did relationships with the party apparatus in Conservative Central Office. Alongside Tom Strathclyde, Bill Cash, Owen Paterson and David Maclean, I was involved in a sequence of increasingly bizarre manoeuvres to keep the ship afloat. It wasn't until close to the end of Iain's time, when Tim Montgomerie came to run his office, that a degree of orderliness was imposed. Nor was Iain able to match William Hague's commanding presence when tangling with Tony Blair in the House of Commons. And these defects convinced a substantial part of those amongst the parliamentary party who had voted either for Ken Clarke or for Michael Portillo that Iain was not the right man for the job. The resulting plots led to his downfall.

But all of this masked the fundamental strategic shift that Iain was rightly trying to achieve. By 1997, when Iain had become shadow Secretary for Social Security, he had already been profoundly influenced by Frank Field. At that time, despite the fact that he and Frank were on opposite sides of the House of Commons, he had been determined to do whatever he could to help Frank reform the welfare system so that it stopped being a dependency trap, locking people into unemployment. As soon as Iain became Leader of the Opposition, he widened this ambition into a general programme to prevent anyone in our society being, as he put it, 'left behind'. This became the centrepiece of his strategy. The passion with which he pursued this programme intensified as he visited hard-pressed Glasgow housing estates and other parts of the country where he found families, indeed multiple generations, whose life chances had been dramatically affected by continued unemployment, welfare dependency and, in many cases, chaotic lifestyles.

Iain is a genuinely original thinker, in the sense that his politics emerges not from a textbook but from somewhere deep in his being. He didn't adopt his drive for social reform out of some calculation that it would be electorally beneficial, but rather because he (like me) had come to the conclusion that the cycle of deprivation was genuinely the biggest problem facing our society at that time. He felt (and repeatedly said to me) that the Conservative Party, if it wanted to govern the country, needed to put forward a serious programme to address that problem. But Iain is also conscious of the way that political parties are perceived, and he could see clearly what so many others had missed – that the attachment of the party to free market theory had unnecessarily become a reason for placing far too little emphasis on social justice, and that this in turn had given the party the appearance of callousness. As Theresa May famously put it in a speech at one of Iain's party conferences, 'they call us the nasty party'. Because Iain was a thorough-going Eurosceptic and an unabashed free marketeer (and perhaps also because he was clearly identified with the socially con-servative section of the party) he wasn't at all cowed by accusations of 'unsoundness'. Coming from the right, he felt he had the moral au-thority to lead the party into social reform and the capacity to take the right of the party with him. In addition, he was able to carry social lib-erals like David Willetts and me – because we saw that his programme would at last enable the party to slay the dragon of social injustice that we had so clearly failed to slay since the days when David and I had been in Mrs Thatcher's Policy Unit.

It was therefore with his full backing that I used my time as shadow Home Secretary to promote a social reform agenda of my own. This I developed in a series of speeches which centred on the concepts of 'the neighbourly society' and 'the conveyor belt to crime'.

The idea behind my advocacy of the 'neighbourly society' was that the conditions for social well-being come about not by chance but when children grow up in a society where they acquire the right values from an early age. I argued that the system of criminal justice works only to the extent that most of us don't actually need to be constrained by it on a daily basis because we are fundamentally well disposed to-wards our fellow citizens most of the time. We are, in short, generally 'neighbourly'. And I argued that it was where this neighbourliness had broken down, where children were being brought up with different, less pro-social, assumptions and values, that society was at risk from crime and disorder.

The concept of the 'conveyor belt to crime' was a natural sequel to this analysis of the need for a neighbourly society. My thesis was (and remains to this day) that – while there is undoubtedly a small fraction of serious law-breakers who are either psychopathic or organised professional criminals – the great bulk of those (mainly young men) who fill our prisons are in fact neither psychopathic nor determined professionals: they are young people who have been grossly damaged, alienated and often partially deranged as a result of chaotic home backgrounds, poor education, and drug and alcohol dependency. They find support and comradeship, if they find it at all, in gangs which all too often act as surrogate families. In short, they are the classic products of Keith Joseph's cycles of deprivation. They are on a conveyor belt that they cannot stop.

These two concepts drove me – again with Iain's full and enthusiastic backing – to focus on two particular elements of the solution: rehabilitation and the voluntary sector. I argued that we needed to mobilise the voluntary sector to rescue children and families from the chaotic and destructive conditions of life in which some of them found themselves; and I argued that we needed to focus on the treatment and rehabilitation of chaotic drug- and alcohol-users to reduce levels of crime and begin to bring the victims of these dependencies back into work and into the mainstream of society. It was commonly thought that this agenda would be rejected wholesale by the Conservative Party as 'too weedy'. But, based on my own experience of the voluntary party in West Dorset, I didn't believe it; and indeed it turned out to be untrue. With help from a brilliant team who gathered around my chief of staff, Robert Halfon, and my press officer, Henry Macrory, I put together a session at the party conference of 2002 at which – to the open surprise of many seasoned journalists – the 'party faithful' enthusiastically accepted our new emphasis on rescue and rehabilitation, and warmly applauded non-traditional and non-partisan speakers such as the remarkable Camila Batmanghelidjh of Kids Company, whose work with massively deprived children in south London had hugely impressed me. I think we proved, at that party conference, what is now widely understood – that the centre of gravity of the Conservative voluntary party is in fact the belief that the state should help people to help themselves and others. Contrary to what is suggested by some parodies of the party, an agenda that focuses on increasing life chances and opening up opportunities for people who have been denied them will, in my experience, always meet with strong support from a Conservative audience.

By itself, of course, my promotion of this agenda was not enough to make a significant difference to the direction of the party. But, as part of Iain's much wider drive for social justice and social reform, I think it did contribute to a substantial reorientation of the party, and to the beginning of an answer to the question that had sat unanswered on my computer screen in 1997. By comparison with this main thrust, the rest of my activities as shadow Home Secretary were of little real interest – though some of them did generate a considerable amount of attention in the media, much of it less than complimentary. I made a series of efforts in Parliament to moderate what were by then becoming somewhat authoritarian tendencies in the Blair government and I opposed campaigns for tougher sentencing by *The Sun* and others; this led to me being excoriated in the tabloids on various occasions. I also made an injudicious and tactless remark that I would sooner beg in the streets than send my children to a school round the corner from me in London which was at that time in a parlous condition; this added to the (reasonably justified) view in the media that I was gaffe-prone. And I suggested that the government should seek to resolve what was at that time a considerable crisis in the system for processing asylum claims by emulating the Australian system of offshore processing; this was described in some quarters as my 'fantasy island' proposal and was sensibly dropped by my successor, David Davis.

A wrong turning was the decision to oppose Blair's student loans. On this occasion, I was on the right side of the argument. I argued vehemently we should support the introduction of loans as a progressive and equitable system for funding the universities, which were desperately short of cash, at the expense of those who had benefited financially from going to them rather than hard-working taxpayers who had never been anywhere near a university. But being on the right side of an argument doesn't guarantee victory. I lost comprehensively in the shadow Cabinet; indeed, I found myself in a minority of one.

An even more important turning point of Iain's time as leader occurred late in the afternoon on a dark March day in 2003. The shadow Cabinet Room, oak-panelled and under-lit, was even more sepulchral than usual. We met to decide how we – Her Majesty's Loyal Opposition – should vote on the invasion of Iraq. For once, our decision mattered. Enough Labour MPs were likely to vote against the invasion to deprive the Blair government of a majority, but only if we decided to join the Labour rebels in the division lobbies. Was it legal? We had been told it was. Did Saddam have weapons of mass destruction? We had been told that he did. Could Saddam's armies be defeated quickly and easily? We were told they could be. But we had also heard many of our constituents doubting each of these propositions. We knew that there were huge question marks hanging over the evidence of WMD. Many of our backbenchers, and some of our shadow ministers, were not prepared to support the war.

As I sat in that darkling room, surveying the murky scene, I tried to discern what it was that we were really deciding. President Bush had already moved his forces half the way across the world and into position for an attack. He was clearly determined to proceed, come what might. Blair had equally clearly committed British support for the invasion. So what would happen if we Conservatives voted against it? Britain's credibility as an ally of the US would be impaired, perhaps for a generation. The Atlantic alliance, on which so great a proportion of our intelligence and security depends, would be put in jeopardy: the White House had been sending us messages to that effect through the day. But the invasion would still take place. Bush would move forward without the UK. So, I reasoned, the vote in the House of Commons would not be about whether there should be a war against Iraq, but about whether Britain should risk the Atlantic alliance by opting out of the coming war at this eleventh hour.

Once I had put the matter in this way, the question seemed to answer itself: to my mind, it made no sense to risk fracturing an alliance of great value if one could not thereby stop the invasion. No need, then, to ask the further, much more difficult question of whether the invasion was a good idea. No need to ask how certain we could be that the assurances we had been given were well founded. We were voting about our Atlantic relationship, and our duty as a loyal opposition seemed to be to strengthen, not weaken that relationship.

Whether this was the right decision, and whether it was the right way for us to make the decision we were called upon to make, will be questions that remain with me for the rest of my life. It is of course now clear that Saddam did not possess the alleged WMD – and that the invasion was therefore clearly not justifiable on the basis of self-defence. It is also now clear that the invasion itself, the process thereafter of 'de-Baathification' which removed most of the bureaucracy, and the failure to establish any effective government for several years, left Iraq with massive problems with which it and we are still wrestling today. But these are all issues primarily for Blair and his colleagues. The most difficult issue for those of us sat in the shadow Cabinet Room that day remains whether it was right, regardless of other justification, to support NATO at a time when Bush was depending on Blair. Knowing what I know now, I wouldn't have done it.

Alongside these very serious moments, there was some light relief – sometimes of an embarrassing kind. At about four o'clock one morning, I was planning to go to the Netherlands for a meeting in my capacity as a director of Rothschild before returning to the Commons to take part in a debate as shadow Home Secretary for the afternoon and evening. Rothschild had sent a car to take me to the airport for an early flight. I had just emerged from the bath when the doorbell rang. Imagining that it must be the Rothschild driver, I donned a towel and popped downstairs. When I opened the door, it was not the driver but a man with a great deal of grease on his hands, who explained that he and his mate had been trying to mend his car and that my driver had told them that he was waiting for me to come out, so they knew that I must be up – and he was therefore asking whether he could use my loo to wash his hands before they set off.

I said 'yes, of course'. The man came in and I showed him upstairs while his mate stayed downstairs. A few moments later, they both left. It was at this point that I realised my wallet (which I had left downstairs on the kitchen table) had gone. I dashed out in my towel just in time to reach them as they went out through the gate of the front garden, and demanded my credit cards back. Amazingly, they gave them back to me and scampered away.

It was not until I had dressed and got into the car to be driven to the airport that I realised I was also missing my Palm Pilot, which contained my diary and contacts. From the car, I called the local police to report the theft. When I returned to the UK at lunchtime, the media were in full swing. Clearly, some police officer had sold to the newspapers the story that the shadow Home Secretary had been burgled. Within a few hours, as I described the events to reporters (and also discovered that my wife's not very valuable jewellery had been removed – no doubt by the gentleman I showed upstairs), the story had been turned into a matter of intense human interest.

I was unable to understand why the furore was going on quite so long, until I discovered that the rumour was circulating that there was much more to this than met the eye. Apparently, some of the hard-bitten journalists believed I couldn't possibly just have let the burglars in to wash their hands, and must instead have had some sexual liaison or other illicit relationship with them. It is only when we tracked down my Rothschild driver and got him to speak to the reporters in order to confirm my version of events that the fuss subsided.

Despite these various difficulties, in the main I thoroughly enjoyed my time shadowing the Home Office and began to feel that – through the promotion of the neighbourly society agenda – I was able to help make a difference. Unfortunately, it all came to an untimely end when, in a swirl of what later turned out to be unjustified allegations and an increasing sense that Iain could not win a general election, the parliamentary party finally lost faith in Iain's leadership and his position became unsustainable. The rules allowed for a vote of confidence to be held if enough Conservative MPs signed letters asking for one; the requisite number of such letters were deposited with the chairman of the weirdly named 1922 Committee, which represents the parliamentary party; a vote of confidence was held; and Iain lost.

At this point, in October 2003, we faced a major crisis. To lose a leader after the loss of a general election is one thing. To lose the leader in the middle of the parliament is quite another. The headlines were screaming about the implosion of the Conservatives, and it looked quite conceivable that (despite Iain's good work in reorienting the party) we would face an even bigger defeat at the next election than we had in 1997 or 2001. It seemed to me that the only way forward was for the parliamentary party to coalesce around a single candidate for the leadership, and a candidate of unquestionable competence. I reasoned that, if this could be done before anyone in the media had time to draw breath, we might be able to regain momentum. It was with this thought in mind that I had begun discussions with the shadow Chancellor, Michael Howard, once it was clear that the vote of confidence in Iain's leadership was going to take place and that those of us supporting Iain would be sizeably outnumbered by those opposing him. I had agreed with Michael and with my erstwhile boss in the constitutional team, Liam Fox (who was then shadow Health Secretary), that, in the likely event of Iain being defeated, Liam and I would support Michael's candidacy and that we would make an effort to unify Conservative MPs around this proposition. Hence, a very few hours after Iain's defeat, I joined forces with Liam (who represented the traditionalist wing of the parliamentary party) and Stephen Dorrell (who represented its modernising wing) to hold an impromptu press conference outside my office in Speaker's Court at the House of Commons. I think it may have been imagined by some of the many journalists who gathered there that evening that either Liam or I was going to announce our own candidacy. Instead, the three of us made clear that we would be supporting Michael Howard, and urged the whole parliamentary party to do so. The tactic worked. Within hours, David Davis, Michael's main rival, had issued a statement supporting Michael, and this was followed by similar statements from other, less plausible contenders. The race was over before it had begun.

The immediate effect of this smooth and bloodless coup was everything that could be hoped. Michael gave a magisterial speech at the Saatchi Gallery to which I suspected Francis Maude and Nick Boles had heavily contributed. It contained a strong message of party unity, made clear the intention to continue with Iain's social justice agenda and added an acknowledgement of the need to modernise the party's attitudes on social issues. From my point of view, it sounded like a dream combination. Not long afterwards, Michael asked me to be his shadow Chancellor. Unfortunately, I made the mistake of accepting. It seemed like a good idea at the time.

The Conservative Party owes an undying debt of gratitude to Michael Howard. At this nadir of our fortunes, he stepped into the breach, bringing huge professionalism to the task of restoring the party's reputation after all the disunity and plotting that had brought Iain down. In contrast to the problems of Iain's machine in 2001, Michael quickly organised a highly efficient private office headed by Stephen Sherbourne (one of the most charming and unflappable people in politics, who had for a long period been Mrs T.'s political secretary) and Rachel Whetstone (a warm, energetic and talented figure, who had been Michael's special adviser during his period as Home Secretary). Michael also took up John Maples's interesting idea of a smaller shadow Cabinet, imposed an effective discipline on the whole ministerial team, immediately began to attract funding from donors who had deserted us during the previous two years, performed admirably at the despatch box against Tony Blair, and infused the whole of the opposition with huge amounts of energy. I had already watched with admiration his own effective spell as shadow Chancellor, and my respect for his integrity and decisiveness increased further as I worked closely with him as his shadow Chancellor over the succeeding eighteen months. But, while our personal relationship remained excellent, I began slowly to realise that there were two fundamental political problems: despite Michael's tactical and organisational brilliance, his strategy was wrong; and I was in the wrong job.

Michael's speech at the Saatchi Gallery had intimated a combination of Iain's emphasis on social justice for those excluded from the mainstream with the Portillo–Maude agenda of social liberalism and modernisation of the party's attitudes. But, as the time between Michael's uncontested election as leader and the coming general election ticked away, it was difficult to discern much, if any, of the passion that Iain had shown for improving the life chances of those trapped in cycles of deprivation. So far as the criminal justice system was concerned, while we maintained the policies I had advocated for an increased drug treatment and rehabilitation programme and for mobilising the voluntary sector to help cure the cycle of deprivation, these items were given very much a second billing compared to the emphasis placed on increasing police numbers, tougher sentencing and the reclassification of cannabis as a class B (rather than class C) drug. Similarly, in every other area of policy, Michael aimed at clear, definite, tough action. This squeezed out any sense of social liberalism or modernised attitudes. The resulting manifesto, when it came, was short, crisp, well-written and hard-edged – and summed up by its front page, which promised 'more police, cleaner hospitals, lower taxes, school discipline, controlled immigration, accountability'. The tone was unmistakable: we were replaying 2001 – right down to a virtual repeat of William Hague's punchline that 'people who work hard, pay their taxes and do the right thing should be rewarded, not punished'. Unsurprisingly, the result, when that came, was also virtually a replay of the defeat we had suffered in 2001.

Why was I, as shadow Chancellor, unable to exercise any real influence over this strategy? One reason, certainly, was a conscious decision on my part to support Michael in shadow Cabinet more or less regardless, on the grounds that – after the debacle of Iain's departure – the last thing the party needed was disunity at the top. On one or two occasions, I took this to the extent of supporting policies with which I strongly disagreed; but mainly, it meant carefully avoiding any potentially disruptive effort to pull the tone and priorities in directions that Michael would have found uncomfortable. But there was another, at least equally significant, reason that, despite my officially important status in the hierarchy of the opposition, I had no real impact on the general strategy: I was too preoccupied with the problems of my own position and of policy in my own area.

There are very few posts that really put you on the front line in British politics. One of these is shadow Chancellor. Of course, you have no more effect on the administrative activities of government than any other opposition politician – and far, far less than many virtually incognito ministers. But when it comes to the battles in Parliament and over the airwaves, the shadow Chancellor is at the centre of the fray. As shadow Home Secretary under Iain Duncan Smith, I had taken on the real Home Secretary, David Blunkett, with reasonable success – agreeing with him publicly when I in fact agreed with him, maintaining a studious courtesy in Parliament and in the media, and engaging in carefully calibrated attacks on his policies where this was required to sustain my own agendas of social liberalism and the 'neighbourly society'. By and large, it was recognised even by the sections of the media that were hostile to me that what was sometimes called the 'David and Olli show' was a proper example of civilised but vigorous debate between opposition and government. But none of this prepared me adequately for the battle with Gordon Brown, who was then at the zenith of his (mainly unjustified) reputation as Chancellor of the Exchequer. When I became Gordon's shadow, I found that I had entered what, to me, was a nightmare world.

I'm afraid that one of the elements of the nightmare was my experience of Gordon himself. In contrast to the relationship I established with David Blunkett, or the engagement I was later to have with Margaret Beckett when she was Environment Secretary and I was briefly her shadow, I was never able to establish the slightest rapport with Gordon. I just couldn't get through the carapace. No doubt this was in part a failing on my side; but I am not persuaded, in retrospect, that it was really possible for an opponent to find a way through his personal defences in such a way as to establish a personal relationship. On one occasion early in my time as shadow Chancellor, I found myself standing next to Gordon behind the Speaker's chair while both of us were waiting to go into the chamber for Treasury Questions. I thought I would try to break the ice by murmuring a few sweet nothings. No response. Then a colleague of mine, presumably unaware of the fact that I was trying to be emollient, came up to us and, with sublime lack of tact (I take it intentional), said to him, 'Time for a change of job, Gordon?' Since this was one of the many moments when the press was full of Gordon's efforts to displace Tony Blair as Prime Minister, it was predictable that he would be less than amused by such jocularity. But the sequel was nevertheless surprising. Instead of saying anything, Gordon walked silently a few paces across to the Aye lobby, turned, walked the few paces back to the doors behind the Speaker's chair, and then executed a further half-turn and strode, still without a word, into the chamber and towards the government front bench. For the first and only time in my life, I had witnessed a literal rendition of the meaning of the phrase 'taking time out'.

In the chamber itself, I found encounters with Gordon totally disconcerting. As one unkind journalist put it, my rapier was no match for Gordon's tank. Alas, the journalist was right. On the big occasions, when virtually the whole membership of the House of Commons is packed into the chamber for the Autumn Statement or some other similar encounter between the Chancellor and the shadow Chancellor, both Michael Howard before me and George Osborne after me found ways of dealing with the wall of noise generated by Gordon's supporters on the Labour benches and also ways of puncturing, at least from time to time, the bravado and aggression of Gordon's technique at the despatch box. I never did; he had the upper hand on every occasion. Even when my argument was subsequently proved to have been right, I think I can accurately say that I made no impact at the time.

In the middle of the afternoon on 10 December 2003, I rose from the opposition front bench and grasped the despatch box with both hands. As the shadow Chancellor, it was my job to answer Gordon Brown's Autumn Statement on public expenditure. The House was packed. The noise in the chamber was deafening, with Gordon's many henchmen gesticulating and shouting. We had prepared a series of arguments, hoping that they would be relevant to what Gordon announced, and my team had done some quick work behind the scenes during his statement to arm me with further facts for my response. But nothing had prepared me for the atmosphere, which was more like a bear pit than the civilised proceedings to which I had been accustomed in my encounters with David Blunkett when I was shadow Home Secretary.

As I rose, I realised with a thud that the speech I was about to give was the wrong speech. It simply didn't have the punch that is required under such circumstances. The points it contained were broadly right, and some of them would have been of interest in an academic common room, or even to the House of Commons in some of its more reflective moods. But they were calculated to score *nul points* in this nearly hysterical atmosphere. I had watched both Francis Maude and Michael Portillo fall into this same trap, so I should have seen it coming. But rationality and courtesy had got the better of me, and I had a dud speech. So there were two choices. Ditch it, and speak without notes. Or soldier on. I had just a few seconds to decide.

Conflicting thoughts crowded into my head. If I read out the speech, it would be very bad but it would not be a disaster; if I ditched the speech and went solo, it might be much better but it might be much worse – perhaps to the point of catastrophe. In this baying hullabaloo, would I be able to think sufficiently straight to make a coherent impromptu speech of a different kind? Without a text in front of me, would I be able to remember the crucial facts and figures?

As my hands engaged with the wooden surface of the despatch box, my mouth began to speak the first words on the paper I had in front of me. The decision – cowardly as it was – appeared to have been made. I knew it wouldn't be any good. And it wasn't. But it was hopelessly mediocre rather than catastrophic. Some generous and good-hearted colleagues found it in themselves to say something nice about it, which they clearly didn't believe. But on an occasion like this, it's the thought that counts.

This failure in debate was bad enough. What was worse, I was having a devil of a time back home fashioning Conservative economic policy. In some ways, things had moved in a positive direction since my previous foray into this arena as shadow Chief Secretary to the Treasury in the 1997–2001 parliament. Michael Howard and I were in complete agreement that, as well as stoutly resisting any suggestion of joining the euro, we should guarantee the continued independence of the Monetary Policy Committee of the Bank of England if we took office at the next election. We also agreed on the need to maintain the CPI inflation target of 2 per cent. Michael gallantly supported my proposals to introduce independent fiscal forecasting (foreshadowing what later became George Osborne's Office for Budget Responsibility), to increase the independence of the national statistician (a measure subsequently adopted by Gordon Brown), and to move macro-prudential supervision of the banking system back into the hands of the Bank of

England (anticipating George's later creation of the Prudential Regulation Authority as the sister institution to the Monetary Policy Committee within the Bank). Michael and I worked happily together on formulating a serious deregulatory agenda (boosted in the second half of Michael's tenure by the appointment of John Redwood as shadow Deregulation Secretary). In addition, we agreed about the need to complete the James Review of wasteful public spending – which resulted in commitments to freeze civil service recruitment, reduce the public sector payroll by 235,000 and reform or abolish 168 public bodies.

The reductions in waste and bureaucracy were relatively easy to find after several years in which Gordon had effectively lost control of the bureaucratic machine. And this in turn led to fairly straightforward agreement on a public spending programme – admittedly after quite a lot of hard work had been done on the details in close cooperation with George Osborne (at that time, my shadow Chief Secretary). Following the pattern of 2001, we adopted a trajectory of annual public spending growth one percentage point lower than Labour's for the three years 2005/06, 2006/07 and 2007/08. As Gordon had by this stage reached a staggering public spending growth rate of 5 per cent per year, this left us with a projected 4 per cent annual public spending growth rate for the first three years of a prospective Conservative administration. This was enough to achieve public expenditure savings of £12 billion per year by 2007/08, compared with Labour's programme – and yet gave us not only sufficient headroom to match Labour's programmed increases in spending on the NHS, schools, transport and international development but also the ability to outspend Labour on the police, defence and pensions (in line with Michael's overall strategy). Although I had learned from my experiences in 2001 not to speculate about future years beyond 2007/08 in public, I was quite clear that a Conservative government would be able in due course to find further deliverable and politically acceptable savings once we were in office, so that the rate of growth of spending could eventually, later in the 2005–10 parliament, be trimmed back to the growth rate of the economy and thereby deliver balanced budgets.

With monetary policy in the hands of the Bank of England under a sensible inflation target, accompanied by serious efforts to improve the macro-prudential supervision of the banking system, increase the transparency of fiscal policy and prune back the excessive regulation of business, and with public spending being gently brought back under some degree of control, I felt that we had a basis for a sensible, if not particularly exciting, economic policy. But there remained the great question of tax and public borrowing. If we were saving £12 billion per year by 2007/08, how should we deploy that saving – for tax cuts or for reduced government borrowing? It was this question that dogged me.

Both Michael and I were under huge pressure from Conservatively inclined commentators and from Conservative parliamentary colleagues to make promises of tax cuts. The people arguing for such cuts came in two varieties. There were the 'supply-siders', who were enormously impressed by the so-called Laffer curve; they argued that tax receipts could be increased if tax rates were reduced – because the reductions in tax rates would give people greater incentives to work hard and invest more, thereby increasing economic activity. And then there were the believers in Brownian motion; they argued that Gordon Brown's public sector net borrowing (then running at around 3 per cent per year) and public sector net debt (then around 34 per cent of GDP) were both at sustainable levels, and that any money saved as a result of more modest Conservative public expenditure growth rates should therefore be used for tax cuts. The problem was that I disagreed with both of these propositions.

Of course it is true that, as the Laffer curve illustrates, 100 per cent tax rates will produce roughly the same amount of tax (none) as 0 per cent tax rates, because no one will work hard or invest their own money in businesses if the result is that the state snaffles up 100 per cent of the return on that work or money; and it does indeed follow that there is, for each particular tax, an optimisation point at which the rate is set neither too high nor too low but just at the level which will produce the highest possible tax yield. But the rub is that no one knows in advance where this optimisation point will be; so reducing tax rates in the hope of generating increased tax yields is a punt which any Chancellor of the Exchequer should take only when he or she has enough headroom to make a mistake without living to regret it. True, the reduction in the top rate of income tax brought in by Margaret Thatcher and Geoffrey Howe had produced more tax yield from high earners within a couple of years, and George Osborne was later to prove the same point when he refused to implement Labour's last-minute increase in the top rate of income tax after he took over as Chancellor in 2010. But I did not believe that I could convincingly or sensibly rely on such 'supply-side' effects to commit to unfunded cuts of tax rates in 2005, and nor did Michael.

This left us with the question of whether the other Conservatively inclined pundits were right to be saying that we could afford to use any savings we made in public expenditure to fund tax cuts because the public sector net borrowing and net debt were at sustainable levels in 2005. My own view was that, despite apparently being low, these borrowing and debt levels were not in fact sustainable – because I did not believe that Gordon Brown had 'abolished the economic cycle' (as I think he had at least partly deluded himself he had). It seemed to me that, with the economy growing steadily over a long period, Gordon should have been running either balanced budgets or surpluses as he had been in the 1997–2001 parliament, not borrowing 2 or 3 per cent of GDP each year, and certainly not increasing public sector net debt from 28 per cent to 34 per cent of GDP over the 2001–05 parliament. I reasoned that, against this background, an economic downturn in the succeeding parliament would quickly lead to unsustainable borrowing and debt. I therefore argued strongly that we should use the majority of our savings to fund reductions in public sector borrowing rather than to fund tax cuts.

In retrospect, my two regrets are that I didn't argue this even more strongly and that I didn't watch more closely the parallel build-up of borrowing and debt in the private sector, to which the Liberal Democrat finance spokesman, Vince Cable, was drawing attention. As we all now know, Gordon was in fact borrowing recklessly at a time when the rest of the country was doing the same thing – with catastrophic consequences when the inevitable economic downturn coincided with the banking crisis. I cannot claim to have prophesied such doom. But I was at least clear that it was highly imprudent for the Chancellor to be running deficits in the boom years, thereby failing to mend the roof while the sun was shining (though I didn't have the skill to use this perspicuous phrase later fashioned by George Osborne). I should, I now believe, have pressed this further by arguing for a sharper slowdown in public spending growth, and for all of the savings to be applied to deficit reduction. And, while I was at it, I should have pressed for the Financial Services Authority (which Gordon had bizarrely put in charge of macro-prudential supervision) to take steps to restrict the pace of growth in private sector lending. When the chairman and chief executive of the FSA had come to see me about my proposal to abolish it and fold prudential supervision of the banking sector back into the Bank of England, I had been genuinely shocked by their naïve confidence in the modelling that they had done of the systemically important banks. I could not have known at the time what we now know – that by omitting the scenario in which the wholesale lending markets completely dry up, their modelling managed to avoid even investigating exactly the crisis that actually happened in 2008.

At the time, however, I was in no condition to create new monetary battles because I was finding it difficult to get any real support for my fiscal policies – even for the modest cuts in public spending growth that I was proposing, let alone for the proposition that we should devote the majority of the savings to reducing the public sector deficit. The supply-siders said I lacked the guts to deliver real tax cuts, and the Brownian-motion enthusiasts implied that I was a prissy fiscal conservative at a time when there was no need for such prissiness. I eventually reached an agreement with Michael to use £8 billion of the £12 billion saved annually on public expenditure to reduce the deficit, with the remaining £4 billion going on tax cuts (largely for council tax payers and for savers). This pleased no one.

In retrospect, it is clear that just about everything that we proposed as economic policy in the 2005 election was in the right direction – albeit too restrained to meet the full scale of the disaster that hit the economy in 2008. But from the point of view of the politics of the time, I was absolutely conscious that I had failed to persuade anyone of the problems that Gordon was laying in store for the country, and that I had also failed to match him in debate. My period as shadow Chancellor just added one more reason why Michael was not going to lead the Conservative Party to victory in the 2005 general election – a fact that I think we all privately acknowledged, though we certainly didn't admit it.

Immediately after our inevitable defeat, I asked Michael to move me from the shadow Chancellorship into the very different and much lower-profile post of shadow Environment Secretary. Gordon, with his usual political brilliance, characterised this as an unusual case of a politician wanting to spend more time with his merchant bank (the move enabled me to return as a non-executive director to Rothschild, from which I had been forced to retire while shadow Chancellor). In fact, as so often, the truth would have been an even more powerful accusation if Gordon had only known it: I wanted to do another job because I didn't think I had done the shadow Chancellor job very well, and because I thought George Osborne would do it much better (as indeed subsequently proved to be the case). As for the choice of the Environment portfolio, this was my bid to find a new way of helping to transform and modernise the Conservative Party – but that forms part of the next phase of my story.

CHAPTER 5

REMOULDING THE CONSERVATIVE PARTY

At the moment in 2005 when I became shadow Environment Secretary, the Conservative Party's reputation on the environment was at a low ebb.

There was no historical justification for this state of affairs. Mrs Thatcher had put herself at the forefront of global action to deal with environmental risks – making seminal speeches that highlighted both the risk to the climate caused by carbon emissions and the risk to the ozone layer caused by chlorofluorocarbons (CFCs). Building on these speeches, she had established a new international agenda when she took her arguments about carbon emissions to the UN General Assembly in 1989. More or less simultaneously, she had sponsored sustained diplomatic efforts to combat CFCs, culminating in a speech delivered in 1990 to the representatives of 100 countries – which undoubtedly did more than the actions of any other world leader to bring about an international ban on these noxious chemicals. Nor was she operating solo. Four environment secretaries between 1989 and 1997 – Chris Patten, Michael Heseltine, Michael Howard and John Selwyn Gummer – all had distinguished records of attending to the preservation of the natural environment and the enhancement of our countryside.

Not surprisingly, Michael Howard had retained his concern for the environment – including his commitment to global reductions in carbon emissions – when he became leader of the party in 2001. Indeed, William Hague before him had favoured action to sustain and improve the environment as early as 1997 while he was Leader of the Opposition – an attitude borne out by his later activities as Foreign Secretary in the coalition government, when he played a leading role in efforts to promote global reductions in carbon emissions, to arrest global deforestation, to protect international wildlife and to eliminate the illegal trade in ivory.

So it was remarkable that, in the years between 1997 and 2005, and notwithstanding two party leaders with strong environmental interests, the Conservative Party in opposition had failed to produce a single memorable contribution to environmental policy; indeed, in some quarters within the party, disregard for ecology and nature and beauty was seen as a test of being 'sound' or 'one of us' (those dreadful words again). There was the implicit (even if never quite the explicit) idea that anyone sufficiently equipped with free market machismo to count as 'one of us' would gaily bulldoze and concrete over any part of the globe, regardless of its beauty or ecological significance, in the cause of unconstrained economic growth.

I had increasingly come to the conclusion that this simply had to change. Admittedly, the direct effect of an opposition on an area of policy like this is slight; so the attitude of the Conservative Party did not have any immediate, practical adverse effects on the en-vironment itself – and the Blair governments had certainly taken environmental issues sufficiently seriously to maintain the rhetorical momentum created by Mrs Thatcher in the late 1980s. But I could see real administrative and political dangers if we continued to downplay environmental issues in the new parliament. Administratively, the danger was that the Blair (and soon thereafter, the Brown) government would feel entitled to relax on environmental issues because the principal opposition was so feeble in this area, effectively leaving the 'green agenda' to be championed enthusiastically but relatively ineffectively and sometimes unrealistically by the Liberal Democrats or the Green Party. Indeed, there were already signs of this trend beginning to establish itself in 2005, since the Blair governments – despite their welcome rhetoric – had in fact made no significant impact on carbon emissions other than through a serendipitous one-off change in the industrial production of the adipic acid used to make nylon. Meanwhile, politically, it seemed to me that by stepping away from the environment we were not only concealing some of the best instincts of Conservatives but also reinforcing some of the worst images of ourselves as philistine proponents of 'free-market-theory-gone-wrong', thereby giving our detractors another basis for describing us as the 'nasty party'.

On the last evening of the 2005 general election, when the votes had all been cast, Michael Howard had called me to discuss what he himself should do if we lost the election, as by then seemed almost certain. We had agreed that it would be a huge benefit for him to set a delayed date for his departure so that the party could take a proper amount of time to select a new leader. Although many colleagues had criticised Michael when he announced his intention to do this, on the grounds that he was imposing a relatively long period of uncertainty on the party, I think it is clear from the sequel that in this, as in so many of his other actions, he did what was in the long term the right thing with splendid disregard for any short-term effect on himself. But the future beneficial consequences of his action were not, of course, visible in the early days after the inevitable election defeat had occurred. What was visible was that those of us who formed his interim shadow Cabinet were going to have more than six months in the job before a new leader could make his or her dispositions. I was determined to use those six months to establish both new Conservative policy commitments on the environment and a new reputation for the Conservative Party in this field.

So far as chunky policy was concerned, I wanted to focus on climate change. I had read enough of the literature surrounding the science to feel confident that Mrs T. had been right to highlight the risks. I use the work 'risks' advisedly. I did not know enough to be certain that the majority of scientists in the various relevant fields were right to be as worried as they were about the long-run effects of high levels of carbon emissions on climate change; nor did I put much faith in some of the more lurid and unbalanced accounts given by some commentators about the effects of climate change on economies and societies across the globe; still less was I inclined to buy into the quasi-religious fervour of some of the more extreme environmental groups who wanted to use the threat of climate change as a basis for rejecting market economics and returning to a mythical medieval state of bliss. But it nevertheless seemed to me that it would be unwise for mankind to ignore the risk that unrestricted carbon emissions might cause climate change of a kind that could in turn cause significant economic and social changes with possibly severe effects on global security and stability. Clearly, if we were to respond to this by reducing carbon emissions, we would need to do so in a way that maintained energy security and kept energy costs within reason. But the work of Nicholas Stern and others, together with my own long involvement in the energy industries while working at Rothschild, had persuaded me that the costs and risks of moving progressively towards a low-carbon economy were not in fact as great as was imagined by the sceptics.

So I came to the conclusion that the Conservative Party should adopt and promote a strong policy of carbon reduction. Of course I was aware that, by itself, the UK was responsible for only about 2 per cent of global carbon emissions and that we could not therefore make significant changes to the amount of global risk just by progressively decarbonising the UK economy. But I reasoned that, by adopting a world-leading policy in the UK, we could obtain the moral authority to argue much more effectively for international action both with our European and transatlantic allies and with world leaders as a whole.

The question therefore was: how best could we Conservatives push the UK into this position of global leadership? It was at this point that a combination of Zac Goldsmith and Tony Juniper came to my aid. Zac, who in 2005 had not yet entered Parliament, helped to shape and finance some critical modelling work that enabled us to get a handle on what rate of decarbonisation was feasible at modest economic cost and without threatening our energy security. Meanwhile, Tony (who was at that time running Friends of the Earth) came up with a plan to have all the political parties sign up to a Climate Change Bill that would require the UK government to move to a low-carbon economy over a set period of years. Putting our modelling together with Tony's idea for a Bill enabled us to produce a carefully calibrated proposal. This recognised that there would be costs involved in decarbonisation, and that it would always be open to political opponents to use those costs to cause significant political problems for any party that tried to lock itself into a policy of decarbonisation. But I sought to solve that problem by obtaining agreement from all the political parties. I believed that if we all signed up and passed the legislation for a long-term decarbonisation programme unanimously, then none of the parties would be able to point a finger at whichever party was implementing the programme in government at any given moment. And this, I hoped, would produce long-term policy stability, on which industrial investors would be able to rely.

The Climate Change Act that eventually emerged has today many supporters and many detractors. I remain convinced that it was an important building block (though of course no more than a building block) in the establishment of a more universal global successor to the Kyoto Treaty – and, although UKIP's opposition to it has subsequently deprived it of some of its attributes as a political insurance policy within the UK, I think it has by and large given us the stability of expectation required for long-term low-carbon investment. So I think it can be claimed, so far at any rate, as a significant success. But to put it in place required two things beyond our own work: I needed to get the other opposition parties to sign up to it; and I needed to persuade the Blair government to turn it into a government Bill.

The first of these objectives proved fairly straightforward except for one unexpected glitch. I had sailed smoothly through meetings with all the other opposition parties, and had prepared the text of a press release announcing cross-party support for the proposed Bill. At the very last moment, however, as we were about to issue the release, I had an urgent call from Ian Paisley (senior). As a conscientious leader of the Democratic Unionist Party, he had been reading the final text and had, he explained to me, come across a wholly unacceptable paragraph in the paper that accompanied the press release. I anxiously enquired where in the paper this unacceptable paragraph appeared. He explained that it was in the very first page. 'But Ian, the first page is just a historical throat-clearing.' 'Exactly,' he said. 'It asserts that climate change has been occurring for millions of years. I cannot accept a paper that makes such an assertion.' I realised, with huge relief, that the problem lay not in a difference of policy about the future but in the contrast between, on the one hand, the geophysical chronology as portrayed by modern science and, on the other, the timetable of Creation as established on a biblical basis by Archbishop Ussher in the seventeenth century. The offending, irrelevant paragraph was duly removed, and we proceeded to publication with support from all opposition parties.

My efforts to bring the Blair government into the fold were less straightforward. Despite considerable manoeuvring and the support of all other parties in the House of Commons, I had not managed to persuade Labour to support the Bill by the end of 2005, when I ceased to be shadow Environment Secretary. It was clear that Tony Blair and his colleagues were hesitating about whether the costs of mandatory progressive decarbonisation would be too great to bear. I therefore went with my successor as shadow Environment Secretary, Peter Ainsworth, to see the newly appointed Environment Secretary, David Miliband, in order to make a further push. He was pretty obviously attracted to the idea of the Bill, but understandably reluctant to let it be an initiative foisted on the government by the opposition. He smilingly and rather disarmingly gave us to understand that while he could not, as he put it, 'prevent consensus breaking out', he intended that if the Bill were to be taken forward it should be taken forward by him and not by us. I was happy to settle for that, as was Peter, who entirely shared my sense of mission about the Bill.

But I didn't think that promoting decarbonisation and the Climate Change Bill were enough to change the misperception of the Conservatives as a party that had no real interest in the shape of the world around us. So I decided also to engage in some philosophising – always a high-risk strategy in politics. My theme was that politics should be conducted 'as if beauty matters', and my point (which happens to be abundantly true) was that (a) beauty does matter and (b) politics is usually conducted as if it doesn't. Of course, this speech (despite quite wide coverage) was nothing like enough to get through to a mass audience – and it wasn't until David Cameron and Steve Hilton got to work on much more politically perspicuous ways of making the point that we eventually brought home to people the fact that Conservatives do actually care about how the world around them looks and feels. But in the restricted circles of those who write and think about the politics of nature and architecture I think my endeavours did register slightly, and I have found that there continues to be some niche interest in this topic ever since.

These beginnings of serious changes in the party's positions on both 'hard' and 'soft' environmental issues were, however, just one part of what I hoped we could achieve when I backed David Cameron's campaign for the leadership. By the time I came to make the choice to support David, I had worked quite closely with three party leaders. I had also seen at increasingly close hand what had gone wrong in different ways for each of them. So I had a pretty good handle on the characteristics that a leader needed to possess. I wanted someone who would combine modern, socially liberal and environmentally conscious attitudes with a serious and unremitting effort to improve the life chances of people caught in cycles of deprivation; and I wanted someone who would see sensibly regulated free markets, sound money, balanced budgets, welfare reform, school reform, rehabilitation for prisoners and addicts and full employment as powerful engines for delivering true social justice in a prosperous, modern economy. It seemed to me then – and has continued to seem to me since – that David Cameron was a person who combined the characteristics required for leadership with the determination to remould the Conservative Party in precisely this way.

It has to be admitted that, at the start of the long leadership campaign, this view was not widely shared. Indeed, with the notable exception of George Osborne, there was at the start no other member of the shadow Cabinet who appeared to agree with me. When David launched his bid at the magnificent headquarters of the Royal United Services Institute in Whitehall, George and I had to do the introductions because there wasn't anyone else of equivalent seniority in the party to do so. Even at this remove in time, I can very clearly remember standing on the stage, staring out at the audience (which consisted of virtually the entire community of UK political journalists together with a thin sprinkling of our exiguous band of parliamentary supporters) and thinking to myself, 'Well, this is clearly a hopeless cause, but at least I am in the right place.' This sense was reinforced a little later in the lobby of the House of Commons by Chris Grayling, who was then running Liam Fox's leadership campaign and who has always in my experience acted as a perfect gentleman; he gently (and obviously entirely sincerely) described my support for David Cameron as 'thoroughly decent' but 'Quixotic'. I wish I had had the wit to reply that the genuinely Quixotic act would be for the Conservative Party to elect anyone other than David: we had done quite enough tilting at windmills of one kind or another between 1997 and 2005. But of course that is the kind of clever response one doesn't usually think of until later. At the time, I just put my head down and hoped for the best – without much genuine hope.

Very surprisingly, bit by bit, things turned our way. Of course, the main reason for this was David himself. His potential for leadership shone out. It became clearer and clearer that he had the capacity to connect not just with the party membership but with a far wider audience to a degree that William, Iain and Michael had not been able to match. It also became apparent that David had a ready-made political support network of very high quality. Andrew Feldman, who was later to transform the party's finances as party chairman, came on board immediately to garner funds and manage the financial side of the campaign with huge aplomb. The admirable Ed Llewellyn and the highly sensitive and unflappable Kate Fall, who were to be the political mainstay of David's private office during five years of opposition and

six years of government, were available to deal smoothly and effectively with every subtle issue of organisation and to manage the dizzying
complexity of relationships with which any leader of the opposition has
to wrestle. A highly competent trio of George Eustice, Gabby Bertin
and Liz Sugg were there to organise properly the multiplicity of David's
public appearances and conduct the often difficult relationships with
the media. And David's unbelievably energetic strategist, Steve Hilton,
sprinkled his stardust, turning everything that might otherwise have
been pedestrian and forgettable into something interesting and memorable. It has become fashionable, recently, to decry this group around
David as a 'chumocracy'; but the fact that it was, and remained for
many years through enormous ups and downs, a group of friends as
well as a group of colleagues was not a disadvantage. On the contrary,
this closely integrated network of highly talented and highly dedicated
individuals gave David from the start the huge benefit of loyal support
on which he could rely absolutely. He knew that the trains would run on
time – leaving him with the space and time to make the key decisions
about the destinations to which they should be sent.

The details of the leadership campaign and how it was won have
been written about elsewhere. But what I have not seen adequately described is the parallel effort that went into establishing groundwork for
the conduct of the opposition if and when we won.

Once David had been selected by the parliamentary party as one
of the last two candidates and was largely occupied touring the country seeking votes from the party members, these parallel preparations
began in earnest. George Osborne, Steve Hilton, Ed Llewellyn, Michael
Gove (then a new MP) and I met regularly to devise a draft programme
for the first hundred days – putting ideas to David for approval or
adjustment as we went along. This was, I think, the crucible within
which many of the main lines of what followed were first developed.

The programme incorporated just about everything that I had hoped the party would do at this stage in its long march back to electability.

From my own point of view, as someone primarily interested in ideas and policy rather than presentation and hand-to-hand politics, the centrepiece of the plan was the Policy Review. This review was established immediately after David was installed as Leader of the Opposition, and my job in the shadow Cabinet was to be its chairman. Our purpose in creating the review was threefold: we wanted to identify the main areas on which the party would focus over the years leading up to the coming general election – and thereby signal what kind of party we wanted to be; we wanted to get some serious, considered policy analysis done in each of these areas – bringing in grown-up experts from relevant areas of the public, commercial and voluntary sectors to increase the credibility both of the analysis and of the party itself; and we wanted to buy ourselves a sensible amount of time in which we could avoid premature policy commitments that we might later come to regret (by giving ourselves the ability to reply to almost any question of policy that the issue in question would be considered during the course of the Policy Review). To achieve these goals, we set up six separate policy groups, each with its own chair or chairs – and we asked those chairs to work out ways of involving the widest possible array of experts.

To take forward the work that I had begun on environmental policy, we secured John Selwyn Gummer and Zac Goldsmith as chairs of our group; they quickly accumulated a vast team of colleagues from a whole range of relevant disciplines and set to work investigating every aspect of environmental policy from house-building to climate change. Rereading their work in later years, I have been repeatedly surprised by the depth and continued relevance of much of the analysis. A striking example is the section of their mammoth report that deals with the water cycle. Many of the proposals (for example, the spread of sustainable drainage systems) have since become mainstream elements of government policy. But it is only now, almost a decade later, that we are at last beginning to see the implementation of other ideas contained in this section – such as the emergence of science-based catchment management plans to reduce flood risk by slowing down the flow of some parts of our rivers while easing it in other parts.

Four policy groups were established to deal, respectively, with national security (under Tom King and Pauline Neville-Jones), public service reform (under Stephen Dorrell and Pauline Perry), international development (under Peter Lilley) and the economy (under John Redwood and Simon Wolfson). Each of these made a major contribution. The national security report established the basic framework of a National Security Council, which was to be the most important innovation in the machinery of government in 2010: for the first time it brought together the ministers who had responsibility for domestic security, energy security and resilience with those who had responsibility for defence, foreign policy and international development in a continuing weekly conversation chaired by the Prime Minister, with the heads of the intelligence agencies and the armed forces as well as relevant senior officials also around the table. Together with the appointment of a National Security Adviser heading a new National Security Secretariat, the establishment of the council was designed to enable us to make more coherent decisions both about day-to-day operational issues and about the allocation of budgets to the various departments or agencies involved in security, stability and resilience at home and abroad – something that was woefully lacking under the Blair and Brown governments. Meanwhile, the public service reform report began the long march towards increasing the responsiveness of the major public services to the needs of the people that they are meant to serve; the international development report set out the main reforms required to ensure that a party already committed to achieving an overseas aid budget equal to 0.7 per cent of gross national income would be able to manage and direct that budget in a way that made it an effective contributor to humanitarian relief, public health, education and enterprise in poor countries; and the economic report focused on the main investment and deregulatory decisions that an incoming Conservative administration would need to make.

But it was the sixth group, concerned with social justice and headed by Iain Duncan Smith, that ultimately made the biggest difference of all. In two magisterial volumes, entitled *Breakdown Britain* and *Breakthrough Britain*, Iain and his team plumbed the depths of the cycle of deprivation and made a series of programmatic proposals to tackle the social crisis that it represented. The argument was that some families were caught in a deadly combination of debt, drugs, poor education, unemployment and broken relationships – with each of these afflictions reinforced by all of the others in a vicious circle that virtually ensured the transmission of deprivation from one generation to the next. Set in the context of David Cameron's socially liberal, environmentally conscious and highly competent leadership, Iain's powerful analysis brought back to the fore all the best features of his own time as Leader of the Opposition and helped to bring the whole party enthusiastically behind a programme of social justice. At last, the balance between free market prosperity and social justice that Keith Joseph had unsuccessfully sought to promote all the way back in the 1980s had become a mainstream Conservative preoccupation.

Through the work of these six groups, the Policy Review served the purposes for which it was intended; it not only bought time for David Cameron to establish a new tone without making untoward detailed policy commitments, but also provided an analytical basis on which we could build a new policy programme for a government of the kind that we wanted to form. What it did not do, however, and what it was not intended to do, was deliver the policy programme itself. So, in late 2007, midway through the parliament, we began to build a set of detailed and costed policies in a series of Green Papers on which I worked with each of the relevant shadow secretaries of state as well as with Steve Hilton, a small policy unit that Steve and I had formed, and George Osborne's talented shadow Treasury team.

But, before this work could begin, we faced a different problem. After many false starts, Gordon Brown had at last in the spring of 2007 managed to oust Tony Blair and install himself as Prime Minister. For a brief period, he enjoyed a considerable honeymoon with the electorate and it seemed distinctly possible that (in an era before fixed-term parliaments) he would call a snap election to capitalise on this early popularity. Amongst other much more serious problems, this entirely wrecked my summer since I had to produce a draft manifesto in case of an autumn 2007 poll. This was very much a matter of making bricks without straw – and, even after my spectacularly bad first draft had been much improved by Steve, we really didn't have anything satisfactory to offer David and the rest of the shadow Cabinet. It was simply two years too early to produce a document of this kind. As a result of the Policy Review, the analysis was there; but the policy programme wasn't yet. And it showed.

It was at this point that David and George first demonstrated that they had what Ken Clarke accurately described as 'big match capability'. Our party conference was set to follow Labour's in the autumn of 2007. We knew that all the journalists would come from Labour's event full of stories about how Gordon Brown and Ed Balls were poised to wipe the Tories out. We were well behind in the opinion polls; our four-year programme of policy development had been abruptly halted in midstream; our draft manifesto was sadly lacking substance; and we were facing a new Prime Minister riding the crest of a wave. Things could hardly have looked worse.

In the sunlight – surrounded by the glass walls of David Cameron's office at Conservative Campaign Headquarters high up in Millbank Tower – George proposed a daring measure to give the party something to cheer: raising the inheritance tax threshold for a married couple to £1 million. There was a certain element of the piquant – because George and I had crossed over one another. Some years before, in 2004, when I was shadow Chancellor and he was shadow Chief Secretary to the Treasury, I had proposed essentially the same step as a means of proving our determination to reduce taxes without costing us too much in the short term. He had persuaded both me and Michael Howard that it was the wrong thing to do, because inheritance tax was paid by so few people. But now it was George who was proposing the move – on the grounds that it was the only thing that would sufficiently energise our troops at a time when we needed them to be energised more than ever. And I (having learned from the old George) was opposing the measure, on the grounds that it would benefit only a few and would diminish the force of our emphasis on social justice.

David Cameron, as always, let me make the argument. But he settled in favour of George's view. A few days later, it turned out that George was definitively right. At the party conference, he brought the house down with his promise to raise the inheritance tax threshold so that only millionaires would have to pay the tax. Then David made the speech of his life at the end of the conference. Within a couple of days, the tables had turned. Our opinion poll rating bounced upwards. Gordon let it be known that he wasn't going to hold a snap election after all. And, because of the unwise briefings given by his inner circle to the journalists, we were able to claim with extreme plausibility (and accuracy) that he had 'bottled it'. I believe we even produced some bottles to ram the point home.

From my point of view, this unexpected turn of events had two very important consequences. The first was that we were no longer faced with immediate defeat at the ballot box and the consequent, inevitable, collapse of the whole Cameron project. The second was that we now had a chance to complete the work we had begun by constructing the detailed Green Papers that would realise the potential of the Policy Review's analysis and give us a solid substantive basis for a proper manifesto containing a properly developed Programme for Government.

On the Saturday after the conference, while driving with my wife to do some long-delayed shopping in the lull after the storm, I received a call from David Cameron, instructing me to lay down tools on the draft manifesto in order to begin work on detailed policies. The rainclouds had lifted.

The time we spent developing the Green Papers was by far the most satisfying episode of my time in opposition. I felt that we were, at last, setting about the serious task of preparing for government, against the background of a tone and strategy that were civilised, liberal and realistic – capable, in other words, of attracting the sensible, middle-ground voters who had deserted to Blair but who were certainly capable of moving back to us now that Gordon Brown was Prime Minister and past his honeymoon period.

Everywhere we looked, there were opportunities to establish new lines of policy based on the analysis of the Policy Review groups. With Greg Clark and Greg Barker, I worked up an energy policy based on a sensible mix of generating technologies and on the new, interactive technologies of smart grids and smart meters to achieve a secure balance of the electricity and gas systems at times of peak load as well as what we hoped would be significantly enhanced domestic and industrial energy efficiency. With Chris Grayling, I put together the basic structure of a new payment-by-results Work Programme, to help get people back to work by using the energies and skills of the private and voluntary sectors, but with the providers, rather than the taxpayer, taking the risk of success or failure. With Nick Herbert, I developed a parallel policy of payment by results for the rehabilitation of prisoners from the moment just before they leave jail, using the private and voluntary sector to get them into homes and jobs rather than just abandoning them to their own devices with the occasional visit to a probation officer. With John Howell, I developed the first version of a new system of neighbourhood planning, to try to move away from the institutionalised warfare of the traditional systems of 'development control' and thereby overcome the culture of 'nimbyism' that was doing so much damage by preventing young families from getting the homes they needed. With Michael Gove, I constructed a programme to enable parents to find good schools in areas where education was still sadly lacking – with a huge expansion in the number of academies and new free schools and Ken Baker's university technology colleges, as well as a system of pupil premiums to help make it more attractive for good schools in relatively prosperous areas to go in search of pupils from deprived backgrounds, rather than just drawing on middle-class children whose parents could afford to buy homes in affluent neighbourhoods.

While we were doing all of this work in the eighteen months following the 2007 party conference, two other huge evolutions in Conservative policy and one political earthquake were occurring. George Osborne was wrestling with the consequences of the growing financial crisis. Iain Duncan Smith's Centre for Social Justice was developing radical ideas about a new system of Universal Credit. And the expenses scandal hit Westminster.

From my personal point of view, the expenses scandal was a complete nightmare. The *Daily Telegraph* published a massive front-page story about me and other members of the shadow Cabinet. In my case, the *Telegraph* report strongly suggested that I had made a claim for repair of my tennis court. In point of fact, the claim in question was for repair of a water pipe that used to run under the tennis court on its way from the mains to my house in Dorset. The pipe itself had been replaced without in any way affecting the tennis court; but the builder's invoice, which the *Telegraph* had seen, unfortunately referred to the location of the pipe – and this was quite enough to give the tennis court story what journalists call 'legs'. Everywhere you looked, there were pictures of my house and... the tennis court.

From an official point of view, all was well. The auditors in due course determined that the claim was legitimate, and I was offered (though, to avoid further stories, I did not accept) a refund of the amount of the claim, which I had paid back when the story broke. And in my own constituency, where the local papers let me explain the full facts, there was no real trouble. But of course the world will never believe this. Outside the constituency, I am forever to be known as the politician who made a claim for repair of his tennis court. These are the tribulations of political life.

Much more seriously for my fellow citizens, the signs of coming financial problems were emerging in the second half of 2007, with the issues surrounding sub-prime lending in the US and the inability in the UK of Northern Rock to access funding from the wholesale markets on which it relied. By early 2008, with the collapse and nationalisation of Northern Rock, it was becoming clear that we were heading towards a full-blown financial crisis. Against this background, one could begin to see the likely dire consequences of Gordon Brown's failure in the previous few years to heed the warnings about excessive borrowing, either from Vince Cable regarding the private sector or from me as shadow Chancellor regarding the public sector.

As Her Majesty's Loyal Opposition, we were faced with two major challenges. The first was to avoid any suggestion that, through pessimistic analysis or sniping from the sidelines, we were ourselves contributing to the growing crisis. This was relatively easy to achieve – and, despite significant temptations, George managed to maintain a tone that rendered the government's occasional efforts to paint us as the villains of the piece almost wholly ineffective. But the second challenge was much more difficult to meet: George had to find a way of moving off the slogan of 'sharing the proceeds of growth' which he had adopted as a means of avoiding the bear traps into which I had fallen in two successive elections.

George had correctly observed that, both as shadow Chief Secretary and as shadow Chancellor, I had come unstuck because I had given Gordon Brown the opportunity to accuse the Conservative Party of planning a terrible destruction of the public services. As George saw more clearly than I had been able to see, Gordon could make these wholly untrue accusations stick on the spurious, but superficially plausible, grounds that an incoming Conservative government would never be able to make the public expenditure savings I was planning to make in the way I was planning to make them, and would therefore be forced instead to make the savings by slashing spending on the NHS, schools and other key public services that the whole nation wanted to see protected. So George's response when he became shadow Chancellor was to point out that he didn't need to cut public spending at all – he could just use the 'proceeds of growth' rather differently from Gordon, using some of the extra tax revenue derived from a growing economy to reduce borrowing while using the rest of the extra tax revenue to increase public spending.

During the early years of the 2005–2010 parliament, this strategy of 'sharing the proceeds of growth' looked enormously promising as a way of pursuing a responsible fiscal strategy without exposing the opposition to the same attacks that had been made so successfully by Gordon in the elections of 2001 and 2005. But by late 2007, it was becoming clear that there was likely to be a problem – namely, that there might not be any 'proceeds of growth' because there might not be any growth. And by late 2008, though the scale of what was hitting us was still being missed by almost all of the commentators, it was pretty evident to those of us at the core of the Cameron project that there was going to be a very serious recession indeed. This was a real crisis. We were locked into a strategy that was designed to avoid repeating the mistakes and vulnerabilities of the past; and now that strategy was exposing us to a whole new set of mistakes and vulnerabilities.

So George had to shift both the spending plan and the slogan. In one of the most accomplished manoeuvres of this kind that I have witnessed (and for which I don't think he has ever really been given sufficient credit), he turned the whole thing around. By focusing on the fact that Gordon had 'failed to mend the roof while the sun was shining', George enabled himself to accept that the so-called automatic stabilisers of reduced tax revenues and increased welfare payments should be used to avoid deepening the recession in the short term while at the same time explaining why he, as an incoming Chancellor in 2010, would need to institute a serious programme to reduce both public expenditure and public sector deficits in order to restabilise the economy in the long term.

The result of this changing fiscal stance was that the opposition Green Papers were all developed on the basis that none of them could cost a single penny of increased public expenditure. This, I am convinced, is one of the reasons that so much of the work done in preparing the Green Papers survived the test of time when we came to put a great part of them into effect in the years after 2010.

But there was another consequence of the coming public expenditure squeeze: we needed to find some way of making tight control of public spending compatible with getting people back to work – a problem that was evidently going to be even more severe as a result of the recession. Chris Grayling's Green Paper on our new Work Programme was certainly going to be a step in the right direction. But it equally clearly wasn't going to be enough. We had to find some means of ensuring that, in this coming recession and its sequel, we didn't see a repeat of the ghastly increases in unemployment that we had seen in the 1980s, with millions of people trapped in welfare dependency and unable to get jobs that would pay enough to make it worthwhile for them to work.

Enter Iain Duncan Smith, stage right – or maybe one should say stage left. After completing his huge Policy Review analysis in *Breakdown Britain* and *Breakthrough Britain*, Iain had redirected the work of his Centre for Social Justice onto the design of a welfare system that would finally put an end to the unemployment and poverty traps. This produced remarkable results. He now proposed a complete change in the system of working-age benefits for the able-bodied – replacing tax credits, unemployment benefit and housing benefit with a new, single Universal Credit.

This radical proposal was based on a series of fundamental insights. The first, and in some ways the most important, was that the route out of poverty is work. This may sound trite. But it was a principle that had been wholly ignored by – had indeed been positively undermined by – the welfare state for decades. Iain pointed out that, if the way out of poverty was work, then the welfare system should reward people for all work, any work, however little it might at first be. Under the existing system, this was far from the case. If someone unemployed took a few hours of work a week at low pay, they would often lose the whole of what they earned in reductions of benefit – and of course they would normally have some costs involved in getting to work and in equipping themselves to do the work. So they had no incentive at all to do a small amount of low-paid work as a route back into the workforce. Under Iain's proposed system of Universal Credit, this would change: every unemployed person would have a strong incentive to move into a small amount of work even at the minimum wage, because they would not any longer lose all (or anything like all) of what they earned in benefit reductions.

Iain's second insight was that, to achieve this new incentive for small amounts of work at low pay and to ensure that people continued to have reasonable incentives to increase the amount earned through work as they went further up the work ladder, we needed to bring together all of the existing working-age benefits into one seamless system. Iain spotted that this would enable us to establish a single rate of withdrawal of benefit as your income rose, rather than confronting benefit recipients with the existing vast web of different withdrawal rates for different benefits.

The third insight was that, once the working-age benefit system was redesigned into a single system of Universal Credit, with clear rewards for every hour worked and for every extra pound earned, the role of the Jobcentres would change fundamentally. They could now become places where the staff, instead of just acting as benefit police, helped the clients to identify extra work that they could do to improve their incomes. The Jobcentres would become advisers on the route out of poverty – and thereby come together with the Work Programme. Eventually, once the new system of Universal Credit was fully in place and the Jobcentres became what their name implied, the need for the Work Programme might evaporate entirely.

From the start, I was hugely enthusiastic about this radical approach to welfare reform. I believed that, without costing the taxpayer a single penny (indeed with the prospect of gradually saving the taxpayer huge sums in out-of-work benefits), Iain's new system could genuinely eradicate the unemployment and poverty traps that had played such a malign part in fostering Keith Joseph's 'cycle of deprivation'. I wasn't able to get the idea of Universal Credit incorporated as a commitment in the 2010 manifesto because George and his team (though they, too, could see the potential advantages) were wary of the possible administrative difficulties involved in introducing such a radical reform and wanted to let the Treasury go through it in detail before a new government adopted it. But I did at least reach agreement that it would be examined in fine-grain detail as soon as we got into office.

With the Green Papers published, and the spending and welfare plans developed, I thought that we were at last in a position to have a proper manifesto drafted. The main lines of the programme were clear. To bring down the deficit, we would have an emergency Budget, a public sector pay freeze, reductions in public sector pensions and dramatic cuts in the administrative overhead of the public sector. To regulate the financial system properly, we would restore the Bank of England's supervisory role. To tackle carbon emissions, we would introduce new measures to encourage investment in low-carbon energy production, smart grids and smart meters. To improve the life chances of children, we would encourage parents to create new free schools, provide a huge increase in health visitors, as well as in early intervention and parenting support, and create a new generation of apprenticeships. We would improve the NHS by decentralising it and opening up competition while preserving the all-important principle of healthcare free at the point of use. To tackle 'Breakdown Britain', we would seek to reduce welfare dependency (a hint at Universal Credit) and introduce the Work Programme and rehabilitation programmes for offenders; social enterprises, charities and voluntary groups would deliver not only these but also other public services aimed at tackling deep-rooted social problems; and this would be backed up by powers for employee-led cooperatives to bid to take over public services, as well as by a new bank, funded from unclaimed bank assets, to provide new finance for neighbourhood groups, charities and social enterprises. And there would be a new National Citizen Service to give sixteen-year-olds skills to be responsible citizens, as well as a new system of neighbourhood planning.

What this lacked was a slogan that could capture the shift we were trying to engender – from an unaffordable and inefficiently bureaucratic public sector to a much more open-textured society in which the energies of every kind of community and voluntary group could be mobilised to deliver much more cost-effective and much less bureaucratic services at a human scale that could tackle social problems with more chance of success. It was Steve Hilton, as so often, who came up with the right phrase – the Big Society. The manifesto that he and James O'Shaughnessy drafted was built around this theme of 'small state, big society', and it managed to present all of the careful policy work of the past five years in a coherent and interesting way. At last, I felt we had found a way of showing that free market Conservatism had a heart as well as a head.

However, despite an initially favourable reception from the media, the manifesto and its Big Society theme didn't really work as a way of winning the election. It arrived on the scene too soon before the election to get fully into people's minds; and it didn't quite have the oomph that a slogan needs to carry you through an election.

But the big problem of the election wasn't the failure of our Big Society theme to light bonfires around the country. The big problem was that, at a time when the electorate was more than willing to get rid of Gordon Brown and the Labour government, the exciting new feature of British politics wasn't David Cameron (by this time well known and pretty well understood) but the Liberal Democrat leader, Nick Clegg, of whom almost no one had previously heard and who suddenly burst onto the scene as a fresh-faced and attractive figure of the middle ground. Clegg-mania came rapidly into existence after a TV debate which made people 'lose their hearts to that nice young man', as one of my erstwhile Tory constituents in Litton Cheney dispiritingly put it when I knocked on her door during the weekend after the debate in question. Gradually, as the election wore on, the Clegg-mania somewhat dissipated and the risk of Conservatives in constituencies like mine losing their seats to Liberal Democrat challengers receded. But it was clear that, even with a further swing back to us over the last couple of weeks, we were going to be hard-pressed to get an overall majority in the House of Commons.

It was at this point in the middle of the election that David asked me to work with George and William Hague to prepare secretly for a possible post-election deal with the Liberal Democrats.

I had already spent quite a long time in the weeks leading up to the election reading the policy papers produced by the Liberal Democrats, the work done by the free market liberal Orange Book group, who were the main influence on Clegg, and of course the Liberal Democrat manifesto itself. This enabled me to produce a rapid analysis of the considerable overlap between Clegg's programme and our own and also provided a basis for guessing which of the items of contention between us would really matter to the Liberal Democrats.

It was clear to me that the large degree of convergence between the Liberal Democrat programme and our own arose not from political expediency but from the fact that the Orange Book Liberals had a world view very similar to that of the Cameroon Conservatives. It therefore seemed more than possible that, if we didn't get an overall majority, we could propose an arrangement with the Liberal Democrats. I assumed that this arrangement would be one in which – in return for certain policy commitments on both sides – the Liberal Democrats would agree to vote with us on our Budgets and on any motion of no confidence in the House of Commons, thereby keeping a Conservative government in being for as long as the arrangement held good. (In retrospect, the fact that the Liberal Democrats were able to work with us, and that they might well have been able also to work with Labour, makes clear the extent to which the social liberalism that was at the core of the Orange Book Liberal Democrat agenda had become common ground between all three major political parties at that time – and thereby helps to explain the extent to which UKIP was later able to capitalise on the sense of disenfranchisement felt by many socially conservative voters, including the voter whom Gordon Brown memorably described as a 'bigot' during the election campaign.)

I therefore prepared a draft agreement for a 'supply and confidence' arrangement, together with a negotiating brief laying out what I expected to be the main trade-offs. George, William and I met at William's house to discuss these initial drafts, after which I did some further work on them before sending them over to David and Ed Llewellyn. Following one further discussion, they were put into a locked cabinet while we waited to see how the last few days of the election would pan out.

I maintained my hopes (and bet on the result) – partly because I thought we were at last ready to govern, with or without help from the Liberal Democrats; and partly because I thought the electorate were likely to see Labour as having lost the right to govern. Admittedly with a little help from us, Tony Blair had been one of the most electorally successful party leaders in British political history; he had understood and preserved the essence of Margaret Thatcher's free market legacy; and he had at the same time made Britain a better place – with the establishment of the minimum wage, the extension of Thatcher's Family Credit into a full-blown system of tax credits, and the introduction of a whole series of measures that increased opportunities for women and ethnic minorities and protected the rights of gays and lesbians. This was the positive side of the ledger. But on the negative side, the combination of the dubious process leading to the Iraq War and Gordon Brown's reckless overspending had left the country distrustful, demoralised and adding to its debt at an alarming rate. Gordon's own relatively brief period as Prime Minister had served merely to bloat the bureaucracy further, bringing no solution to the fiscal implosion and offering the country Blair without the charm. I couldn't see any real reason to suppose that the electorate would now want to entrust him with the task of solving the crisis that he, as Chancellor, had done much to cause.

CHAPTER 6

NEGOTIATING THE COALITION

As the future of my own seat was in some doubt, I spent the final couple of days of the campaign firmly located in West Dorset drumming up what support I could. The media were still predicting my demise. Because I have followed a set routine of canvassing in particular places day by day in election after election, I am pretty well able to compare the response in a particular street or village with the response from the same place at the same point in previous campaigns – and, over almost a quarter of a century, that has proved a reasonably reliable guide to the eventual result. On this occasion, the responses I was getting on the doorsteps in the last hours of campaigning led me to suppose that I would in fact be likely to scrape by, despite the media speculation. But of course one inevitably doubts the veracity of one's own canvassing; there is a terrible temptation amongst canvassers to display optimism bias, no matter how much the candidate tries to persuade everyone to avoid this; and the candidate himself or herself is equally prone (if not, indeed, more prone) to suffer from false optimism.

So I arrived at the count in a state of considerable uncertainty. I could see the TV cameras set up to record the moment of my defeat.

And I could see the expected large piles of Liberal Democrat votes from Dorchester (which always gets counted first, and has traditionally had an in-built Liberal Democrat majority). As on so many previous occasions, I contemplated the possibilities of a different life outside politics, and reflected rather sadly on the thought that I might never, after all that had passed, find my way back to Downing Street. And there was also, as on each previous occasion, the sense that losing the seat would somehow reflect on me personally. Of course, one knows that none of this (win or lose) actually has much to do with the candidate: the country is, very sensibly, making a decision largely about a government rather than about an individual MP. But, however much one knows this as a matter of psephological theory, it's difficult fully to believe it at the emotional level.

However, by around two o'clock in the morning, the situation was improving – as I had hoped (though not confidently expected) it would. The Conservatives in the villages had turned out as my doorstep canvassing had led me to believe they might, and the blue piles on the tables at the centre of the hall were growing significantly larger. It was with very considerable satisfaction that I saw the TV crews begin to pack up their gear: clearly, they had concluded that they were not going to get the decapitation that alone justified their presence. But, even at this stage, I imagined that the result would be close. It was not until right at the end that I was able to believe that my (admittedly small) majority had doubled.

Clearly, the national trend had turned in the last stages of the election. And it was to this national scene that I turned my attention as I drove back to London with my ever-tolerant and rather sleepy wife. As we neared the capital, the tide of results made me increasingly hopeful that we might, after all, be able to form a government.

By the time I joined David Cameron and his team in Conservative

Campaign Headquarters shortly after sunrise, it was beginning to be clear that we were indeed going to be decisively the largest party in Parliament. But it was also becoming clear that we would be around twenty seats short of an overall majority. The work I had done with William Hague and George Osborne on preparing for a negotiation with the Liberal Democrats was going to come in useful.

There have been various studies of the intense discussions that took place during the days that followed. Inevitably, those of us who participated in those discussions on the Conservative negotiating team had a partial view: we couldn't know what was going on between the Liberal Democrats and Labour; and we weren't of course privy to the undisclosed thoughts of our Liberal Democrat counterparts. But some features of the landscape as seen through my eyes do seem to be missing from the pictures so far painted.

To begin with, there was the question of structure. In our highly secretive internal discussions during the election itself, David, William, George, Ed Llewellyn, Kate Fall and I had all assumed that the best we would be able to achieve with the Liberal Democrats would be a 'supply and confidence' arrangement of the sort that I had drafted. We had never discussed the issue with shadow Cabinet colleagues, let alone the wider parliamentary party; but I had assumed that a full coalition of any sort would be a difficult thing to sell – though it certainly seemed to all of us that coalition would be a vastly better solution (both for the UK and for us) than any mere agreement. So when David asked Steve Hilton to write a speech for him to make at the St Stephen's Club, specifically offering to form with the Liberal Democrats a 'strong, stable' government based on a 'new politics', he specifically identified a 'supply and confidence' arrangement as one possibility – and his 'comprehensive offer' to go further carefully avoided any direct mention of a full coalition.

I was completely astonished when all the members of the Liberal Democrat team responded to my draft agreement by making clear that they wanted a full-blown coalition rather than a 'supply and confidence' arrangement. During spare moments in the election campaign, I had read a good deal about the history of coalitions, and all of it had convinced me that the long-term self-interest of a minority party almost always lies in maintaining maximum distance from its partners rather than in being dragged into a marriage. This also tallied with what I had gleaned from discussions with counterparts in Sweden and the Netherlands. So I reasoned that the Liberal Democrats would never agree to go beyond an arrangement.

When it became apparent that they were instead seriously requesting a full coalition, there seemed to be only three possible explanations: either they were unaware of the implications of the historical and international precedents for their own long-term future; or they were so determined to obtain ministerial office that they were disregarding the long term; or they were focused on producing the best possible government under the circumstances rather than on their own party interests. As the people we were dealing with were clearly well informed, and as they had been content to remain for years in a party with no obvious route to ministerial office, the first two explanations seemed implausible. I was therefore driven to the conclusion, right at the start of the negotiations, that we were talking to a group of politicians whose main aim was actually to produce and be part of a workable government.

This conclusion, which I never had occasion to revise in the succeeding five years, was absolutely fundamental. It seemed to me to define the whole of our negotiating strategy. If they were aiming principally at workable coalition government, then this opened up a whole series of possible solutions to otherwise quite intractable problems.

For example – on grounds of workability – we should be able to 'park' certain disagreeably contentious issues by agreeing that the Liberal Democrat ministers and MPs and peers would be free to abstain when the relevant legislation came to Parliament. The parliamentary arithmetic produced by the election meant that, with the Liberal Democrats abstaining, we Conservatives would have a substantial majority in the House of Commons and a fair chance of winning votes in the House of Lords. And sure enough, the Liberal Democrat negotiators were happy to sign up to this method of dealing with some hugely contentious issues such as university tuition fees and nuclear power stations – both of which I had originally assumed we would have to forgo or trade off in order to get any sort of deal.

Apart from the fact that the Liberal Democrat negotiators – Danny Alexander, David Laws, Chris Huhne and Andrew Stunell (two of whom were to become personal friends) – were all people with serious conceptions of government, there was, I think, another reason that the prospect of a truly workable and long-lasting coalition appealed to them. They seemed to me at the time to be making, and indeed were shown subsequently to have been making, a fundamental political error about the question of the voting system for the Westminster Parliament.

During my preparations for the negotiations as chair of the party's Policy Review, it had become clear to me that the single biggest aim of the Liberal Democrats was going to be to obtain a change in the voting system and, in particular, the replacement of the traditional first-past-the-post system with the alternative-vote (AV) system. It was Chris Huhne who most explicitly set out how the Liberal Democrat negotiating team saw the relationship between the change in the voting system and the consequences of entering into a fully-fledged coalition government with us. He explained that, after several years of coalition with the Tories, the more leftward-inclined of his voters in Eastleigh would be all too likely to desert him and vote either for Labour or for the Green Party; and he added that what would save him would be the repeated rounds of voting under an AV system – where voters rank the candidates in order of preference, and the votes cast for losing candidates are then redistributed to higher-placed candidates until eventually one candidate has over 50 per cent. His view was that the votes in Eastleigh of those who deserted to Labour or Green in the first round would be redistributed to him in subsequent rounds and would in the end get him over the 50 per cent mark.

Our analysis was that a shift to AV might well have significant advantages of this kind for a centrist minority party – though our psephological experts were careful to point out, first, that the effects of a new system on voter behaviour in particular constituencies (and hence on the outcomes of elections) were highly unpredictable and, second, that under certain circumstances an AV system was actually likely to produce even bigger overall majorities for the party with the largest vote share than the first-past-the-post system.

I have never personally been attracted to any form of proportional representation. As Jim Callaghan had explained to me when I visited his office in the House of Lords as a very junior opposition spokesman all those years ago in 1998, the first-past-the-post system is far more likely to enable voters to chuck out a government they don't want; it also forces parties to make internal coalitions before the election – thereby giving the electorate a clear choice between competing propositions rather than leaving it up to politicians to form governments behind closed doors after the election. Both of these seem to me to be monumental advantages of first-past-the-post politics. And, even so far as purportedly proportional representation systems go, AV seems to me about the most cack-handed, as it doesn't even guarantee proportional results. But I didn't think in any case that there was much chance of the electorate supporting a move to AV. Alerted to the complexity of these matters by my long-past work on Roy Jenkins's proposals for AV+ in 1997–98, I had looked quite carefully at the evidence showing what voters felt about the choice between voting systems. The quantitative and qualitative results of polls and focus groups showed that, whereas a referendum could well produce a majority in favour of a loosely defined system of proportional representation, once you explained to voters the detail of how the AV system actually worked, you got a huge reaction against it.

It pretty quickly transpired that the Liberal Democrat negotiating team either hadn't seen this evidence or didn't believe it. So, to my further astonishment, instead of insisting on the immediate introduction of AV for the next election, they were happy to sign up to a promise from us that we would have a referendum on whether to introduce AV. Just to make sure that there was no misunderstanding between us, I said to Danny Alexander that we were agreeing to implement the legislation for an AV referendum together, and we were agreeing to hold an AV referendum together, but that the aim of Conservatives during the ensuing referendum campaign would be to oppose AV and to beat the hell out of the Liberal Democrats proposing it. Danny readily agreed that this was exactly how their negotiating team understood the situation. I forbore to add that, based on the work I had done with Labour MPs and peers on AV+ all those years ago, I was pretty confident that the Labour Party would also be out there trying to persuade voters in the referendum to have nothing to do with AV.

Once the really big dividing lines had been resolved or parked, it was pretty clear that we were going to be able to form a coalition government. But it was also clear that, to make the coalition work, we were going to need to agree very rapidly on the detailed mechanics of Cabinet government and on the detailed Programme for Government. We all agreed that these things would be best done after the basic coalition agreement was signed. So the discussions on both of these fronts went on after David Cameron had been to the Palace and had agreed to form a government. While he and Nick Clegg busied themselves with appointing a ministerial team, and very senior ministers like George Osborne in the Treasury and William Hague in the Foreign Office set to work on their portfolios, I set about negotiating the detailed structures of coalition Cabinet government with Jim Wallace as well as a new Programme for Government with Danny Alexander.

In order to waste no time, Jim and I began our work on the Cabinet committees from the first night when David entered No. 10. As none of us yet had offices of our own, we went with some senior Cabinet Secretariat officials to the 'snug' in 12 Downing Street. This room was reached by going down a long corridor through No. 11 and past a very strange U-shaped array of desks and screens, from where – I was told – Gordon Brown had directed operations sitting with Peter Mandelson, Shriti Vadera and other key figures at the centre of his administration. How they could hear themselves think with the screens on all over the room, I don't know. But it seems that Gordon would withdraw into the 'snug' when he needed to get away from it all.

The centrepiece of the 'snug' at that time was a rather beautiful walnut dining table. We gathered around this table and started discussing the arrangements for coalition decision-making. As we did so, my eyes were irresistibly drawn downwards to the surface of the table; its highly polished walnut surface was covered in small pock-marks. Eventually, it became clear to me that they were almost certainly caused by Gordon's pen as he brought it thumping down on the table. Oh my God, I thought, the stories about what life was like in the Brown regime are all true.

By contrast, my discussions with Jim were completely cordial. He had been intimately involved as Deputy First Minister in the Scottish government coalition between Labour and the Liberal Democrats, so he had direct personal experience of what was needed to make a coalition function smoothly. We quickly agreed on an arrangement in which, while Conservatives would have a large majority in each Cabinet committee (as in Cabinet itself), there would be a Coalition Committee with equal numbers of Conservatives and Liberal Democrats, and all the other Cabinet committees would have either a Conservative chair and a Liberal Democrat deputy chair or vice-versa, with a right for the chair or deputy chair to refer any decision to the Coalition Committee.

In practice, this right of referral was never used and the Coalition Committee met on only a very few occasions in the succeeding five years. But this was exactly what we hoped would happen. The point of the arrangement was to guarantee that neither side could bludgeon the other into particular decisions. We hoped this would provide a basis upon which informal discussion between the two sides of the coalition could be used to resolve tricky issues without either party feeling disadvantaged. And this is indeed the result that the system produced. Around the formal mechanics, a Venn diagram of overlapping informal discussions took place – bilaterals between David Cameron and Nick Clegg; 'quads' (especially about budgets) between David, Nick, George Osborne and Danny Alexander, sometimes expanded to include me and (in the later years) David Laws; regular weekly discussions between me and Danny, and (again in the later years) between me and David Laws; and a whole series of informal discussions within and between departments that involved ministers from the two sides of the coalition.

The key to the whole operation was trust – or, as Jim Wallace put it, a rule of 'no surprises'. This meant each side being up-front about disagreements, so that the issues were brought out into the open as early as possible. It also meant continuous discussion – talking, talking, talking, so that there weren't hidden undercurrents creating grounds for mutual suspicion. Of course, the functioning of the system also depended on the personalities of those involved. On this, we had more than a bit of luck. In my experience, the three crucial politicians on the Liberal Democrat side – Nick Clegg, Danny Alexander and David Laws – were people that one could trust and like. There were inevitably disagreements; but it was impossible to doubt either their fundamental decency or their willingness to engage in open and honest argument without that ever descending to personal antagonism. Moreover, the detailed disagreements occurred against the background of a fundamentally similar view on most issues other than the European Question: the differences of attitude to domestic politics between these Orange Book Liberal Democrats and those of us at the centre of David Cameron's machine were never so great as to become intractable.

My regular Sunday evening phone call with Danny Alexander and my regular breakfast early on Tuesday mornings with David Laws were occasions to which I looked forward. We could get through an enormous range of coalition business with almost unvarying good humour, and even when there was a real bone of contention the discussion would usually throw up a solution or at least a way of moving towards a solution. I became totally confident that what was said in those discussions was not going to be twisted, reported out of context or used for narrow party political purposes. These were people who, besides being intelligent and rational, had turned out to be as devoted to making the coalition work as I had thought they were during the opening negotiations that had led to the formation of the government.

These Liberal Democrat colleagues were also highly tolerant of my personal failings. I never heard a word from them, for example, about the regrettable incident of the papers in the park. In contrast to the repair of the water pipe during the expenses saga, I really had done something wrong – and the *Daily Mirror* used more or less the whole of its front page to tell the nation that I had been disposing of confidential documents in the bins in St James's Park. Of course, the story was not quite as lurid as the *Mirror* had suggested. The papers in question were not secrets of state, as a reader of the *Mirror* would have assumed. Rather, they were photocopies of letters from constituents that I had been answering by dictating replies to my secretary while walking round St James's Park in the early mornings.

Nevertheless, I was made thoroughly aware by the Information Commissioner that I should have shredded the photocopies securely, rather than tearing them up and placing them in public bins, because I had a legal obligation as a registered data-handler to protect any personal data sent to me by constituents. I had to sign a declaration that I would do so in future, and this was placed on the Information Commissioner's website. As David Cameron rather tellingly put it, using the bins in the park was 'not a sensible way' to dispose of copies of constituency correspondence. I was crimson with embarrassment – but, apart from a little gentle teasing, the Liberal Democrats made nothing of it.

Would the mechanisms established with Jim Wallace in those first few days of the coalition have worked with a different cast of characters – less intelligent, less rational, less decent, less aligned with Cameron's Conservatives? My guess is that they would not. We had designed a system which could very easily be made to work by people who had a strong mutual desire to make it work in the interests of good government; but I doubt that the system would have prevented things going wrong if the key players had been fundamentally at loggerheads. The people mattered at least as much as the system. Nevertheless, the speed

– just a few days – with which Jim and I agreed the new structures (and had them approved by David Cameron and Nick Clegg after they were documented and polished by the Cabinet Office and No. 10 officials) did in itself contribute to the smooth functioning of the coalition. Instead of months spent arguing about the shape of the table, we were able to engage right away in discussion of the substantive policy issues.

The main protagonists in the discussion of the new Programme for Government were, on the Liberal Democrat side, Danny Alexander and Nick Clegg's virtually omniscient policy adviser Polly Mackenzie; and, on the Conservative side, Steve Hilton, James O'Shaughnessy and me. By the time we began this discussion on the second day of the coalition government, I had obtained an office overlooking Horse Guards Parade – so it was there that we met over several further days to crunch through the two manifestos (ours and the Liberal Democrats') to arrive at a common programme.

As I look back on it now, I am amazed at the ease with which we were able to put together a document that essentially guided the domestic activity of the UK government for the next five years. We were, of course, very much helped by the fact that the most contentious issues had either been resolved or parked by the original coalition agreement negotiated in the 120 hours of discussions leading up to the formation of the new government. We were also much helped by the fact that the there was a large amount of overlap between the two manifestos. The extent to which we had on each side read and understood the underlying policy papers of the other side was also a distinct advantage; Polly and James, in particular, seemed to have a synoptic knowledge of both manifestos. Nevertheless, this sort of detailed programme formation takes many weeks in some countries that have had much more experience of coalition than we have in the UK – and I think it was as much of a surprise to the media as it was to us how fast we were able to crack through several hundred specific policy commitments and get them documented.

As we did this foundational work, I became increasingly conscious that – together with the structures that Jim Wallace and I had designed – the resulting Programme for Government was going to have one effect that I had not in any way anticipated.

Normally, when a new government comes into office, its manifesto has a certain standing in Whitehall. It is, after all, the basis upon which the incumbent Prime Minister has just fought and won a general election. But the extent to which individual ministers and ministries do actually implement the strict terms of the manifesto is variable – and there is certainly nothing in the constitution to prevent a government from adding liberally to its manifesto once in office if it can obtain sufficient parliamentary support for doing so. By contrast, as we developed the Programme for Government in the first few days of the coalition, it became increasingly clear that the status of this document was going to be very different from that of a normal manifesto. The Programme for Government was, in effect, a contract between the two sides of the coalition. Its guardian was, ultimately, the Coalition Committee, composed of equal numbers of ministers from each party; and any decision not to implement any part of the Programme, or any move to add to the Programme, could come about only by further 'contractual' agreement between the parties.

It seemed to me that this, in turn, was bound to have a profound effect on the relationship between the Cabinet and the official Whitehall machine. Throughout Whitehall, I could sense a strong desire on the part of senior officials to make the coalition work; it is in the fine tradition of the British civil service to work with just about any result thrown up by our democracy, and it was clear to me from the things that were said to me by a wide range of permanent secretaries, directors general and directors that they regarded the workability of a coalition government as a test of the flexibility and maturity of the civil service machine. They could all see that the Programme for Government was a contract between the two sides of the coalition – and, as such, something that could not be enlarged, reduced or altered without explicit consent from both parties. So they, too, felt bound by the document. And they wanted to get it implemented in order to make the coalition government work. In other words, wholly to my surprise, through the Programme for Government the politicians had produced a method of making the civil service machine stick firmly to the script, in a way that manifestos cannot normally do.

But we had a further way of making the machine do what we had set out to do. In the closing months before the general election, Francis Maude, Steve Hilton and I had run an exercise with our shadow Cabinet colleagues to produce departmental 'business plans'. These were intended to identify the practical steps that each department would take to implement our manifesto and Green Paper commitments, as well as the timetable for taking these steps. So we entered government with a fully developed programme of action, department by department. But of course this action programme reflected only Conservative policies. I therefore ran an exercise with Danny Alexander, Polly Mackenzie, Steve Hilton and James O'Shaughnessy as well as a team of Cabinet Office officials, immediately after the Programme for Government had been agreed, to adjust the Conservative departmental business plans so that they fitted the Programme rather than just the Conservative manifesto. Because the Programme for Government was more detailed and more specific than our manifesto had been, and also because we were able to engage officials around Whitehall to a degree that had been impossible when in opposition, these new 'business plans' represented a significant improvement on the originals. They became a reliable basis for monitoring the implementation of the Programme for Government, month by month.

There was, however, a further challenge: we needed to establish some central mechanisms to help us perform this monitoring role, and to enable both David Cameron and Nick Clegg to get direct advice on policy issues rather than just relying on the papers which would no doubt flow in from the various ministers and departments. On this front, we made two early mistakes – both later corrected.

So far as the monitoring of performance by the departments against their 'business plans' was concerned, I was keen to move away from using the Delivery Unit, which had operated under Gordon Brown. Unsurprisingly, this unit seemed to have a Brown-style culture of micromanaging public services from the centre; whereas the policies in our Programme for Government were designed to create structures within which public services would, so far as possible, be made more efficient by competition and by more direct accountability to the service-users and to local communities. What we needed – or at least what we thought we needed – was a group of officials who would help us simply find out whether those policies were being implemented as per the 'business plans'.

It turned out that getting rid of the Delivery Unit wasn't as easy as it sounded. For some while, Whitehall (and especially the Treasury) fought back. But eventually we did succeed in this ostensibly simple task. Then we hit the much more difficult question: how would we get a group established that would do the task we wanted done with energy and effectiveness right across Whitehall? This proved to be much more difficult than I had anticipated. Although various officials in the Cabinet Office and in the Policy Unit stepped up to the plate, and we did manage to do several rounds of checking on the implementation of the 'business plans', it wasn't until half way through the period of coalition government that I agreed with Jeremy Heywood and Danny Alexander – and we then collectively agreed with David Cameron, Nick Clegg and George Osborne – on the formation of a dedicated Implementation Unit, separate from the Policy Unit. This turned out to be exactly the right move, one that we should have made at the very beginning. The new Implementation Unit, with its dedicated staff focused wholly on implementing our programme, and with none of the culture of micromanagement that characterised the Delivery Unit, at last gave us a real grip on the monitoring and reporting system.

By the time we had got this bit of the structure in place, I had discovered an even more important problem, which the Implementation Unit (and, thereafter, an expanding number of mini-Implementation Units in departments around Whitehall) also helped us to address. The dreadful truth was that the government machine as a whole had remarkably little accurate real-time information about its own activities. Danny Alexander put this beautifully when he likened being a minister to sitting in a huge combine harvester observing what had happened to the field behind you in the rear-view mirror. We had plenty of statistics but, with the exception of some of the economic stats, all the data was wildly out of date. You could find out what had gone right or wrong a couple of years ago; but you couldn't find out what was happening now.

The need for real-time information became clearer and clearer as the years of coalition progressed. Increasingly, we needed to know not just whether the legislative and administrative actions set out in the Programme for Government and the departmental 'business plans' had been done but also – even more importantly – whether they were beginning to have the effects that they were intended to have. It also became clearer and clearer that officials in departments and agencies were singularly disinclined to collect and disseminate real-time information about their own operations. Partly, no doubt, there was a natural fear that this would expose those running the operations to un-welcome scrutiny from their own ministers, the centre of government and, worse still, Parliament and the press. But I formed the impression that the problem was, in general, inertia rather than conspiracy. Real-time data in usable, analysable form just wasn't a commodity in which Whitehall had in general been trained to deal; so collecting it and analysing it was a task that caused disruption, required large amounts of energy and diverted hard-working officials from getting on with business as usual. But of course, as soon as business as usual went wrong in some way, they were all too often flying blind because they had no up-to-date facts in a usable format on which to base any effort to analyse the problem they were encountering. And trying to formulate an appropriate solution to a problem that hasn't been properly understood is a mug's game.

In early 2014, we had a prime example of this phenomenon. I was sitting in my meeting room with my colleague James Brokenshire and officials from the Passport Agency. James (who is a 'steady pair of hands' and consequently gets all the worst jobs – including, nowadays, that of Northern Ireland Secretary) at that time had the thankless task of being minister for immigration. Amongst many other horrors, this meant that he was the minister for passports. We had a problem. After many years of functioning pretty smoothly, the Passport Agency had developed a queue, and some people were waiting a long time for their passport to be renewed.

The strange thing was that, when I had first become aware of this problem as a result of complaints from some of my own constituents (and had then confirmed with other MPs that they were having similar experiences in their constituencies), I had been assured by the Passport Agency that there was no real problem. They were, they said, very close to meeting their target for processing passports – and they could prove it. But now I had investigated the discrepancy between the statistics presented by the agency and the anecdotes from MPs – or, rather, my officials in the Implementation Unit had investigated it. They had discovered a very interesting situation. It turned out that the Passport Agency statistics were right: it was perfectly true that they were not far off their target for processing passport applications within a given average time. But the target was barmy – or at any rate, barmy if used as the *only* target.

The Implementation Unit had patiently explained to me that if a few passports each day were put in a 'to do later' pile and the rest of the passports were processed within the target time, then the average time of processing passport applications as a whole would be pretty close to the target – but the pile of 'to do later' passports would grow and grow, and if you happened to be the proud owner of one of the passports in this 'to do later' pile, it was of absolutely no comfort to you to know that other people were doing OK. This is what the Implementation Unit called 'a stock/flow problem': the flow will look just about alright on the statistics for quite some while, but the stock of people waiting a long time will gradually increase to the point where it begins to cause mayhem.

My first task at the meeting was to agree with the Home Office and the Passport Agency that this was the nature of the problem. This didn't take long. The next problem was to work out what to do about the situation. It wasn't rocket science: we needed some more people to help process the stock of overdue passport applications, and some more computer terminals for them to do this at. With the help of the ever-resourceful Cabinet Secretary Jeremy Heywood, we were able to find the people, because we had built up a little army of apprentices trained in just this sort of processing task. The agency just needed to find the computer terminals.

We got this sorted out fairy quickly. But I remained amazed at the way in which the very tools that were meant to have given us early warning of a problem had in fact enabled the agency for some while to hide the problem. If nothing else, I learned that targets and indicators are useful in bureaucracies only if they are well enough designed to tell the people looking at them what they need to know rather than what the bureaucracy in question wants them to think.

Once the Implementation Unit started to collect usable real-time data, a range of administrative problems that had seemed intractable suddenly began to look soluble, while others that remained problematic were at least open to analysis and proper discussion at the centre of government – and, indeed, with departmental ministers. When we drilled down into the data, we could begin to see, for instance, why the numbers of reservists in the armed forces weren't rising as fast as we had hoped: from the stage-by-stage figures each month, we could see the fall-off rates at each stage of recruitment and we could at least ask the right questions to find out what caused so many people to drop out at each stage. Likewise, when we began to get clear real-time analysis of what was happening at each stage of diagnosis and treatment for specific diseases, we were able to identify that an endoscopy bottleneck was having a profound effect in the NHS – and dozens of other NHS bottlenecks started coming to light as we went into other aspects of the data. Serious, disaggregated, up-to-date statistics showing the time taken to go through the various stages of the planning process from putting in a planning application to completing a building likewise threw up completely unexpected opportunities to speed up the whole process. A relentless enquiry into the parallel and sequential operations involved in widening trunk roads revealed that we could in some cases halve the elapsed time. And so it went on. Danny Alexander and I (who shared first-line responsibility for the Implementation Unit) were both absolutely persuaded that the collection and analysis of real-time data – though incredibly boring for most of the media, and indeed for most politicians – was a critical component of improving the operations of government that most affected our economy and our citizens. From the start, David Cameron and Nick Clegg (to whom the Unit ultimately reported) were similarly enthusiastic about the value of such information; gradually, an increasing number of our Cabinet colleagues also began to use the unit and its departmental replicas as a way of finding out what was really happening in government.

One of the reasons why the Implementation Unit and its approach gained ground rapidly was that, when it came to monitoring the implementation of the Programme for Government and improving the administrative operations of government, there was an identity of interest across the coalition. By contrast, the development of new policy in response to changing circumstances – which had been the domain of the Policy Unit not only during my time with Mrs Thatcher in the 1980s but also through the Major, Blair and Brown years – inevitably raised the question: was the coalition government a single entity when it came to developing new, post-Programme for Government policy? Or should the coalition for this purpose be regarded as two parties, each with its own agenda to develop?

At the start of the coalition, in our new-found enthusiasm and camaraderie, we had hoped that even the process of new policy formulation could be done jointly. But as time wore on, we discovered that this initial enthusiasm for unified policy formulation was somewhat naïve. The effort to construct a single Policy Unit, first under a combination of political special advisers and permanent civil servants, and then as a purely civil service function, didn't really work – because it just wasn't possible for a group nominally serving both the (Conservative) Prime Minister and the (Liberal Democrat) Deputy Prime

Minister to command the confidence of either sufficiently to have the kind of access and relationship that a successful Policy Unit requires. In this case, the dictum that you can't serve two masters turned out to be applicable.

As we moved into the closing phase of the coalition, and each of the two parties began the process of thinking about its policy programme for the coming election, the impossibility of operating a single Policy Unit came into stark relief. This provided the necessary shock therapy, and led to the problem being solved in the only way it could – by creating a unit of Conservative special advisers and civil servants, under Jo Johnson, which served only the PM, with a separate bevy of Liberal Democrat special advisers and private secretaries offering policy advice to the DPM. I can't speak for the DPM part of this arrangement; but there is no doubt at all that Jo's team quickly regained the sort of standing that the No. 10 Policy Unit had enjoyed in the days before the coalition, and they did an excellent job in bringing together a serious policy programme for what turned out to be the next government.

Inevitably, this did also produce a small fluttering in the dovecotes so far as the wider civil service machine was concerned. In the days when we were trying (not very successfully) to operate a single Policy Unit, the relationship between that unit and the Cabinet Office – and, in particular, with Jeremy Heywood, then the PM's permanent secretary – had operated very smoothly. Each side of this bureaucratic relationship understood the other, and the information flow between them was reliable. But once Jo Johnson and his team had begun work on a Conservative-only policy programme, there was bound to be a considerable need for the unit not to share information that might find its way through the Cabinet Office into the various departments and thence, quite possibly, through Liberal Democrat departmental ministers and special advisers, back to Nick Clegg's office. I couldn't see any way of avoiding the need for such Chinese walls – and, in what was otherwise an extraordinarily close day-by-day working relationship, I simply had to fend off enquiries from Jeremy about the progress of policy-making by the Conservative side of the coalition.

With this one exception, cooperation with Jeremy was a mainstay for me throughout the coalition years. It quickly became apparent that, to get things done, what I needed was not only continuous and direct access to David Cameron and George Osborne on our side of the fence and to Danny Alexander and David Laws on the Liberal Democrat side but also some means of making sure that the messages I was trying to convey to Whitehall were consistent with the messages that were being sent by the centre of the civil service machine to the most senior departmental officials. It also rapidly became apparent that, through continuous email and face-to-face discussion with Jeremy in addition to the daily meetings in David's study which he and I both attended, it was possible to arrange for Jeremy and me almost always to be despatching exactly such coordinated messages into the Whitehall machine. I could then use my regular discussions with the Liberal Democrats at the centre to ensure either that these messages from 9 Downing Street and the Cabinet Secretary were in line with what Nick Clegg's office would be feeding into the machine or that, where there were differences between the two sides of the coalition, these were acknowledged so that the officials across Whitehall didn't experience unexplained hold-ups of a kind that could otherwise rapidly erode confidence in the capacity of the centre to make decisions. It is impossible to prove, but I am pretty confident that this nexus of relationships, and the continuous dialogue it engendered, were critical to the remarkably smooth operation of the coalition. If the two halves of the political centre hadn't been kept in synch not only with one another but also with the central apparatus of the civil service, there would have been either stasis or warfare; in practice, there was movement and – generally – peaceful coexistence.

Just as the workmanlike relations between David Cameron and Nick Clegg (and indeed between George Osborne and Danny Alexander at the Treasury) were fundamental to this smooth operation, I think Jeremy Heywood's character and particular brand of intellect really mattered for the success of the coalition. A Cabinet Secretary who had wanted to play games of his own, or who had simply been ineffectual, would have made it nearly impossible to identify and resolve the inevitable tensions between the two sides of the coalition. The politicians at the centre obviously needed to work together; but if the most senior civil servants in the various departments across Whitehall hadn't received direct information from their central apparatus about what the central politicians had discussed and agreed (or agreed to park), the opportunity for confusion – which always exists between the centre of government and the individual departments – would have been refracted into endless and ultimately stultifying disputes between Conservative and Liberal Democrat ministers within the departments. Moreover, speed of communication can be vital in defusing what can otherwise escalate into crises of unmanageable proportions. The fact that Jeremy was a completely unpompous user of immediate, concise emails, texts and phone calls rather than a producer of long, mellifluous 'Rolls-Royce' civil service memorandums meant that, working in parallel (where necessary, also with Ed Llewellyn and Jonny Oates in the PM's and DPM's offices), he and I could often resolve coalition policy issues almost before they had arisen.

Of course, none of these mechanisms could remove real-world differences between the two sides of the coalition. Although, in general, the surprise was how few serious differences crystallised, I did become heavily involved in three sagas – each of which involved long-running negotiations arising out of fundamental divisions of opinion across the coalition that could not simply be smoothed away. The first concerned student loans; the second was about EU justice and home affairs arrangements; and the third was the 'small matter' of UK energy policy.

In many ways, the argument about student loans was the easiest of the three. One early summer day in 2010, I was sitting at my table in 70 Whitehall (this was in the days before I moved across into 9 Downing Street). A guards band was playing in Horse Guards Parade below my eighteenth-century sash windows. A couple of floors down, Nick Clegg occupied a much grander office, as befitted the Deputy Prime Minister and leader of the Liberal Democrat side of the coalition government. From time to time since we formed the coalition, I had been invited to descend in person in order to discuss a particular issue. But, on this occasion, Nick called me on the telephone – perhaps he was on one of his peregrinations to rally the troops or making a speech somewhere. He was clearly in a certain amount of inner anguish.

He wanted to discuss the question of student loans and student fees. The Conservative side of the coalition had signed up to implementing the recommendation of John Browne's review by raising the cap on student fees, with an accompanying rise in the value of the soft loans made available to students. The Liberal Democrats, by contrast, had spent much of the preceding election campaigning against a rise in student fees, and all fifty-seven Liberal Democrat MPs elected in 2010 had signed a pledge saying: 'I pledge to vote against any increase in fees in the next parliament and to pressure the government to introduce a fairer alternative.'

Agonisingly for Nick Clegg, he had now been fully briefed by officials and by the universities themselves on what would happen to their finances if the student fees were not increased. As a rational administrator, he could see that the case for injecting more funds into the universities was overwhelmingly strong; and he could see also that there was no way on earth that the government was going to be able to meet the necessary expenditure out of taxpayer funds, given the extreme fiscal emergency with which we were grappling in the early years of the coalition. So he had become persuaded that the right thing for the country was to increase the student fee.

But of course there was his wretched pledge to contend with. If ever there were a time when the Liberal Democrats were in a position 'to pressure the government to introduce a fairer alternative', this would have been it. Now, unexpectedly, they *were* the government – or at least part of it. As I listened to Nick on the phone, I could feel him wrestling with this conundrum. He was trying to find a way – any way – of reconciling his new-found sense of what it was right to do in the national interest with his pre-election commitment.

I was, of course, only too happy to help him find adjustments in the policy that would allow him to support the increase in the fee while arguing that the proposal was nevertheless a 'fairer alternative' to what John Browne had proposed. But surely such fig leaves wouldn't be enough? They would evidently be torn away by the media in a matter of minutes. And yet, as his conversational convolutions unfolded, it became increasingly clear to me, more as a matter of emotional intelligence than as a result of any definite intellectual apprehension, that Nick might actually be about to persuade himself that he could and should support the increase, notwithstanding the pledge.

As I struggled to avoid any hint of disbelief or even surprise on my part, I reflected privately that this was probably a significant turning point in the fortunes not only of our universities but also of the Liberal Democrats. I had nothing but respect for Nick's open-mindedness in coming to a conclusion so different from the one he had presented to the electorate just a short time earlier. But I simply couldn't see how he would explain the abandonment of the pledge to the hundreds of thousands of students who constituted one of the mainstays of the Liberal Democrats' electoral success. Of course in policy terms it was the right decision, but this had blinded him to the fact that, politically, *he* wasn't in a position to make it. The rest, as they say, is history.

Even more than student loans, the EU was bound to be a dividing line between us. On the Conservative side in Cabinet (with the notable exception of Ken Clarke), opinion ranged from nascent 'Euro-outers' through strong Eurosceptics to milder Eurosceptics, whereas the Liberal Democrats around the Cabinet table were mainly people whose political formation was bound up with belief in the EU. When you came right down to it, there really wasn't much that basically divided Danny Alexander's politics from mine, except on this issue. From my point of view, whether it was advantageous to remain in the EU at all was a matter of fine balance, and the right question about almost any new proposition from the EU was how we could best prevent it becoming yet another Trojan horse for expansionist interpretation of the treaties. Like the majority of the electorate (as it turned out), I retained far more faith in the institutions of our ancient nation state than in the structures of Brussels and Strasbourg; so the EU was for me a pill worth swallowing only because of the economic advantages of the internal market. For Danny, by contrast, the starting point was always enthusiasm about the European project, and the right question was how we could further that project without interfering unduly with free markets and prosperity. As far as he was concerned, the nation state was always in danger of descending into a nationalism that would impede trading and cultural exchange and cause international instability. He saw the pooling of sovereignty within the EU not only as a way of guaranteeing access to a world-scale market, but also of giving Europe a powerful voice in the world, and (perhaps most importantly of all) locking in the principles of liberal democracy and human rights across the Continent. For him, it was all upside.

There were plenty of times when the discussion of particular negotiating positions on particular draft directives or other EU matters gave rise to short-term disagreements that we had to resolve between us. But the fundamental difference of view on the EU between the two sides of the coalition became something of much wider and more immediate importance when we had to decide how to deal with the opt-out from the Justice and Home Affairs (JHA) 'pillar' that the UK had obtained in a protocol to the 2008 Lisbon Treaty.

Under Maastricht and its successor treaties, and particularly after the Lisbon Treaty, the EU had gradually developed both a substantial body of regulation and a significant set of new institutions and organisations operating in the field of criminal law. But, under the 2008 opt-out, Britain could decide which of the new regulations in this field to adopt and which such institutions or organisations to join. Over the years, successive UK governments had adopted or joined some and opted out of others. But the Lisbon settlement had a further provision: by May 2014, the UK had to make a final decision about which of the (by then) 130 EU directives and organisations in the JHA field we would accept and which we would opt out of. So this was a decision on a highly significant European issue that the coalition government had to make, notwithstanding the fact that the two sides in the coalition came to it from very different points of view.

In late 2012, Danny and I began to discuss this looming challenge. Predictably, neither of us wanted, or felt in any way empowered, to compromise any future negotiations; so, equally predictably, our opening positions were rather far apart. Danny argued that we should opt into all 130 EU JHA measures; I argued that we should opt into none of them at all. Clearly, some basis for narrowing this gap had to be found.

To achieve a solution, quite a lot of different constraints had to be met. In the first place, I had to agree with Danny that items which no one in Whitehall or the various security agencies thought had any practical merit should be removed from his shopping list. This was relatively straightforward – because Danny, ever rational, could see that there really wasn't any point in having an argument about opting into something that all the experts couldn't see any point in joining.

Next, Jeremy Heywood needed to get all the experts in the various agencies to take a view on the measures which were really of practical benefit to the UK in fighting crime and terrorism – and I needed to discuss the outcome of that expert review with Theresa May (then Home Secretary), Chris Grayling (then Justice Secretary), Dominic Grieve (then Attorney General) and William Hague (then Foreign Secretary, who would become a key player once we got to the stage of dealing with the EU Commission, Council and Parliament rather than our own internal coalition dynamics).

While I was having this discussion with Conservative colleagues, and of course keeping David Cameron informed of the evolving picture to ensure that he was happy with the direction of travel, Danny was off doing his own work with his Liberal Democrat colleagues and having his own discussions with the various experts. The result, inevitably, was that he came to somewhat different conclusions than I did about which of the measures really were useful – and also about which of the measures were positively dangerous because of the extent to which they intruded on our ability to make our own decisions in our own Parliament about our own criminal law (which, for me and Chris Grayling, was a 'red line').

Nevertheless, the basic ground rule that we would opt into only those items that were of real practical value to law enforcement agencies, combined with the various consultations on each side of the coalition fence, did massively reduce the numerical gap. Depending on exactly how you did your sums, there was a remaining difference between us of around thirty measures, with a clear centre-point between us that would involve ditching ninety-five of the measures and opting into only thirty-five of them. Based on my experience of the many smaller items that we had negotiated over the past few years, I was pretty sure that Danny would trade off roughly to this centre-point. As I happened to know from my discussions with Conservative colleagues, this would also be roughly in line with what the Home Office and the Ministry of Justice thought would be the sensible outcome from the point of view of practical law enforcement. Given that the measures included within the thirty-five would not include any that seriously intruded into our ability to make our own criminal law, I was content to settle on that basis. So, ultimately, were both David Cameron and Nick Clegg.

This still left us with a slightly tricky negotiation with the EU Commission and the other member states, who had some remaining negotiating power since they could refuse to allow us to make selective opt-ins. But it seemed to me clear that, in terms of our internal coalition discussion, this was not too much of a problem – since, under the Lisbon settlement, the result of any refusal by the Commission or member states to allow us the thirty-five opt-ins would simply be us exiting all 130 measures automatically in December 2014 and then having to negotiate separately some alternative set of practical arrangements to replicate the effects of the thirty-five desirable measures. I therefore came to the conclusion that, once the thirty-five opt-ins were identified and internally agreed within the coalition, the whole matter could be removed from the coalition negotiations and handed over to Theresa May, William Hague and David Lidington (the legendary Europe Minister) to achieve a final agreement with the EU institutions and states – which they promptly did with consummate skill.

Energy policy was a whole different ball game. There were all sorts of problems tangled up with one another. The Programme for Government had announced that we were going to be the greenest government ever – and, whatever else, this clearly had to mean a significant decarbonisation of the electricity supply industry. On that, the whole government was agreed. But the question was how to achieve this decarbonisation of electricity supply while keeping the lights on and preventing customer bills from rising too high.

What made this a particularly difficult conundrum to resolve was that the structure of the electricity supply market was fundamentally ill-adapted to the world we were in. The basic idea of the market rules was that all the electricity plants offered prices at which they would generate electricity in a given half-hour on a certain day. The system operator would then call on the plants in ascending order of price up to the point at which supply for that particular half-hour matched demand in that half-hour. All the plants were then paid the 'clearing price' bid by the most expensive plant operating in that half-hour.

In theory, the result of this bidding system would be to ensure that, across all 17,520 half-hours in a year, each of the plants needed by the system would get at least enough revenue to meet its capital and operating costs – since any plant that couldn't get under the clearing price often enough to keep sufficient revenue coming in would quickly be closed down or mothballed; meanwhile the generating companies would quickly spot that they could make money by opening new plants if the system was getting tight and clearing prices were rising.

Unfortunately, there were several reasons why this neat theory wasn't true in practice. The most important of these was that we were subsidising all sorts of low-carbon generation (including renewable energy from wind and sun as well as nuclear energy) and were thereby distorting the economics of the system. This had two notable effects that became more and more apparent as the years of coalition government wore on: there was less and less gas-fired generation coming onto the bars despite the fact that we needed such plant to keep the lights on when the sun wasn't shining and the wind wasn't at the right speed to make the wind turbines generate; and the costs to the electricity consumer caused by the high prices for the gas used by the existing gas-fired plant combined with high subsidies for renewable energy were becoming, by the end of the parliament, a real political issue, which the Labour leader, Ed Miliband, was ruthlessly exploiting.

Finding a sensible way through this mess – which could combine progressive carbon reduction both with high-capacity margins of plant to keep the lights on, and with low or at least relatively stable prices for the customer, was never going to be easy even for a single-party government. But adding in the element of intra-coalition negotiation made the resolution of the triangle of requirements horribly difficult to achieve.

I found myself at the centre of two simultaneous battles: one between the Treasury and the Department of Energy & Climate Change (DECC) about the level of subsidies (and hence consumer prices), and the other between ourselves in Downing Street and the combined forces of the Treasury and the department about what was needed to keep the lights on. As the DECC was in the hands of Liberal Democrat energy secretaries, while the Treasury had both Conservative and Liberal Democrat Cabinet ministers and Nos 9 and 10 Downing Street were occupied by Conservatives, we had what we had always sought to avoid – a nightmarish cat's cradle of inter-departmental and intra-coalition disagreements.

My constant fear was that, if I didn't keep on the *qui vive* at all times, someone might produce a purported solution that would keep down prices and keep the carbon reducing but in a way that would turn the lights off. There were some positively ghastly moments when my allies in the No. 10 private office and I discovered in the middle of one August that a large amount of plant on which we had been relying for the coming winter was actually going to be unavailable due to engineering problems, and we had to take rapid remedial action to get the National Grid to contract for more power through the inter-connections to France and the Netherlands. There were also huge debates about a new capacity market. We did eventually bring in this new market so that we could gradually commission the extra plant needed to create a more secure capacity margin and keep the lights on; but not without major opposition from people around the Treasury who were worried about building in extra costs. There were intense discussions about the rate of subsidy for renewables, not helped by the fact that the DECC consistently failed to keep abreast of the fast-reducing construction costs in onshore wind and solar power. And there was a continuing dispute between the two sides of the coalition about how many onshore wind turbines could be built without causing unsustainable damage to the landscape as well as unsustainable local opposition in the places where turbines the size of jumbo jets were being erected.

Disentangling one issue from another in the midst of this Spaghetti Junction of concerns was no laughing matter. As David Howell has trenchantly pointed out, we certainly didn't find a satisfactory long-term energy strategy during the coalition years. But it was, from my point of view at least, enough of a miracle that we just about managed to keep a cap on consumer prices, keep the lights on, make progress with the negotiations for new nuclear power plants and keep carbon production falling all the way to 2015. I don't think we could have done it if the coalition relationships at the centre hadn't been so strong.

By comparison, the challenges we faced on Universal Credit and the NHS were caused almost exclusively by the government's encounter with the real world rather than by intra-coalition differences. Universal Credit was one of the Conservative ideas that the Liberal Democrats were more than willing to buy into. The problem was that the Treasury did not agree. Treasury ministers and officials were worried both that the combining of all the working-age non-disability benefits into one seamless system of credits would be hugely difficult to implement in practice and that the new system would, in some way not yet anticipated, lead to expanding rather than contracting welfare bills for the taxpayer.

Unfortunately, it was clear that direct discussions between George Osborne and Iain Duncan Smith were not likely to prove productive – the relationship between them just wasn't going to sustain a prolonged and detailed negotiation about a fiendishly complicated topic like this. The first phase therefore consisted of me going off into a side room at Chequers with George's and Iain's leading special advisers, Rupert Harrison and Philippa Stroud respectively, in order to agree some ground rules within which the Treasury would allow the Department for Work & Pensions (DWP) to develop the proposals into a working system. This was duly achieved; I was then able also to agree relatively easily with Danny Alexander – and, through Danny, with Nick Clegg and Steve Webb (the Liberal Democrat minister in the DWP) – that the development of the programme should proceed as agreed with Rupert and Philippa. We also agreed, crucially, that the new credits would be introduced very, very gradually, starting with trials for just a few thousand claimants and with back-up arrangements to ensure that these claimants got the right amounts of money even if all the new systems failed.

But this proved to be just the start of a much longer saga. We had Cabinet committee meetings in which ministers lined up to support the Treasury's scepticism and Nick Clegg (who was in the chair) was therefore unable to conclude definitively in favour of the programme; the best I could do was to prevent the whole thing from being brought to a permanent halt then and there. Then we had massive problems with the development of the computer systems required for the new unified credits, just as the Treasury officials had predicted. There was trench warfare between Francis Maude's Cabinet Office IT gurus and their counterparts in the DWP. To this day, I don't know which of them – if either – was right about the best way to do the computing; but I do know that reaching an eventual, much-delayed roll-out of the new systems took massive upheavals, new project managers (several times over), endless meetings at which Danny and I tried to distinguish what mattered from what didn't, and the use of manual systems for processing even the simplest claims until we were confident that the computers could deliver the right answers.

Throughout this arduous struggle to liberate the prisoners from the stone, I was determined not to lose faith in Iain's vision – of a unified structure within which even the first hour of work would be worthwhile for the person doing it. I continued to believe that if we could realise that vision, the Jobcentres would gradually become places where people were genuinely helped progressively from welfare into ascending amounts of work. And that would be transformative – putting an end for ever to the ghastly scenes of the 1960s, 1970s and 1980s when people had just been marooned on the rolls of the unemployed.

Luckily, that view was shared across the coalition. And this made it possible – notwithstanding all the massive practical problems and all the inter-departmental battles – to keep moving forward. Eventually, creaking and groaning, the new system did deliver the first real-life trials. It was positively inspiring to go to a Jobcentre in Hammersmith and talk to the staff whose claimants were the first in the country to have switched over to Universal Credit. They told me that, for the first time in their careers, they were actually doing the task they had come into the service to do. Instead of being mainly benefit police officers, they were able to have the conversations they had always wanted to have with their clients about the routes back into work, and hence the routes out of poverty.

But Universal Credit wasn't our biggest headache. By far the bigger worry was how to get the NHS to meet the huge challenge of providing affordable, world-class healthcare for an ageing population. As I look back on it, I am more troubled by my own failure to understand the true nature and scale of this problem than by any other aspect of my time in government.

The origins of this misunderstanding lay in the work we had done from the opposition benches during the 2005–10 parliament. Our policy group on improving the public services, led by Stephen Dorrell and Pauline Perry, had looked in some detail at the real problems facing the NHS as a result of the increasing age of the population – and had rightly concluded that an increased emphasis on public health and on integration of healthcare with social care would be needed to meet the massive challenge of burgeoning costs identified by the Wanless Review. But, when we came to write our opposition Green Paper on healthcare, entitled *NHS Autonomy and Accountability*, the title alone was enough to indicate that the emphasis had shifted: instead of concerning ourselves with the huge pressures on the system caused by caring for the elderly, we had moved to the question of the structure of the NHS.

Broadly, the proposals in *NHS Autonomy and Accountability* were modelled on the operation of the utilities providing services like energy and water to the public – but with the taxpayer, rather than the patient, picking up the bill in order to preserve the sacrosanct principle of providing healthcare free at the point of use. The idea was that an independent board (now known as NHS England) would allocate funds within the NHS on the basis of a mandate provided to it by the secretary of state; these funds would then be used by 'commissioners' in each locality (strategic health authorities and primary care trusts) to buy healthcare services from independently run NHS foundation trusts and other qualified service-providers; patients would be free to choose amongst all qualified service-providers, with 'tariffs' following the patient to the provider of their choice; the money provided by the commissioners through the tariffs would be used by the providers to meet the cost of treatments certified as value for money by the independent National Institute of Health and Clinical Excellence; a new quality inspector (now known as the Care Quality Commission) would guarantee standards by disqualifying any inadequate service-provider; and a new economic regulator (originally called Monitor but now known as NHS Improvement) would ensure that all the service-providers competed fairly for patients. In this way, *NHS Autonomy and Accountability* would, we believed, create an efficient 'social market for delivery of effective high quality healthcare to NHS patients'.

Having wrestled with the real-life challenges of the NHS alongside two successive secretaries of state for six years, I can now confidently state that the picture presented in *NHS Autonomy and Accountability*, though entirely well intentioned, was woefully naïve. It failed to recognise that the central issue for the sustainability of the whole system was (and still is) the ability of the combined forces of the NHS and the adult social services to provide the integrated care that is needed by the frail elderly. Any model that focuses on elective surgery and other treatments for the younger and generally fitter part of the population – as *NHS Autonomy and Accountability* did – is bound to miss this fundamental point.

But of course *NHS Autonomy and Accountability* was a purely

Conservative document. So, when the coalition was formed, there had to be a discussion with our Liberal Democrat colleagues about how far its proposals should be adjusted. Most unfortunately, this was exactly the discussion we did have when we constructed the coalition's Programme for Government. Instead of going back to the fundamental question of care for the frail elderly, which had rightly preoccupied the policy group, we started with *NHS Autonomy and Accountability* and asked what needed to be added in order for the Liberal Democrats to be happy. Basically, apart from absolutely sensible commitments to increase NHS spending in real terms each year and to cut massively the number of administrators (both of which would have happened anyway), the only changes to the 'social market' model advocated in *NHS Autonomy and Accountability* demanded by Danny Alexander and his team were the addition of local councillors to the boards of primary care trusts, and a reinforced commitment to patients' rights to change their GP. Although we weren't exactly sure how these could be made to cohere with the proposals of *NHS Autonomy and Account-ability*, they seemed innocuous in principle, so we accepted them and asked the combined Conservative–Liberal Democrat ministerial team at the Department for Health to work out the details. True, our coalition partners also led us to insert some useful references to what turned out to be three much more central issues – expansion of urgent care services, the improvement of procedures for discharging patients from hospitals, and home adaptations or other means of enabling the elderly to remain in their own homes; but none of these were properly worked out because the Liberal Democrats hadn't done any serious work on them during their time in opposition and nor (after the completion of the policy group's review) had we. The result was that the NHS section of the Programme for Government sent over to Andrew Lansley (the Health Secretary) and his Liberal Democrat minister of

state, Paul Burstow, in mid-May 2010 was essentially a slightly less coherent version of the naïve proposals contained in our *NHS Autonomy
and Accountability* document.

At this point, I was preoccupied with other pressing matters that
had to be resolved during the first few weeks of coalition government.
I caught up with health policy only in June, when Danny Alexander
and I received the first draft of a White Paper produced by Andrew
Lansley and Paul Burstow, entitled *Equity and Excellence: Liberating
the NHS*. It was clear from this draft that during the intervening weeks,
Andrew and Paul had been puzzling over two issues that had been left
unresolved by the Programme for Government: how to reconcile the
Liberal Democrat proposal for 'GP commissioning' with our proposal
for commissioning to be done by the primary care trusts; and how to
achieve the massive savings in administrative overheads which were
crucial if we were going to be able to accommodate the fast-rising costs
of caring for the elderly.

Their solution to these two problems was to do precisely what we
had committed ourselves not to do – a top-down reorganisation. To
avoid a conflict between different types of commissioner within the
NHS, and to reduce the layers of bureaucracy, they proposed that we
should abolish the strategic health authorities entirely, and put the staff
of the primary care trusts into new 'clinical commissioning groups',
run by GPs. As the eventual published version of the White Paper put
it, these groups would 'devolve power and responsibility for commissioning services to the healthcare professionals closest to patients: GPs
and their practice teams working in consortia'.

It is a matter of public record that, when these proposals were published, they caused a gradually increasing groundswell of opposition.
It is also a matter of public record that Danny Alexander and I were
asked to look into them, and that we did so, and that we reported that

the administrative changes were likely to work mechanically and to produce the savings forecast. And it is a matter of public record that the opposition within the coalition backbenchers was eventually bought off to a sufficient degree through a 'review' process that resulted in some minor adjustments. Finally, it is a matter of public record that the transition to clinical commissioning groups was achieved reasonably smoothly and that the administrative overheads were indeed drastically reduced, thereby enabling the finances to add up in the short term.

What has not attracted so much attention but is, alas, a matter of fact is that this reorganisation left us and – more importantly – left the NHS with no solution to the fundamental challenges that are caused by an ageing population. These real-world challenges were not even seriously addressed, let alone resolved, by the proposals for a 'social market' that had been put forward originally in *NHS Autonomy and Accountability* and that still formed the essence of the structure envisaged by *Equity and Excellence: Liberating the NHS*.

The crunch came in the last two winters of coalition government – by which time Jeremy Hunt had taken over from Andrew Lansley as Health Secretary. The shoe was beginning to pinch, because the bulk of the savings in administrative overheads had been made already, and the pressure on the system from the rising costs of care for the elderly was beginning to grow. The visible manifestations of these pressures were the lengthening queues of patients at Accident and Emergency units and the rising number of beds being 'blocked' by elderly patients who were medically fit to leave hospital but who couldn't be found the residential care or the package of domiciliary care required to enable them to do so.

As we struggled through those winters, with endless meetings and conference calls to investigate what was going on in the hardest-pressed areas, including on Christmas Day, it became clearer and clearer to me that the whole picture of the NHS as a social market just didn't fit the facts. The truth is that there are actually two distinct kinds of thing going on in the healthcare system. One is a system of GPs, A&E, maternity care and elective surgery for the young and basically fit. In principle, this side of NHS healthcare could operate as a social market, with GPs and independent foundation trusts competing for these patients and with the taxpayer's money following them to the GP or hospital of their choice. Even then, there would be some pretty tricky issues about how to maintain viable A&E and maternity services in an area from which a high proportion of the funding drained away because young and fit patients opted to have elective surgery at hospitals in another area; there would also be the thorny issue of how to ensure that the GPs had sufficient incentives to be available at times when patients actually needed them, and that they performed or purchased for their patients enough timely screening and diagnostics to produce rates of survival from serious disease that could match what is achieved in more successful countries.

But the real problem is that there is a second healthcare system – or rather un-system – which is meant to provide care for the frail elderly. It is this system that actually absorbs most of the cost of the NHS and adult social services. And – as Stephen Dorrell and Sarah Wollaston quite rightly pointed out but I didn't understand until later – it is purely fanciful to portray this as something that can operate on anything like the social market model proposed in *NHS Autonomy and Accountability* or *Equity and Excellence: Liberating the NHS*. What is needed, instead, is an arrangement within which some integrated entity can provide a complete package of health and social care for each frail elderly person, which has the aim (and actually has the effect) of enabling that person to remain well and at home for as long as possible. As we went through the winter crises of 2013 and 2014, it became abundantly clear that this was absolutely the only way in which we were ever going to prevent an all-too-predictable cycle of disasters: frail elderly people are insufficiently well-equipped and looked after at home; then they are rushed into A&E; then they are admitted to hospital; then they become frailer in hospital; then they return home, often after delayed discharge and often with insufficient care; then they fall or become ill again, with another rush to A&E, another admission, and finally another delayed discharge – but this time into phenomenally expensive residential care which neither the elderly person themselves nor their relatives want.

Once all this did become clear, Jeremy Hunt, Danny Alexander and I set about trying to find some solution that would bring about the indispensable integration of healthcare and adult social services for the elderly which we so evidently lacked. The basic problem was, of course, that both sides of the system – the NHS that provided the healthcare and the local authorities that provided the social care – were by this time under severe financial pressure because, despite small real-terms increases in NHS budgets and significant pay restraint, the total costs of both systems were rising faster with the increase in the elderly population than the budgets could accommodate. As a result, the NHS was reluctant to invest money today in more social care even if this would reduce healthcare costs in the long run; and the social care providers were so focused on meeting their immediate obligations that they had little or no capacity to think about how they could invest preventatively to break out of the vicious circle.

We tried to solve this conundrum by introducing a Better Care Fund that would enable the social services to receive extra funding from the NHS if they could use that to keep more frail elderly people well and at home, thereby reducing costs for the NHS. But, despite two successive efforts to get this to work in the last two years of the coalition, we didn't manage to produce much actual change in the money flows or in the level of social care provided for the frail elderly. Gradually, it became clear that this was a problem which was going to have to be left for the next government to solve.

So the coalition's efforts to address the fundamental challenges facing the NHS left us with no real improvement on the situation we had inherited in 2010. We dramatically cut the administrative over-heads of a service whose bureaucracy had been ludicrously bloated during the Brown years. By doing so, we kept the system broadly stable during years when cost pressures were rising much faster than budgets. But the basic issues remained wholly unresolved.

If one steps back from these great difficulties in the NHS, and indeed from the knotty details of energy policy, Universal Credit and the Justice and Home Affairs opt-out, what does the whole of the coalition's tenure in office look like?

When we originally reached agreement with the Liberal Democrats, any number of commentators assured us that the government would be unstable and incapable of taking action. But the doom-mongers didn't have the satisfaction of seeing their miserable prognoses come true. When one looks at the performance of the coalition government across the board, I think it is difficult to resist the conclusion that it was sane, pragmatic and stable. The structures we had set up enabled us to work together in a business-like way. I found I could have sensible discussions not just with Danny Alexander, David Laws and Nick Clegg, but also with other Liberal Democrats in government. As in any group of ministers in any government, there were inevitably differences of view. But I found myself as often allied with as opposed to Vince Cable, Chris Huhne and Ed Davey on different elements of industrial and energy strategy, and (even if Chris and Ed could sometimes be slightly choleric) I certainly found them a great deal less difficult to deal with than seems to have been the case when Blairites were dealing with Brownites in the previous Labour government. I had a happy time cooperating in endless meetings with the very energetic Norman Baker to make Whitehall greener and cheaper by using energy, paper, water and air travel more efficiently; our problems in this field were all with rather slow-moving permanent secretaries rather than any intra-coalition friction. You could guarantee a perfectly sensible discussion if you picked up the phone to middle-ranking ministers like Simon Hughes, Jo Swinson or Norman Lamb. And it was always possible to do business efficiently and constructively with the senior Liberal Democrat apparatchiks like Polly Mackenzie and Jonny Oates.

From my own point of view, there were in fact considerable advantages to coalition. As anybody could see, the effect of a durable parliament-long alliance between Conservatives and Liberal Democrats was that we had a convincing majority in the Commons and a decent chance of winning votes in the Lords. In both respects, that represented an improvement on the situation of many single-party governments. Of course, there was the downside that we had to reach agreement on the details of all legislation with our Liberal Democrat colleagues before we could get the assured majorities; but that involved negotiating with people whose broad outlook was pretty similar to mine – at least in the case of the Orange Book Liberals, who dominated the Liberal Democrat side of the coalition; and it also meant that we weren't anything like as reliant as some single-party governments have been on our own hard-liners. The deep truth is that all parties are coalitions and, although I agree to some extent with what almost any of my Conservative parliamentary colleagues would think about almost anything, I certainly had more in common with some of my closest Liberal Democrat coalition colleagues than I did with some of my most ideologically distant fellow Conservatives. If it came to a choice between having to negotiate the details of legislation with

Danny Alexander or David Laws and having to negotiate with Conservative colleagues like Peter Bone or David T. C. Davies (for both of whom I have considerable personal respect, but with whom I agree about relatively little), then I know which I'd generally have picked as the preferable counter-parties.

There were just two episodes where the basic harmony of the coalition broke down. The first of these was during the saga of the Leveson Report. The origins of this episode lay in the appalling behaviour of some of the newspapers – with phone-tapping and goodness knows how many other forms of behaviour that went beyond any civilised person's view of what was reasonable activity for press hounds. As more and more murky goings-on came to public attention through the hearings held by Lord Justice Leveson, the demand for reform of the rules governing press conduct increased, particularly from Hacked Off (the organisation formed by Hugh Grant and others to put the case on behalf of victims of press intrusion). The result was a magisterial report in which Leveson made a large number of recommendations, including – critically – that the newspapers should set up a new system of free arbitration so that people who had been libelled could get redress (including front-page apologies and proportionate damages) without having to pay the huge fees involved in taking a libel case to court.

The arrival of this report created a considerable problem for the coalition. David Cameron had more or less committed himself in advance to implementing whatever Leveson recommended, and he also had some considerable sympathy with the general principles that Leveson was advocating; but he was very reluctant to see Parliament turned into a vehicle for statutory regulation in this area (on the very reasonable grounds that, once we went down that road, it would be difficult to prevent increasingly illiberal constraints on important aspects of the freedom of the press). By contrast, Nick Clegg was much influenced by Evan Harris, a former Liberal Democrat MP and one of the leading lights of Hacked Off. Clegg had come to the conclusion that Leveson could safely and properly be implemented via legislation. It was a strange reversal of roles, with the Liberal leader more concerned about protecting the conservative principle of personal privacy and the Conservative leader more concerned about the liberal principle of keeping the press free from statutory regulation.

As I sat in David's kitchen on the night before the report was due to be published, it became clear to both of us that we had the makings of a major intra-coalition bust-up. I went in search of Paul Jenkins, the government's senior lawyer, in the hope that he would bring his highly creative intelligence to the task of finding a solution that both sides of the coalition could live with. The result of a series of conversations with Paul was the proposal to square the circle by using a Royal Charter rather than direct statutory regulation. The idea was that such a charter would embody the Leveson principles, and under it we would create a body that would certify whether the independent press regulator was implementing the principles – and we would then legislate to ensure that newspapers were subject to the prospect of horrible costs and damages in court if they libelled people after having failed to sign up to a charter-certified regulator. The effect of this would be to give a strong incentive for the newspapers to cooperate with a charter-certified regulator and set up a free arbitration service exactly as Leveson had recommended, but without Parliament establishing any direct statutory control over what the press published. The only legislation that would be needed from Parliament would be changes to the law on costs and damages in libel cases – areas already covered by statute, and not taking politicians into the terrain of determining what the press could or couldn't report.

Meanwhile, Nick Clegg and his Liberal Democrat colleagues began manoeuvres of a most unusual kind. They started working not with the Conservative side of the coalition but with Hacked Off and the Labour Party – and indeed started using the Labour/Liberal army in the House of Lords to pass amendments to government legislation that would, if enacted, have created much more statutory interference with the press than the Conservative side of the coalition was willing to countenance. I could see, all too easily, where this was heading. If we didn't watch out, we would have not only an unholy alliance forming between Nick Clegg and the Labour leader, Ed Miliband, but also a situation in which the government would have to withdraw all sorts of Bills on a whole range of topics, which could otherwise be used to carry amendments on Leveson that we couldn't accept. If this carried on for any serious length of time, our whole legislative programme would be compromised and the damage to the coalition would become irreparable.

I therefore began, in conjunction with the Culture Secretary, Maria Miller, a long series of multilateral negotiations – with Labour, with Hacked Off, with the newspapers themselves, and with our Liberal Democrat colleagues – in an effort to reach a solution that would keep the coalition together. To begin with, this all looked as if it was heading in the right direction, since I was able at a relatively early stage to agree with all parties that the Royal Charter approach was a reasonable one. But as soon as we started discussing the detail of what was to be in the Royal Charter, the problems began.

The Liberal Democrat side of the negotiation was led by my old sparring partner Jim Wallace; as usual, he was thoroughly reasonable and entirely charming to deal with. I'm pretty sure that, left to our own devices, we would have come up with an agreed solution very quickly. But unfortunately Nick Clegg was unwilling to agree to anything to which the Labour Party (represented by Harriet Harman and Charlie

Falconer) were unwilling to agree; and I could see that Harriet and Charlie were going to be unwilling to agree to anything that Hacked Off wouldn't accept. Although Harriet was surprisingly flexible, Charlie was fairly difficult about the whole thing and kept coming up with spurious but ingenious crypto-legal reasons why the structure we were proposing might not work. Meanwhile, it was difficult to tell whether the extremists in Hacked Off were more or less unreasonable than the hard-liners in some of the newspapers. Basically, Hugh Grant and the more intransigent amongst his colleagues seemed to believe that all concerns about the freedom of the press were simply not worth talking about; and the most hard-line newspaper types seemed to believe that they ought to be allowed to go on libelling people with no effective system of redress.

At the last moment, I got wind of the fact that the Liberal Democrats were sitting in Ed Miliband's office. It was clear that they were discussing whether to vote with Labour in the Commons the next day on an amendment that would have forced the government of which they were a part to withdraw one of its Bills. Luckily, I managed to get a message through to Nick Clegg that we should talk more before he took this dangerous step. I was asked to go late at night with my officials to a meeting with him and Ed Miliband. As I walked into the office in the Commons that was now occupied by Ed, in which I had spent so many hours with Michael Howard and David Cameron during our period in opposition, I had a strange sense of unease, particularly when I found representatives from Hacked Off sitting there. It seemed to me unlikely that we were going to be able to avert catastrophe. But it gradually became apparent that both Ed and Nick were in fact in the mood to compromise, so long as the essence of the Leveson principles could be retained. Perhaps they had become as worn out by Hacked Off as I was.

Just in the nick of time, we struck a deal that I felt sure David

Cameron could live with, which was broadly in line with the proposal that Paul Jenkins and I had made. This involved changing the law on costs and damages in libel cases to give the newspapers incentives to join an independent regulator which had been certified by a Royal Charter body as compliant with the Leveson principles – but left the decision about when to implement the new rules on costs in the hands of the next government. Many of the newspapers were incandescent, because the version of the Leveson principles embodied in the charter included the provisions they most disliked – a free arbitration service for libel claimants and front-page apologies for those libelled. But David, when I called him in the early hours to seek his approval, was content as I had imagined he would be; the split in the coalition was mended; and David's commitment to implement Leveson was fulfilled, but without any direct statutory regulation of the press.

Apart from the close call of the Leveson negotiations, the only other really rocky patch in the coalition dynamics was when we had to deal with the bizarrely twinned issues of the Boundary Review and the reform of the House of Lords. In principle, these two issues had nothing whatsoever to do with one another. The reform of the House of Lords to make it a largely elected chamber was a hugely controversial constitutional issue that the original Coalition Agreement and the coalition's Programme for Government had committed the government to tackling. The Boundary Review, by contrast, was simply a matter of bringing the map of parliamentary constituencies up to date with recent movements in population so that the size of the electorate in each constituency became broadly similar, instead of having MPs in northern England and Scotland representing much smaller electorates than those in the south. This, too, had been agreed between the coalition parties.

In neither of the governing documents of the coalition was there the slightest suggestion of any connection between the fundamental reform of the House of Lords and the tidying up of the parliamentary boundaries. But of course there was high politics involved in both measures. For Nick Clegg and his colleagues, the reform of the Lords represented a significant step forward: they had long campaigned for an elected chamber, and the achievement of this goal was the one major constitutional reform left on their agenda after AV had been rejected by the electorate. By contrast, the Boundary Review was likely to give a boost to Conservatives by creating more constituencies in the south while being at best neutral for the Liberal Democrats.

Unfortunately, by an oversight on the Conservative side of the coalition, we had failed to ensure that the Boundary Review would be implemented automatically as soon as the independent Boundary Commission reported. Instead, the Act setting up the Boundary Review (which had been taken through the Commons by Nick Clegg himself) allowed for the boundaries to be changed only after a further, confirmatory vote in both Houses of Parliament. When it became apparent that many Conservative backbenchers were strongly opposed to the proposals for a largely elected House of Lords put forward by the government, Nick Clegg and Danny Alexander made it quite clear to us that this was a major problem for them. They told us that they were not going to be able – and pretty evidently they weren't even going to try – to get their backbenchers to give the necessary confirmatory vote for the new constituencies proposed by the Boundary Commission unless we could also get our backbenchers to vote for the government's proposals on the reform of the House of Lords.

I therefore began an intensive round of discussions with Conservative backbench colleagues. I didn't know whether to cheer or cry. Those who opposed an elected House of Lords were almost all doing so out of high principle. They believed that an elected second chamber would jam up the constitution, making it nearly impossible for a government with a majority in the Commons to get anything done – because the second chamber, based on proportional representation and therefore usually with no overall majority for any party, would flex its democratic muscles and block legislation from the Commons. Of course I didn't agree with them about the demerits of this system of checks and balances – which seemed to me to work pretty well in the US Congress. But I knew better than to have an argument about principles with colleagues whose constitutional views were entrenched. So I tried to persuade them instead that the Liberal Democrats were just not going to vote for the boundary changes if we didn't vote for the reform of the House of Lords and I reminded them of the obvious fact that the interest of the Conservative Party lay in having a confirmation of the Boundary Commission's conclusions, since this would eliminate the bias of the current boundaries in favour of Labour. Splendidly, though to my mind foolishly, colleagues such as Malcolm Rifkind and Jesse Norman (and many others) gave me to understand in no uncertain terms their utter disdain for this pragmatic argument. I was given polite but devastatingly firm lectures about the need to put constitutional principle before party advantage. It was a strange mixture of reactionary constitutionalism, high principle and political myopia.

I had to report to David Cameron that there was no way we were going to get either the Liberal Democrats or our backbench colleagues to modify their stance to the slightest degree. We were going to lose both the House of Lords reform and the boundary changes. The coalition dynamics had come into conflict with the dynamics (or rather, the statics) of the Conservative parliamentary party and the result was... nothing.

Both the Leveson saga and the saga of House of Lords reform illustrate the fundamentally transactional nature of a coalition government.

Coalition works only when both sides either share a view or feel that they are getting what they bargained for in the original agreements. When that didn't happen because we had different views about things that hadn't been sufficiently spelled out in those original agreements, there were none of the underlying bonds of loyalty which, in all but exceptional circumstances, will pull a single-party government through even big ideological bust-ups.

But, whatever one thinks about the relative advantages of coalition as opposed to single-party government, it is certainly true that at the centre – or at any rate from the perspective of 9 Downing Street – almost all of the time other than during the Leveson and House of Lords sagas it felt like a functional rather than a dysfunctional operation. What is more, it felt like a sane and stable administration. Over five years, we stuck together; we fought off efforts by the SNP to destroy the Union; we brought the nation's deficit back into something much nearer to a sensible state and restored the stability of the financial system that underpins the economy; we reduced the scale of bureaucracy sharply across the board and mitigated its regulatory impacts on British business; we sustained the NHS, improved the universities and the schools, hugely expanded apprenticeship, and set in motion vast and overdue programmes of investment in road, rail and broadband; we made serious efforts to improve rehabilitation for prisoners and drug addicts; to address deep-seated social injustices, we began crucial reforms of taxation, welfare, pensions and savings; we increased employment and decreased unemployment. There were many difficulties, and much was left less than perfect. But all in all, we expanded opportunities for people to climb out of poverty and increased the opportunities for Britain to sustain prosperity in an ecologically and socially responsible way. And all of this was achieved against the inheritance of the worst fiscal and economic crisis any of us had lived through. Judged not just by the prophecies that accompanied the formation of the coalition but by comparison with all sorts of governments across a considerable period of time, it was not a bad record.

That was the basis on which we entered the 2015 general election.

CHAPTER 7

THE CABINET OFFICE

During the early hours of 8 May 2015, I began to see the blue-labelled bundles of Conservative votes pile up very satisfactorily on the tables in the sports hall at Dorchester, confirming the news coming in from other parts of the country that, despite opinion polls consistently showing another hung parliament, we were in fact witnessing the unexpected return of a Conservative majority government. Although I had become more confident about the local result after trudging through West Dorset villages over the previous three weeks (and had indeed bet George Osborne a good dinner that my majority would again be doubled) the scale of the shift (my majority actually quadrupled) came as a relief and a surprise – though this was tinged with some sadness that trusted and valued Liberal Democrat colleagues like Danny Alexander and David Laws had gone missing, not just from government but from Parliament, punished by the electorate for doing the right thing. Undoubtedly, for them to form a full coalition with us in 2010 was in the national interest; but it turned out to be very much not in the interest of the Liberal Democrats who had done it. Politics is a tough business.

As I surveyed, still somewhat disbelievingly, the votes for me occupying more and more of the tables at the centre of the hall, I asked myself: why, despite the tumbles and stumbles, was I so glad to have spent so much of my life in politics?

Part of the answer, certainly, is the joy of having had a role in the governing of a country. One can be swept along in the tide of ideas; or one can try at the deepest level to influence the nature of that tide. But if one is incapable of the leaps of intellect required to shape the philosophical or scientific foundations of the age, and yet reluctant just to be carried along, then there is a third, tantalising possibility – to be one of those who help to translate certain ideas into practice in an effort to improve the condition of society. I have had the extraordinary good fortune to be able to spend most of my adult years engaged in that pursuit.

But it isn't just being part of the route march to a better society that makes a life in politics so enjoyable. It's also the sheer thrill of living in a constantly shaken kaleidoscope. As the patterns form, shatter and re-form, they generate an extraordinary intensity of experience and of memory. Like playing tennis at Wimbledon or dancing a *pas de deux* at the Royal Ballet, a political life yields a sequence of heightened moments – a few of historical significance, others that stick in the mind for more particular and individual reasons like the tunes and poems of youth.

These moments are not restricted to the high politics of Westminster, Whitehall and the world beyond. Some of them occur in the heat of election campaigns. I recall, in particular, the rather unfortunately warm moment when I arrived at my election headquarters in Hackney North & Stoke Newington during the 1987 general election. I had departed the previous night after finishing, with much assistance from the stalwarts of the Conservative Association, the individual labelling by hand in pen and ink of tens of thousands of my personal manifestos addressed to the electors in the constituency. The envelopes containing the documents were then placed in sacks provided by the Royal Mail's free general election postal service.

As I came the next morning to the point on the road outside the headquarters, I could see that there was something wrong. Gradually, I focused on the fact that what was wrong was the headquarters building itself. Not to put too fine a point on it, the building wasn't there any more. It – and all the hand-addressed election manifestos within – had been burned to the ground. It was considered to be a case of arson, and it seemed at least possible that whoever had done it might have been associated with, or perhaps inspired by, a now defunct organisation known as Class War. Class War (though not directly participating in the election on the grounds that elections were bourgeois conspiracies) had been campaigning actively under the perspicuous slogan 'We will bomb, blast and burn every bourgeois out of Hackney'.

In more recent years, campaigning in West Dorset has typically been a rather softer and more cuddly experience. In the middle of the 2005 general election, I found myself knocking on doors one sunny evening in the delightful surroundings of Burton Bradstock – a coastal village, largely built of stone and thatch. My aim as usual was to persuade some Conservatively inclined voters who might not otherwise bother to vote for me to do so on polling day. It is a pleasant enough task in these highly congenial circumstances, but the rate at which I obtain extra votes, if any, is usually low.

On this occasion, I came to a house at the corner of the street. I knew this house. In previous elections, it had sported a Liberal Democrat poster. To my surprise, on this occasion there was no sign of any Liberal Democrat enthusiasm. Instead, the occupants had placed a copy of my election address in one of their windows.

I was intrigued – and rather excited. As a candidate defending an exceedingly thin majority, any sign of drift to the Conservative camp, however slight, was more than welcome. I decided to ring the bell and enquire into the cause.

'I was just wondering—'

No sooner had I begun my usual spiel than I was interrupted. 'Well, we aren't Conservatives; but we really thought that on this occasion, we had to support you.'

'So grateful… but… why?'

'Come and see.' And, with that, they took me into their kitchen, where I found a litter of tiny brown-and-white Cavalier King Charles spaniels almost identical to our own dearly beloved dog, who had shared my election photo as he did all other aspects of our family's life.

Whoever said that election addresses don't make any difference?

But of course it isn't just in elections that my engagement in West Dorset has had its characteristic moments. Many of them have been located in the ostensibly humdrum life of the constituency member. Like any other MP, over the years, I have become a part of my constituency, and it has become a part of me. This was not entirely predictable. In 1995, so far as I could be classified geographically, it was as a Londoner. I was born in London; I had contested two London seats; I had lived more of my life in London than in any other place. And I felt, as I still feel, entirely at home in London – not only the historic London in which I had grown up but also the modern, culturally and commercially vibrant cosmopolitanism of what is now unmistakably a great world city. By contrast, my knowledge of the countryside in 1995 was slight. Accordingly, when I was first selected as the candidate for West Dorset, this was greeted with a certain amount of hilarity by metropolitan friends and acquaintances – including the cartoonist in one national newspaper who rather disobligingly drew a cow with 'helpful' arrows indicating the front and the rear of the animal (presumably intending to suggest, with some justice, that I was not at that time an expert on rural affairs). But one does not have to have roots in a place to come to love it; and in the years since 1995 the plain fact of the matter is that I have come to love the coastal triangle of old England that lies between Lyme Regis to the south-west, Chesil Beach to the south-east and Sherborne to the north. This is God's own country.

The strands of memory that stretch over twenty years as the local member provide a composition of recollections so rich that they could occupy an entire volume. But some in particular gesture towards the character of life in this blessed part of our land. As the year progresses, I go from one West Dorset town or village to another each Friday, holding a surgery in a local hotel or village hall, so that I am in all corners of the constituency over the course of the year. My constituents book in to see me about a wide range of subjects – sometimes bringing very specific problems that they are having with a particular public agency or public service; sometimes representing a town or parish that has a communal problem with traffic or flooding or planning or something of that sort; and sometimes raising a national or international issue that they want to discuss with their MP.

But there are also *sui generis* visitors, and Mr Bean is most definitely one of these. He is a local hero, of a most unusual kind. Mr Bean and I were in contact for many years, ever since he made contact with me to raise his concerns about litter in Chickerell. At first, I was somewhat sceptical: to those with experience of city streets, the small town of Chickerell, near the coast at the far south-east of my constituency, hardly looked like a place with a serious litter problem. But Mr Bean gradually persuaded me – and, more remarkably, he gradually persuaded the people of Chickerell – that they did indeed have a litter problem. And he used true Big Society principles to achieve an improvement in the situation. A team of volunteers was established;

leaflets were printed up ('find a bin, and put it in'); he won himself a place on the town council as the anti-litter candidate; he promulgated his message in the schools and in the local media.

In due time, Mr Bean appeared to tell me the good news. It had all worked – and he could prove it. Whereas the annual litter pick in previous years collected many bags' worth of litter, this year's pick had yielded only an exiguous return on the effort of scouring the town because the culture had changed and the litter wasn't being dropped in the same quantities any more.

Mr Bean is an exemplar of the Big Society at work. But he is just one amongst the countless examples that I have come across over my years in West Dorset. The pub in Shipton Gorge is a classic case. It is no ordinary pub. It is West Dorset's first-ever community pub. Some years back, a group of villagers from Shipton Gorge came to see me about the fact that their pub was about to close. Shipton (named 'Gorge' not from a feature of the landscape but from the family who held the manor in medieval times), gloriously situated in the hills above Burton Bradstock and the sea, is a small village that has no real centre of communal life other than its pub. So I was keen to help. The owners of the establishment, who had been unable to make a go of it, were somewhat sceptical about the suggestion that the villagers could create a viable business out of it, but were willing to allow them to try. The results have been miraculous. As so often in West Dorset villages, there turned out to be inhabitants with every necessary skill. The musty and forbidding interior has been lovingly turned by voluntary but highly skilled craftsmen into a bright, airy and inviting pub. The food has become excellent. The atmosphere is friendliness itself, and the business is booming.

Up and down the constituency, there have been instances of the same Big Society spirit yielding the same results – the community shop in my own village of Thorncombe, a project first discussed in my garden, is now the most beautiful small shop in England (with prizes to show for it); the community libraries have continued traditions of bookishness in villages where these would otherwise have disappeared; and so it goes on. But nothing beats the community pub at Shipton Gorge – except perhaps the service on Remembrance Sunday in Sherborne Abbey, which I have attended regularly for twenty years.

The proceedings begin outside the abbey itself, at the war memorial on the edge of the ecclesiastical grounds. The Reverend Canon Eric Woods, the vicar of Sherborne with Castleton and St Paul's and rector and surrogate of Lillington and Longburton, officiates. The old soldiers come round the corner from Cheap Street, marching towards us, preceded by the town band and the colour party. The command to halt is given. The martial music ceases. The parade turns towards us. One by one, the old soldiers first, the wreath-bearers come up to the memorial, place their wreaths, salute, turn and return to the parade. The Territorial Army, the Cadets and Sea Cadets, the Canadian Army, the US Air Force, the police, the fire brigade… they are all there. At the culmination of the laying of the wreaths, the band strikes up.

The parade proceeds into the abbey: the fan vaulting and the magical reredos lit by sunlight; the colours brought up to the altar; 'Oh God, our help in ages past'; the sermon from the army chaplain; the ancient brigadier ('they shall grow not old … at the going down of the sun and in the morning we will remember them'), and the young cadet ('when you go home, tell them of us and say, for their tomorrow we gave our today'); the Last Post and the lowering of the colours; the Reveille and the raising of the colours.

As those hymns are sung, those prayers said in Sherborne Abbey, the wars we remember differ from one another in kind. There is the inexplicable lunacy of the First World War – battles of unimaginable horror fought for no apparent reason, paving the way for the totalitarian monstrosities of communism, fascism and Nazism across half the world. Then we remember the Second World War – in which the free world removed the monsters responsible for one totalitarian nightmare by praying in aid the monsters responsible for another of them. Then the Cold War, brought to an end not by conquest but by the implosion of totalitarian socialist planning and the triumph of free market economics. Finally – so far – the battles fought, sometimes with at best tenuous justification and effectiveness, against enemies complicatedly connected with the forces of a much more old-fashioned religious totalitarianism.

But all of these reflections quickly give way to the feelings that are generated by the practical effects of an election on a practising politician. For me, the result of the election meant a return to the Cabinet Office – and hence to the centre of government. Of all the departments of state, the Cabinet Office is probably the least well known and, even to many with knowledge of Whitehall, the most mysterious. It exists partly to provide the Cabinet with a secretariat that can ensure the smooth running of the political machine and partly to provide the civil service with an organising centre. In one sense, it is not really a ministerial department at all – since the Cabinet Secretary (a civil servant) presides over the Cabinet Secretariat and is usually also (as at present) the head of the civil service. It contains other very senior officials such as the National Security Adviser and the chair of the Joint Intelligence Committee, who answer directly to the Prime Minister for the functioning of the National Security Secretariat and the Joint Intelligence staff. And there are also senior officials in it who are more or less outside ministerial control as they have an independent and quasi-judicial role in checking up on whether ministers are obeying the Ministerial Code, and in ensuring that the proprieties of government are observed.

From the 2015 election onwards, in addition to having the meaningless title of 'Chancellor of the Duchy of Lancaster' (a duchy which contains the Queen's private estates, and actually runs itself without ministerial interference), I was nominally in 'overall charge' of the Cabinet Office. But, in practice, to the extent that any minister really exerts influence over this mysterious department, it was my friend Matt Hancock who took over the running of the place, from Francis Maude (who had moved to the Lords after the election). So the great bulk of the ministerially supervised activity of the Cabinet Office – the administration of the civil service, the coordination of government IT, the setting of civil service pay and conditions and so forth – were handled, throughout my time in the office, first by Francis and then by Matt. This left me free, from 2010 onwards, to work with the Cabinet Secretariat, the National Security Secretariat, the Civil Contingencies Secretariat and latterly the Constitution Unit and the Implementation Unit (as well, of course, as the team at No. 10) to turn the aims and policies of the government into action on the ground.

In some ways, this was a natural sequel to my work in the shadow Cabinet during our years in opposition – but with one great difference. Oppositions don't actually do anything. Governments *do* things. So, from the time when I became shadow Home Secretary, my principal aim in opposition had been to help a succession of leaders to move the Conservative Party towards a particular ideological position – social and economic liberalism, tempered by a commitment to social justice and environmental stewardship, both globally and nationally. By contrast, in government – both during the coalition years and during the majority Cameron administration after spring 2015 – my principal aim was to help David Cameron produce effects in the real world that were consistent with that brand of liberal Conservatism, by translating policy into practice. And, for this journey, the parts of the

Cabinet Office and of the No. 10 machine with which I worked were the right vehicle.

The opening stage of translating policy into action is to legislate. Accordingly, my first task in 2015 was to sit down and write a draft Queen's Speech, setting out the legislation that would be necessary to implement our manifesto pledges. I realised with a thud that, although I had a full set of draft coalition agreements which I had prepared at clandestine meetings with David Cameron, George Osborne and Ed Llewellyn in the later stages of the 2015 election, I didn't have even the first draft of a legislative programme for a majority Conservative government. Like everyone else, I had been sufficiently misled by the polls to have discounted even the possibility of an outright Conservative majority government.

The tone of our 2015 manifesto had been solidly Cameroon – modern, compassionate, one-nation liberal Conservatism of the sort that David had been advocating since 2005, with no concessions to the reactionary right or the socially conservative brigade. But, apart from the commitment to renegotiation and referendum on the EU, the substance was consciously low key. Rather than offering any bold new departures, our aim was to build on the fiscal, economic and administrative progress we had made in the coalition years. We had therefore promised the voters not a trip to the stars but a series of practical outcomes to enhance public services, improve the economy and make society more just – proper seven-day access to NHS GPs; more good primary schools; three million apprenticeships; a tax-free national living wage; no higher-rate taxes for those earning less than £50,000 a year; no inheritance tax for those leaving less than £1 million; the roll-out of Universal Credit to make work pay for all; thirty hours of free childcare to enable more mothers to enter the labour market; 200,000 new starter homes, a right to buy for housing association tenants and more house-building to enable people to become homeowners; and the triple lock on state pensions so that pensioners could look forward to steadily rising incomes.

Unlike the first session of the coalition government, fulfilling these bread-and-butter promises was not going to involve a particularly heavy legislative programme – because most of the required legislation was already in place. What was principally needed now was a large amount of implementation work to bring about effects in the real world. Nevertheless, we clearly needed to agree quickly on the shape of the relatively small amount of legislation that the manifesto did demand, and I worked through much of the first night after the election to produce a working text by the next day. I suppose the adrenalin of the election victory kept me going through what was by then forty-eight hours without a noticeable amount of sleep.

The second task was to put together proposals for David Cameron for how the central machinery of government should be run now that we were in single-party mode. The Cabinet Secretary, Jeremy Heywood, and I came rapidly to the conclusion – soon afterwards agreed by David and George Osborne – that we should substantially change the structures within which we had operated from 2010 to 2015.

During the coalition years, there had been a need for continuous collective discussion to resolve policy differences. But we were now ministers from just one party, all committed to the same manifesto. Clearly, there still needed to be systems for the resolution of detailed policy issues through formal clearance of papers in Cabinet committee clearance rounds – but (other than in the National Security Council, where decisions had to be made week by week in response to changing international circumstances) we didn't need to have endless policy meetings: the papers could be circulated for comments from each ministry, and the officials in the Cabinet Office's excellent Economic and Domestic Secretariat could then broker solutions to any inter-departmental wrangles before the chair of the relevant committee signed off on the agreed text. With the departure of the Liberal Democrats, almost all of the Cabinet committees were now being chaired either by David himself or by George or me, so it was relatively easy for us to ensure that they operated in the way we envisaged.

But there was a different test. Given that many of our most important implementation challenges could be met only through close cooperation between departments, what we needed was some mechanism to bring those responsible for each major project together in a setting where we could focus on action rather than policy debate. So Jeremy Heywood and I proposed the establishment of ten implementation task forces, which would have no role in deciding new policy but would be concerned exclusively with successful implementation of specific manifesto commitments. To avoid a game of Whitehall whispers (in which it is all too easy for action points to get lost as they are transmitted from one layer of the administration to the next), we proposed to include senior officials and other experts around the table alongside the relevant ministers. Another important difference was that the task forces would be serviced not just by the Cabinet Secretariat but also by the Implementation Unit so that they could provide data showing the progress that had or had not been achieved since the previous meeting.

In the succeeding year, the implementation task forces had a mixed record. Some worked very well and made significant progress. Others turned into talking shops. It very much depended, as always, on the particular chemistry of the people attending, and on the extent to which the minister chairing was able to focus the discussion on facts, problems and solutions rather than descending into futile generalities. I see that Theresa May's new government has reduced the number of task forces, and has correspondingly increased the number of substantive

Cabinet committees chaired by the PM herself. This seems a sensible response to the fact that the new ministerial team is facing huge policy challenges associated with Brexit. For those policy purposes, as with the National Security Council, a Cabinet committee meeting regularly under the chairmanship of the PM is likely to be the most efficient way of conducting business. But in the areas that remain simply matters of implementation and where successful implementation depends critically on inter-departmental cooperation, the task forces remain in place. I suspect that this may prove to be a significant long-term development in the machinery of government.

Once the new structure of Cabinet government was in place and the Queen's Speech was given, I had time on my hands because I no longer needed to spend a large part of each week resolving coalition issues. I was therefore able, in collaboration with two newly acquired and highly effective ministerial colleagues in the Cabinet Office, George Bridges and John Penrose, to expend all my time and energy on the other activities that had occupied me during the coalition years: delivering our manifesto in the areas where the obstacles were greatest; managing crises; and driving forward positive agendas from Downing Street that had insufficient sponsors elsewhere in Whitehall.

A considerable part of my time was, inevitably, spent with Jeremy Hunt, Greg Clark and Treasury colleagues on the integration of health and social care and other critical issues facing the NHS. But this was essentially a continuation of the work I had been doing during the coalition years. In other areas, we were seeking to deliver new agendas – some of which required a large amount of detailed work.

The delivery of the apprenticeship levy was a classic case. For far too long, Britain had been blighted by putting too little emphasis on vocational and technical education. The creation of three million apprenticeships across the years 2015–20 was our chance to remedy this, and the apprenticeship levy was the means to achieve that goal. But a policy that was right in principle and simple in theory could very well go woefully wrong in practice if the administrative systems used to implement it didn't work properly. So I began a process of interrogation to find out whether the officials in the various departments had developed a joined-up system that would guarantee smooth operation of the levy.

There were really two important practical questions: I needed to be sure that someone had worked out how to collect the right amount of money from the right employers to guarantee funding for the number of apprenticeships to which we were committed; and I needed to be sure that the training received by the apprentices would be up to scratch. To my dismay, I discovered that no one in Whitehall had properly sorted out how to run the project. When I asked to see the official who was in charge of the whole thing, rather than one official dropping by, lots and lots of people turned up at 9 Downing Street. It rapidly became apparent that, although each of these senior officials present knew something about some part of the project, there wasn't anyone anywhere whose job in life was to see the whole project through and to know everything about every part of it, so that he or she could make sure that the different parts fitted together. Warning bells went off all over my head. I could just see Whitehall heading towards an administrative disaster with the left hand not really knowing what the right hand was doing. Following active intervention from the indefatigable Jeremy Heywood and his newly installed and highly experienced chief executive John Manzoni, Matt Hancock and I managed to get a single person put in charge of the whole operation. Matt was then able to use the apprenticeship task force to move forward the detailed implementation and to keep track of progress across the various different parts of government.

The next item on the agenda was childcare. Again, the basic policy was very simple: we had committed to providing thirty hours per week of free childcare for working parents. This was a central plank of the Cameron–Osborne platform – enabling more women to participate in the labour market is a crucial progressive step, opening opportunities and increasing social justice for women as well as increasing the productive capacity of the economy. Two talented ministers – Priti Patel and Sam Gyimah – had been put onto the task. So there was plenty of ministerial impetus. But what made the practice a great deal more complicated than the theory was that, in addition to employer vouchers and a few other special arrangements, we already had three major systems of taxpayer-funded childcare in place or coming into place: childcare tax credits for the least well-off parents; fifteen hours per week of free childcare in nurseries for all three- and four- (and some two-) year-olds; and a new system of childcare tax rebates for taxpayers. We needed somehow to knit together the computer and accounting systems for the new childcare provision with all of these existing systems in a way that would enable parents to choose quickly and easily whichever forms of support were best suited to their particular needs.

By early 2016, the reports coming in from the implementation unit were encouraging: they were able to take me through the way that a parent would apply and the way that the money would then flow. It looked as though this might be navigable for the parents, and as if the various systems might work together as intended. We shall see in due course whether that optimism was well founded.

An even bigger issue than the provision of free childcare was the need to provide enough homes for our expanding population to live in. This had been a central preoccupation for both David Cameron and George Osborne since 2010. Massive social problems were being generated by the shortage of housing. I knew very well from experience in my own constituency that, in addition to an extremely worrying and growing problem of homelessness, we were facing the prospect of the lives of many young families being blighted by their inability to buy into their first home and get onto the 'housing ladder'. And this was also inevitably going to cause very serious economic repercussions. One way to write the post-war economic history of Britain was to chart the cycle of booms and busts, engendered, in large part, by the insufficient supply of housing during periods of economic growth. Coming out of the Great Recession of 2008–10, we were determined to put an end to this dreadful cycle by increasing the rate of house-building well before there was any dangerous boom in property prices.

During the coalition years, working alongside Eric Pickles, Greg Clark, Danny Alexander and the No. 10 Policy Unit – and always with strong support from George Osborne in a succession of Budgets – I had tried to use every available lever to push forward the house-building programme. But even the intensive activity in the 2010–15 parliament hadn't been enough to get the rate of house-building anywhere near to the level we needed in order to match demand. We now had an opportunity to go further with the establishment of a new task force headed by Greg Clark (who was installed as the Communities and Local Government Secretary following the election). There were two things in particular that I concluded we needed to drive from the centre if Greg and his task force were going to make the progress we all wanted to make. The first was a new push to liberate public sector land. Knowing that we would get departments to respond effectively only if they were offered financial sticks and carrots, I teamed up with Greg Hands (who had replaced Danny Alexander as Chief Secretary to the Treasury) to take on the three big land-holding departments: Health, Transport and Defence.

David Prior at the Department of Health was keen as mustard to help – and so was his secretary of state, Jeremy Hunt, not least because they both desperately wanted to liberate capital for investment into the NHS. At Transport, too, we had an enthusiastic junior minister, Claire Perry. But the officials at Network Rail, where most of the spare land was lurking, were sublimely resistant. I had various hilarious meetings with them and Claire. We would sit around my table, solemnly pondering a map of some piece of land that was quite clearly of no use to the railway at all; the railway people would begin yet another litany of reasons why this particular patch of earth either (a) couldn't be got at or (b) wouldn't be attractive to any developer or (c) might at some later date be used by the railway for some purpose that they couldn't quite yet put their finger on or (d) was subject to certain legal restrictions that they didn't themselves understand but which it might take their lawyers a long time to find out about or (e) was in fact too small to be of interest or (f) was in fact too large to get planning permission or (g) was something that couldn't be sold for some reason they couldn't remember but which they would go back to their office and find out about… don't call us, we'll call you (not). Eventually, we just settled on a number.

The most important target of all was the Ministry of Defence. I knew from bitter experience in the 2010–15 parliament that the military establishment would bring up its big guns to defend its estates. So I asked the implementation unit to draw up a table of facts about the MoD estate. What came back, all from public open sources, was pretty impressive. Total MoD landholdings were approximately equal to the size of Wales; there was roughly as much land held to support the activities of a couple of hundred thousand army, navy and air force personnel as there had been when we had about ten times as many people under arms in the Second World War; there were numerous golf courses, riding stables and other appurtenances that seemed to serve no obvious military use; and so it went on. Equipped with this rather powerful data, we went to see Michael Fallon and his officials. A little while later we got a serious offer backed by his business-like permanent secretary, Jon Thompson.

Liberating land from the public sector was not, however, going to be enough to get us to the levels of house-building we needed, even after all the changes to the planning system brought about during the coalition years. We still needed to do more to increase the rate at which planning applications were turned into built homes. Once again, the implementation unit delivered the goods: by enquiring closely into the fiddly details, we discovered that the whole process takes on average about two years from the granting of permission to the completion of the first home – and, even more importantly, that without changing any of the individual stages (i.e. just by making things currently done in series be done in parallel and by making things currently done twice be done once) we could reduce the average elapsed time from application to construction from two years to one.

Alongside apprenticeship, childcare and housing, the fourth great cross-departmental challenge was the upgrading of our mobile and broadband infrastructure. This had been a major preoccupation during the coalition years, and it was now brought under the aegis of a task force chaired by Ed Vaizey. Issue number one was the need to make fast broadband service available everywhere in the country. In the coalition years, we had arranged a combination of central government subsidies, county council contributions and investments from BT itself to provide 24Mbps for 95 per cent of premises before the end of 2017. Unfortunately, however, in our enthusiasm to make this giant leap forward, we had forgotten what happens when 95 per cent of the electorate gradually get a hugely improved service. First, the people who get the improvement late in the sequence, after they can see neighbouring areas getting served, complain loudly. And, worse, the people who are in the remaining 5 per cent, who are destined to be left out permanently, become absolutely furious.

As we approached the 2015 general election, it was clear that we needed a universal guarantee of at least a decent speed for all premises by 2020. Despite considerable Whitehall doubts about whether this was really feasible, David Cameron and George Osborne fully backed the drive to get this commitment built into our manifesto, and after the election the task force was duly charged with delivering a new universal service obligation. There ensued a considerable period of semantic debate: what exactly, the various Whitehall luminaries wanted to know, did we mean by a 'universal service'? I'm afraid I may not have been wholly good humoured as I tried to explain in rather plain words that, by 'universal service', I meant a service providing at least 10Mbps download for *everybody*. Ed Vaizey, bless him, did understand exactly what was meant – and the task force proceeded to consult on the real thing. The Digital Economy Bill, which came to Parliament shortly after Matt Hancock took over from Ed Vaizey in Theresa May's new government, gives power to the Media Secretary to establish a genuine all-singing, all-dancing obligation properly in line with what we promised.

But rolling out fast broadband actually proved to be rather more straightforward than getting proper geographical coverage for mobile telecoms. This was a very long-running saga. Right back in 2010, the problem of rural 'not-spots' (where you couldn't use your mobile as you travelled across the countryside) had been an evident deficiency of our system. What made this particularly maddening was that, if you went as a visitor anywhere else in the world, your phone would happily roam from network to network, providing almost seamless coverage as you moved across the terrain – whereas, in the UK, your phone would stick remorselessly to your own service provider's network and refuse to connect you even if you were in a place where some other service provider was providing a perfectly good signal. Cabinet ministers with rural seats like Owen Paterson were incandescent about this problem of 'partial not-spots' – as were many of our backbench colleagues, and hundreds of thousands of their (and my) constituents. The obvious solution was to force the UK mobile operators to allow UK phones to roam between the UK networks, just as foreigners coming to the UK could do.

For reasons that were never really quite clear to me, the UK mobile operators hated this suggestion like poison and were evidently prepared to fight it in court. Sajid Javid (then Media Secretary), Danny Alexander and I decided that the best approach would be to threaten legislation on UK roaming, in an effort to avoid litigation by extracting from the mobile service providers a voluntary agreement which would reduce both partial and total 'not-spots'. After a couple of rather frosty encounters with the chief executives of the mobile companies, we got an agreement – which was then encoded in the mobile operators' licences – under which the operators each guaranteed to provide their own subscribers with voice coverage across 90 per cent of the landmass.

But my activities in the Cabinet Office were not restricted to these domestic challenges. Gradually, as I participated in the meetings of the National Security Council from 2010 onwards, it became clear to me that here, as in the domestic arena, a great part of the task was to obtain first-hand information about what was really happening 'on the ground' – particularly in the places where our military were engaged. I therefore began a series of visits to relevant locations. One of the most revealing of these was my sojourn in Afghanistan with David Richards, then Chief of the Defence Staff. We visited US and UK bases, and talked to our army commanders and civilian administrators, Afghan National Army personnel and a range of Afghan ministers and officials. Shortly before leaving, we paid a call on President Hamid Karzai, the man then at the centre of the whirlwind. I had met the President only once before, at a lunch at Chequers, whereas David Richards – who was present also at that lunch – knew Karzai well as a result of having spent a considerable time as the commander of allied forces in Afghanistan.

In contrast to much of the rest of Kabul, the Presidential Palace was pleasantly laid out, with its gardens and broad avenues. As almost always in the centre of any government, there was an air of tranquillity. We were shown into the President's room, and arranged ourselves around the armchair in which he sat. The conversation ranged widely – from military matters, relationships with neighbouring states and prospects for settlements with the Taliban to English literature, in which Karzai was surprisingly well versed.

As we proceeded with these exchanges, I was wondering whether – and if so, for how long – this rather surreal tranquillity could be preserved. Would Karzai or his successor following the upcoming election be capable of holding even the centre, let alone the periphery, once the US, UK and allied forces of ISAF largely left? How far did this relatively liberal and relatively civilised regime actually have a grip on the levers of power? Would the troops of the Afghan National Army whom we and our allies had been training remain in place? Or would they melt away? And would Karzai himself actually hand over power permanently to whoever was elected in the election, which he was not contesting? Or would this man, who had spent his life putting together shifting networks and alliances, find it irresistible to continue with the power-brokering when he was no longer officially in power?

There was nothing definite in what he said to indicate the answers to any of these questions, and nothing in what we had seen elsewhere in Afghanistan to make me feel certain of any of them either. It was clear from all Karzai's observations that he saw no merit in thinking even a year ahead, let alone five, ten or fifty years. He was living from day to day – willing to deal with all comers, and trusting no one. Would the next day bring the assurance of lasting peace and stability? Most definitely not. Would it bring doom and disaster? One just couldn't know: but at least I concluded that there was no certain doom. It seemed possible, though no more than possible, that what he and we from the West had put in place might be able to hold the forces of barbarism at bay. It was clear that he lived in this hope from moment to moment – and it seemed to me, as I returned to the UK, that this was as good as it was going to get any time soon.

A year or so later, I found myself in one of a heavily guarded convoy of vehicles, making my way from Erbil – the capital of Iraqi Kurdistan – up into the foothills of the Zagros Mountains to see Masoud Barzani, the President of the Kurdistan Regional Government (KRG). The landscape through which we passed at high speed was barren, gaunt and dusty. As inhospitable peaks rose above us and the road became a track, we reached the gates of the compound – part presidential palace, part mountain eyrie.

Barzani is a small, wiry and wizened figure. He had spent, as he explained to me, much of his life engaged in warfare. There was nothing implausible about this; despite his gracious manners, there was something about his bearing that would make me disinclined to take him on in hand-to-hand combat.

In Erbil itself, we found a flourishing city full of construction projects and lively markets; we were somewhat bizarrely entertained to a splendid dinner by the Prime Minister, surrounded by highly cultivated Kurds many of whom had been educated in the UK or US or both. We had meetings with ministers and officials of a sort that might have occurred in many more peaceful parts of the world, discussing issues of economic policy and (the great issue of the day) the allocation of oil revenues between the KRG in Erbil and the federal government in Baghdad.

But here in the mountains, though geographically further from the front line, we were spiritually much closer to the Peshmerga – the highly effective army created out of rival Kurdish military factions, now providing the most sustained and efficient machine for defending the line and recapturing territory then held by Daesh. In Masoud Barzani and his aides we found the centrepiece of Iraqi Kurdish resistance. These are people whose families have been betwixt war and peace – in exile, in power, in conflict – for a century since the defeat of the Ottomans in the First World War, the Treaty of Sèvres, which first gave the Iraqi Kurds a promise of autonomy, and the rebellion of 1923 once it became clear that that promise would be unfulfilled.

My purpose was to discover whether the Peshmerga would hold, and whether all the tensions of the relationship between the KRG and the federal government in Baghdad would ultimately be secondary to the need for unity in the face of Daesh. For once, I found a clear answer. Barzani, though uncompromising in his determination to achieve what he regarded as a fair settlement on the allocation of the oil revenues and uncomplimentary about many aspects of federal Iraqi politics, was very clearly grateful to the West for the delivery of the Kurds from Saddam and equally clearly determined to defeat and destroy Daesh. I was left in no doubt whatsoever that his motive was to promote the interests of the Iraqi Kurds rather than any romance about Iraq as a nation; but there was equally no doubt that he saw those interests as lying in the demolition of Daesh in Iraq, and that he was confident of achieving that aim over however many years it took. This was someone who meant business.

But the National Security Council wasn't just concerned with short-term issues of war and peace. It was equally focused on the UK's long-term strategic relationships – including particularly those with India and China. Soon after joining the council in 2010, I became clear that we needed to do more to foster these relationships across government. I therefore began to travel to both countries, and to immerse myself in a series of issues that affected relations – including visas, inward investment, the place of the City of London as a centre for renminbi- and rupee-denominated security issuance, and inter-governmental cooperation in fields where we had common global interests, such as the ivory trade. My trips back and forth to Beijing, Shanghai, Shenzhen, Nanjing, Hong Kong, Delhi, Bangalore and Mumbai also produced some of the most memorable moments of my time in government.

In 2014, I made my first visit to the Party School in Beijing – because Professor Peter Nolan, from whom I had been taking a series of tutorials about the Chinese bureaucracy, had told me that it was impossible to understand how the 'leading groups' that formulate policy in China transmit that policy through this vast country without understanding the role of the Party School. Now, you can tell a lot about the position that an institution holds in a power structure by seeing its physical position. The Party School is located in the gardens of what used to be the Summer Palace. As we wandered by the lakes and rills beneath the weeping willows, it became clear that this was indeed, as Peter Nolan had instructed me, an institution at the centre of the power structures of modern China.

Some of the buildings in the gardens were relatively unpretentious; others were magnificent. The official guiding me towards the meeting explained that the nature of the buildings varies with the students whom each is designed to accommodate: the grandest provide apartments for the party secretaries and senior ministers; the less grand are to house those of lesser rank – though even these are people of national significance; the cadres of only regional or local importance do not come to Beijing but have their training in regional centres run by the Party School.

I was aware from Peter Nolan's briefing that all officials in the party and government were compelled to attend the school at regular intervals. But seeing the physical reality of the apartments they occupy gave me more of a sense of the scale of the undertaking than I had gleaned from my tutorials. I was reminded of the various habitations disposed around the luxuriant gardens of the Vatican. The Party School, like the Apostolic See, is a place from which the meaning behind the encyclicals radiates to the four corners of the earth.

I entered the grand hall at the centre of the gardens, and was greeted by three professors of the school. I had been told that the senior professors rank with ministers, so I was expecting people of intelligence and acumen. But nothing could have prepared me for the level of comprehension and scholarship. We sat, Chinese-style, in a long gallery, with the professor who was my interlocutor and me in two great armchairs at one end, and his colleagues and my team ranged on either side. Between him and me there was an interpreter, though (as so often in China) it became clear from the professor's occasional interjections that he actually understood my English; my own efforts to learn Mandarin having failed hopelessly, I had no equivalent advantage. We began with some nugatory politesse to break the ice. But soon, before I could begin to ask him anything substantive, he was asking specific questions of a highly detailed kind about particular phrases in the coalition Programme for Government and in speeches that I had practically forgotten giving.

Was this just knowledge acquired for the day, or for show? I decided to find out by responding with replies containing references that would be understood only by well-informed participants in a seminar at our Institute for Government. The professor picked up the references instantly, and launched into a disquisition on UK fiscal consolidation that would have been impressive if coming from one of our own Treasury economists. He was particularly interested in the tapers applying to Universal Credit and their effects on the dynamics of the UK labour market. I was talking to someone who was just about as well informed as I was about the live policy issues in my own government.

When he had exhausted his line of questioning, I had the opportunity in the last part of the discussion to ask him about what I had really come to find out: the nature of the relationship between the Party School and the Standing Committee of the Politburo – the body which, through its 'leading groups', formulates policy for the party and the country. It is, he explained to me, a two-way flow. The strategies of the Standing Committee are transmitted to the party, the ministries and the provincial and municipal governments through the Party School (whose patron is a member of the Standing Committee). But the professors of the Party School also offer analysis and policy advice to the Politburo, alongside various other bodies that I had visited in Beijing. He patiently explained how these two functions interact: it is because the professors are used as the mechanism to transmit strategy to the party that they are able to tailor their policy analysis to fit current strategy and hence to be of real interest to the Politburo.

I have found in China that you have to listen for the silences. The professor wasn't saying – but he was clearly meaning me to understand – that this was not the place where fundamental ideas are formulated. Was he hinting at more, and more unsayable things? Or was he, rather, illustrating to me the hierarchy with which he worked – political strategy driving administrative policy rather than vice-versa? The more I heard him circumnavigate this proposition, the more certain I became that this was indeed his point. Through his statements and his silences, he was offering a more sophisticated version of the cliché that Chinese perspectives are long. Strategy governs; policy conforms. And the enforcement of such a hierarchy is possible because of the discipline of which the Party School is a prime instrument, bringing all the cadres into line with the thinking of the Standing Committee – something unimaginable in the UK. Not for the first time in this China, I found myself passing through recognition of the great similarities between us to the recognition of great difference.

A year later, in 2013, I went with our high commissioner in Delhi, James Bevan, to the white-walled residence occupied by Rahul Gandhi. It was only a matter of months before the Indian general election, and security was tight. The situation was an odd one, because Gandhi was not the Prime Minister (a position occupied by the veteran Manmohan Singh) nor even the leader of the ruling Congress Party (a position occupied by his mother, Sonia Gandhi); but he was nevertheless expected to lead Congress's election campaign. And if (as admittedly seemed less likely than not) Congress had won against an opposing BJP (Bharatiya Janata Party) revitalised by its new leader, Narendra Modi, then it was expected that Rahul would become the de facto head of government.

I was keen to get a sense of this man, whose family had played so pivotal a role in the development of the world's largest democracy since India became independent, and who was in the process of inheriting the mantle that had led to the violent death of his recent forebears. We proceeded through the various security checks and across the courtyards into the light, white meeting room, filled with huge photographs of rural India. Immediately, these photographs, with the press of people everywhere set against the staggering backdrops of Indian landscapes, transported us from the dusty streets of Delhi into a different India, the heartland of the Congress Party.

Rahul Gandhi greeted us with old-world courtesy. Though not tall, he has – as one might have expected – a considerable presence. But it seemed at the beginning of the conversation that he was more of an intellectual surveying the scene than a leader with an immediate practical agenda, still less a messianic mission. He reflected interestingly, if somewhat dispassionately, on the challenges facing India and on the state of Indian politics. He was happy to engage in a discussion of the geo-political relationships with China, with the West, with Islam. It was a pleasant, discursive meander through well-charted, if hideously complex, terrains. He was intelligent, well briefed and of course well connected, but I was discovering nothing about his soul or his mind; it was reminiscent of pleasant but ultimately meaningless evenings in Oxbridge common rooms.

Then, suddenly, there was a step-change. I alluded to the photographs around the walls. We began to discuss election campaigning in rural India and the response of rural Indians to Congress and to other parties. He remained calm and outwardly detached, but the timbre altered; I began to see what it was that he really cared about. It was not the global scene or indeed the new, high-tech India of the cities and the software and the engineers that moved him; it was this other India of which I understand little or nothing – unimaginably populous, ineffably ancient, still in parts unutterably impoverished, half making its way into modernity – with which his life, his family, his griefs and triumphs were bound up. He himself, of course, is a world citizen, an urban sophisticate, educated up to his eyeballs, aware of all the global and Indian high-tech advances; but the centre of his being is in another, much more turbulent and much less sophisticated (or at least much less contemporary) reality. I was getting as close as I would ever get to the paradox and the fascination of the sub-continent: the disjunctions and the connections between what it has been, what it is, and what it might become.

My work in the National Security Council was amongst the most interesting engagements of my time in the Cabinet Office – an outward-looking equivalent to the central domestic agendas. But it was not just these great global and domestic agendas that required attention from the centre. Day by day, new implementation challenges across Whitehall would rear their heads, and it sometimes wasn't easy to keep proper track of all the different challenges. I was very conscious that, if I failed to do so, I would be letting David Cameron down badly. So I was keen to use all the help I could get. Luckily, powerful reinforcements were to hand.

As I look back on my time in 9 Downing Street and on the wide range of the work I was doing there, I am continually reminded of the fact that none of what I did would have been possible without the relationships at the centre of the machine that we had forged in opposition and which lasted largely intact throughout. The knitting together of the Treasury and the Cabinet Office with No. 10 was achieved, not through complicated committees or rulebooks, but through a continuing conversation between a group of people who liked and trusted one another – and who were intensely loyal to David Cameron as Leader of the Opposition and then as Prime Minister. I am not by any means suggesting that this is the only way that a sane administration can be carried on: both Margaret Thatcher and Tony Blair operated very different arrangements. But I do believe that, as well as providing enormous strength and support for those of us involved in it, this nexus of relationships enabled us to make progress towards the goals we had set ourselves. Because we operated on the basis of trust and largely shared instincts rather than rigid dogma or inflexible bureaucratic processes, we could adapt to changing circumstance: I knew that, if the pragmatic approach to achieving a shared aim was to adjust something that had previously been regarded as *de rigueur*, I would be able to put that to David and George and the rest of the team without accusations of failing to be 'one of us'. I also knew that the team around the PM (and indeed the PM himself) was available at all times to help out if I hit a spot of bother; loyalty worked two ways.

At the start of the 2015 parliament, we were joined by Camilla Cavendish, who came in as the new head of the Policy Unit. Steve Hilton and I had been admirers of her intellect and passion back in the days of opposition, and approaches had been made to her to join the team at various stages; but it was only in 2015 that she finally succumbed to the entreaties. As soon as she did so, one could feel the energy she injected into the machine, pushing along all of the important agendas in the various task forces and inserting the Policy Unit into the departments in a highly effective way.

So that we could keep the action across Whitehall broadly on track, Camilla and I took to meeting absolutely regularly with the Cabinet Secretary, Jeremy Heywood, as a threesome. We found that, by continually comparing notes on a whole range of immediate and long-term issues, we could frequently spot issues that one or other of us had missed – and we were often able to work out a way in which, without troubling the PM, we could get the relevant part of government to do what he would have wanted it to do, or to stop doing something we knew he didn't want it to do. As all three of us were also in daily contact with the PM and George, we were also able to make sure, whenever there was any doubt, that we were correctly understanding what was wanted – and indeed bring problems and possible solutions to them as and when they arose, more or less in real time. Time and again, this proved to be an effective way of bringing together the ministerial, the official and the advisory networks in order to produce coordinated action across government. When ministers, special advisers and senior officials were getting the same signals about what the PM wanted from the No. 10 Policy Unit, the Cabinet Secretary in 70 Whitehall and my private office in No. 9, the chance of someone paying attention increased markedly.

Apart from the role that these regular tripartite discussions played in pushing forward the positive agendas, I also found that they were a valuable way to ensure that No. 10, No. 9 and the centre of the civil service were coordinated when it came to handling crises. As David Cameron's odd-job man, I was meant to step in whenever something was going wrong, and it certainly helped to have some powerful friends to deal with these moments – not least because, although the nature of each new crisis was unpredictable, it was certainly predictable that there would be plenty of them. During the coalition years, we had dealt with a steady stream of what could have been very destabilising problems – and throughout my time in Downing Street, at least 50 per cent of the reason for my existence was to make sure that such problems were contained or addressed with sufficient speed to avoid them becoming full-blown crises with lasting consequences for the government's long-term reputation and for the country as a whole.

The first bombshell was the imminent threat of a strike by the drivers of fuel tankers in 2012. It was indeed this episode that brought me into the arena of crisis management, crisis prevention and resilience planning. The issue was simple: the whole nation's fuel supplies – and more or less the whole of our economy and society – depended on a few thousand tanker-drivers turning up for work. This, of course, was not new. Tony Blair had faced disruption to fuel supplies during his first term in office, and the severity of the consequences was therefore well understood. The response of the Whitehall machine to the Blair episode had been to produce a set of emergency powers, duly enacted by Parliament. As I listened to the officials describing this awesome array, it became abundantly clear to me that these were emergency powers in the sense of powers to create an emergency. What did not exist, it turned out, was any plan to *avoid* or *prevent* an emergency.

The next thing that became evident was that the oil industry was not going to solve our problem without a lot of shoving and heaving from government. Neither the oil companies themselves nor the companies that ran tankers for some of them were particularly concerned about what they called rather grandly 'the externalities' – i.e. the effects on the rest of the economy and society. From their point of view, a few days without petrol would have had only a modest effect on one year's profits. Nor was the Department of Energy & Climate Change able to produce a workable solution. They had their awesome powers. But they didn't have any tanker-drivers.

I gradually realised that the only way in which we were going to be able to prevent a crisis was by getting help from the one set of people who *did* have tanker-drivers, who *would* cross picket lines, and who *were* capable of planning and executing a complex logistical exercise in real time: namely the army. Enter General Parker – a splendidly dry and business-like character who had seen action in many parts of the world and whose son was a war hero in Afghanistan. Gradually and painstakingly, the general built up a full plan for training and deploying military tanker-drivers in the event of a strike, with all the ingredients necessary to ensure that even if the public was slightly inconvenienced there would be no major or catastrophic disruption of fuel supplies. I also took steps to ensure that the cadre of trained drivers would be kept in being permanently, so that the plans could be dusted off and the necessary personnel mobilised quickly if a strike were threatened at any time in the future. I have no material doubt that the fact that we were prepared in this way to prevent a strike leading to an emergency was one of the things that persuaded Unite to negotiate a settlement with the haulage companies. So, in the end, the preparations had the best effect of all: they prevented the need to take any exceptional action whatsoever.

Learning from this episode, I subsequently ran an exercise across Whitehall to identify any other areas of national life in which the country might be held to ransom by a small number of key workers – and set in hand actions to ensure that, so far as possible, we were prepared to deal with these as well, again without precipitating an emergency. But of course it was a great deal easier to predict and deal with these human acts than with acts of God or nature. And it didn't take long before we found ourselves in the midst of a serious biological threat – in this case, from Ebola.

When I first read about the Ebola outbreak in Liberia, Sierra Leone and Guinea at the beginning of 2014, I imagined that it was a west African problem, and hence an issue for the Department for International Development (DfID), the World Health Organization (WHO) and the national governments of the three countries concerned. But, as I followed the mounting numbers of reported cases for a few weeks, I became increasingly concerned that we were dealing with something much bigger. I did a back-of-the-envelope calculation, which showed that – at what was then an exponential rate of increase – the epidemic could wipe out colossal proportions of the west African population (and eventually of much wider populations, including our own). So it was clearly essential to mobilise action; and the regional WHO apparatus did not seem to be acting at anything like the required speed.

I began to have a series of discussions with the government's Chief Medical Officer, Dame Sally Davies, and a committed group of officials from the DfID and the Department of Health. This led to a series of conference calls and meetings with the director general of the WHO in Geneva, Margaret Chan, and also with members of the US administration, the major drug companies and the NGOs who were active in the field. Once my colleagues in the DfID and the Foreign Office had agreed with the US and French authorities on a split of primary responsibility (the US in Liberia, the French in Guinea and the UK in Sierra Leone), Justine Greening (then Secretary of State for International Development), MoD ministers, Sally Davies's team and I gradually cranked the UK machine into full-scale action, involving the military and DfID in Sierra Leone as well as a large team of brave and expert medics from the NHS, and a small but effective monitoring group in the Cabinet Office that enabled me to provide David Cameron with reliable real-time information on the spread of the disease, the establishment of a rudimentary public health system and the building and staffing of therapeutic centres in Sierra Leone.

Going to meetings of the WHO in Geneva was an eye-opener. It was clear that Margaret Chan and her colleagues were massively shackled by a combination of international diplomacy (with literally hundreds of people turning up at each meeting from all over the world) and an inability to override the thoroughly useless WHO apparatus in Africa. We urgently needed significant reform of the WHO to give the central apparatus a budget and powers to intervene in global emergencies of this sort. After many months of patient effort – led by Sally Davies and others at our Department of Health and Foreign Office – Margaret Chan subsequently brought much of the necessary transformation about. But at the time it was a nightmare.

I was also really worried by the discovery that we didn't have a pre-established team at the centre of the UK government constantly scanning the horizon for health emergencies in other parts of the world that might affect the UK if not quickly tackled. We clearly needed a unit, to run in parallel with the Civil Contingencies Secretariat, that could perform this function in advance of crises and also, during a global health emergency, do the monitoring and data-gathering job that my ad-hoc team did so splendidly once Jeremy Heywood and I had established it. I'm glad to say that such a permanent team was established in the Cabinet Office in 2015.

But the real essence of defeating Ebola lay in establishing a rudimentary public health system. The most amazing aspect of this whole ghastly saga, as I discovered when I went out to Freetown and some of the rural areas around it, was that Sierra Leone (and, for that matter, Liberia and Guinea) almost entirely lacked such a system. Before going, I had assumed that the main challenge was to establish a network of therapeutic centres that could provide treatment for the thousands of victims of Ebola before they died of it in unspeakable agony. This was what, in a series of cross-departmental meetings chaired by David, we had especially focused on doing; and I was hugely impressed by the extraordinary sangfroid and selflessness of the NHS medics manning the centres that they and the military had established in double-quick time. But I discovered that this was actually the lesser of the two tasks.

This came home to me when I visited the tumbledown warehouse-style buildings in which our troops and Public Health England officials had established command centres, bringing together the local troops and officials to work alongside our experts. As you looked around the great open halls, you saw one team chalking up the addresses at which bodies had been found; another tracing what had happened to the bodies themselves (not least because the dead bodies were maximally infectious so the method of burial was crucial); yet another keeping track of the fate of other inhabitants of the affected houses; and so forth. It was only by doing this boring but crucial logistical work that you could slow down the speed of transmission so as to stabilise the hitherto exponential growth in the disease and eventually bring about a gradual and merciful decline.

I don't think there was anything in my time in 9 Downing Street that taught me nearly as much as the Ebola saga did about the world that we really live in. Anyone who doubts whether we should be devoting significant parts of our national resources to international aid should be asked to witness what I witnessed in Sierra Leone.

By the time we returned from the 2015 election, the threat from Ebola had all but evaporated. But there were plenty of other alarms and excursions in the year that followed.

First of all… floods. If you had asked me in 2010 what I envisaged spending my time as a minister doing, I would not have included hanging out of helicopters to see the pumps pushing water out of the channels that had cut off the Somerset village of Muchelney, or trudging round Yorkshire telephone exchanges and water-works in Wellington boots with Liz Truss on Boxing Day. But these were amongst the joys of being minister for crises. Eventually, I decided that we had to get to grips with the question of why, when we were spending billions of pounds on improved flood defences, we had been surprised, winter after winter, by the overtopping of these defences in different parts of the country – and by the extent of the damage to key local infrastructure like the telephone exchanges and water-works mentioned above. My aim, after one more such Christmas and New Year, was to challenge the Met Office, the Government Office for Science and the Environment Agency to explain what was going wrong with the forecasting of floods. The scientists and modellers from the Met Office are world-class. Likewise, the scientists and modellers from the Environment Agency. So why were the events we had been experiencing out of line with their predictions? Why were we getting occurrences each year that we thought we had been told should be happening only once every hundred years or more?

My suspicion was that we (the politicians and administrators) were misunderstanding something that the scientists were trying to tell us.

But I knew that getting to the bottom of this might be a tricky and pro-longed business. I had the strong sense at the start that the scientists and modellers were wary of a politician intervening in this terrain: no doubt, they were worried that I had some covert plan either to blame them for events beyond their control or to twist the science for some ulterior political purpose.

The body language at the beginning of the meeting was bad. But gradually, as I made clear that I was really trying to understand the truth and nothing more or less, I sensed some of the froideur warming up. I was much helped in this by the Government Chief Scientific Adviser, Mark Walport, with whom I had been through enough different episodes and issues by now for him to believe that I did want the truth.

And then, at last, an important part of the truth did become apparent. As usual, in retrospect, it seemed obvious. The point was that the predictions were all about one specific location: a particular river bank or town or telephone exchange is said to be likely to flood only once in a hundred years. And this prediction is in itself true. But if you have lots of river banks, towns and exchanges, and if there is no particular connection between what causes set A of these locations in river catchment A to flood and what causes set B of these locations in river catchment B to flood, then the chance that some such set of locations, somewhere in Britain, will flood next year is quite high.

So we had all been operating on a false premise for many years, not because the scientists and modellers were wrong, but because we hadn't correctly understood the implication of what they were telling us.

But now the issue was: how do we get to a question that will elicit the answer we need, rather than an answer that doesn't tell us anything very useful? I thought about this for a while, and then suggested that the question to which we really wanted the answer was: 'What would we have to do to ensure that, if the worst rainfall one can reasonably fear will fall in any of the next ten years were in fact to fall in each of the regions of England, and if the worst storms one can reasonably fear will occur in any of the next ten years were in fact to occur in each of the coastal areas of England, our key infrastructure in all of these places would still be safe from flooding?'

'Well,' said the distinguished scientists and modellers, 'that is a good question, but it's not one we can answer.'

Trying to restrain myself from any agitation, I enquired as gently as I could manage why this question (on which depended the well-being of thousands of our fellow citizens) could not be answered.

This was when the bombshell dropped: 'Because', they said, 'the predictions of rainfall and sea storm are made by the Met Office computers, and the predictions of flooding are made by the Environment Agency computers, and there is no link between them.'

So now I knew the real truth. We politicians and administrators had been asking the wrong question and had therefore grossly misunderstood what the scientists and modellers had been telling us. But one of the reasons that no one had corrected our misunderstanding was that the scientists and the modellers knew very well that, if we were to ask the right question, they wouldn't be able to answer it, because their computers didn't talk to one another.

Now I knew also what to do. I wrote down the question. And I asked the scientists and modellers to work out a way of using the two computers together so that they could answer it. Then, and only then, could we begin to develop the defences we needed to stop this all happening year after year. There was as near to a sigh of relief around the room as you can ever hope to get in a meeting of experts, civil service administrators and politicians. I'm delighted to say that after a few more months of hard work, we reached a deal with the various agencies and utilities concerned (now incorporated in a government paper issued after I left office), under which the state of our flood defence infra-structure will be markedly improved.

Then there was the threat of massive disruption to the health service from the junior doctors' strike. Jeremy Hunt and his colleagues proved to be highly competent managers of a very difficult situation. All the planning was done; and the miracle was that, although a lot of elective surgery had to be postponed, the net effect on the Accident and Emergency services was actually positive – because the highly experienced consultants who came in to substitute for the junior doctors were more confident of their diagnoses, referred fewer patients for unnecessary tests and admitted fewer frail elderly patients for unnecessary (and often counter-productive) spells in hospital wards.

Soon after came the crisis precipitated by the prospective sale or closure of Tata Steel's various operations in the UK. This occupied a high proportion of my time during the last few months before the EU referendum – and involved negotiations in both China and the US. At the time of writing, the outcome is still uncertain, though I am increasingly confident that a way will be found to save the great bulk of the remaining steel production in the UK.

Not all of the alarms and excursions were at this macroscopic scale. Sometimes, small items sprang into prominence unexpectedly.

In November 2015, I had to appear before the Public Administration and Constitutional Affairs Committee (PACAC) to defend my decision to give taxpayers' money to the charity Kids Company. I had faced many select committees over my six years as a minister, and had to prepare carefully for all of them. But this one was different. PACAC held a series of highly publicised hearings from various witnesses about Kids Company, and its high-profile chief executive, Camila Batmanghelidjh.

I had spent much of the past couple of weeks going back through every aspect of the events leading up to the collapse of Kids Company, to ensure that I could accurately and comprehensively answer absolutely any factual question the committee posed. In my experience, this is the only way to deal with a parliamentary committee – and on this occasion, given that I was virtually on trial, I needed to be more carefully prepared than ever. In the face of colleagues who are there to raise difficult issues, one cannot duck and weave as one can in debate. Rhetoric does not help; indeed, it will always infuriate the committee. My only weapon was to be so fully informed and so open that, whatever other criticisms they aimed at me (and there were, in the event, many), they at least could not complain about the quality of my evidence.

I had the great advantage of knowing that David Cameron had publicly backed my decision, and was genuinely supportive of it. I also had the advantage that the MPs on the committee, however distrustful they were of my actions in this case, did not have experience of me as a serial liar and were therefore likely to believe facts coming from me to be true, rather than presuming from the start that I would be seeking to mislead them. I also had a clear line of argument (which also happened to be true) that the intention behind giving Kids Company £3 million of taxpayers' funds just before it went bust was to offer it one last chance to put its finances in order.

As the grilling proceeded, I was acutely conscious that my ministerial career was hanging in the balance. Each question carried danger. Each answer had to be precisely right. I didn't have much time to spend thinking about anything beyond the immediate requirement to grasp the next question and provide the next answer. But the thought did cross my mind as I proceeded that I was almost enjoying this: the challenge was considerable, but there was a strong element of a chess game about it – with the difference that both the substance and the outcome mattered a great deal more than in any game of chess I have ever played or will ever play. Masochistic it may be, but give me this any day, compared to the baying hordes of Gordon Brown's cronies or the ludicrous party pieces that all too often pass for debate in the chamber of the House.

But I was determined not to let crisis management in either White-hall or Westminster take over my whole life. I had found right from the start of my time in Downing Street that, regardless of the crises that might be going on at any given moment, it was essential for me to keep pushing also on secondary agendas that weren't sufficiently polit-ically 'sexy' to have attracted more than a line or two in the manifesto (if that) and which might otherwise fall by the wayside due to lack of support in Whitehall. Moving these things forward was in many re-spects more arduous than responding to crises or dealing with the big, central agendas of the government, because you had to generate the energy internally rather than having the need for action thrust upon you by circumstance or political necessity. To take on this task under the new Conservative-only administration, my private office had been complemented by the arrival of the brilliant and endlessly energetic Alok Sharma as my parliamentary private secretary. Together, we drew up a rather daunting to-do list. This included the reform of the energy market; completing the implementation of our commitments to veter-ans and serving military personnel; pressing ahead with the moves to cut red tape; pushing forward the strategy on electric and autonomous vehicles; getting the clean air measures and the work on the fourth and fifth carbon budgets completed; and finishing the process we had begun in coalition to create a 'Blue Belt' of marine protected areas around the Overseas Territories.

The arrival of Amber Rudd as the new Energy Secretary after the 2015 election created an opportunity for a more coherent Conservative-only policy for the electricity supply industry. Amber was determined to agree quickly on a strategy that would keep the lights on and cut carbon while limiting costs for the consumer as far as possible. Through a series of discussions between her, David Cameron, George Osborne and myself, we arrived at a plan that would remove coal-fired plants early, stop subsidising the solar energy that was now economic without subsidies, buy offshore wind at sharply reduced prices, proceed with Hinkley Point C nuclear station, and begin to bring new gas plant and new forms of demand reduction onto the bars through the capacity market. This – when combined with the amount of onshore wind already in existence – was a plan that would deliver the capacity to meet peak demand and provide large amounts of low-carbon energy at affordable costs for the consumer.

But there remained a crucial short-term objective if we were to make this system work: the refinement of the capacity market and of the so-called system balancing reserve, operated by the National Grid. And there was also the crucial medium-term objective of 'shifting the load curve' by reducing domestic demand at peak hours; to do this, the new smart meters we were rolling out to people's homes needed to receive real-time information about half-hourly prices from the Grid – so that they could use that information to turn off electricity-hungry appliances like washing machines at times when prices were high, thereby saving money for households and sparing us the need to build additional power stations. I had been working on these issues with officials from the Grid and from a range of government departments for the previous five years – and that work continued throughout 2015/16. Unfortunately, I wasn't around long enough to see it through; I very much hope that the new team at the new Department for Business, Energy & Industrial Strategy will do so. Certainly, the combination of Greg Clark and Nick Hurd, both of whom understand a great deal about the energy industries, makes me optimistic that we will, by 2020, have a much improved electricity supply market.

Like my concern with energy policy, my preoccupation with the Military Covenant stretched back to the start of the coalition government. In our 2010 manifesto, we had promised to 'restore the Military Covenant and ensure that our Armed Forces, their families and veterans are properly taken care of'. There was a huge amount to be done – and David Cameron was extremely concerned to ensure that we did it. He himself took on the chairmanship of a Cabinet committee on the Military Covenant – but charged me with deputising for him most of the time, and asked me to work with a whole series of departments to make sure that we provided serving military personnel and veterans with crucial improvements like proper married and single living accommodation, dedicated military wards for the wounded, the latest high-tech prosthetic limbs for those who had lost legs or arms, and better access to schooling when service families moved to a new base. I became all too painfully aware of just how important our moral debt was when I visited our military hospital in Afghanistan, and then spoke at the Queen Elizabeth Hospital in Birmingham to soldiers who had lost their legs. As well as pursuing the implementation of all the reforms we had promised with officials in the relevant departments, and going around the country to see for myself what really needed doing for service families, I fostered the establishment of a Covenant Reference Group, formed out of the main service charities, to keep us on our toes. George Osborne then came up with the idea of using fines on errant bankers to fund grants for significant projects put forward by these charities; and I had a huge amount of backing from ministerial colleagues like Andrew Murrison and Mark Francois at the MoD to get the various improvements put in place. I certainly wouldn't want to claim that all is yet wholly as it should be; but I found my work on the Covenant Committee one of the most satisfying parts of my time in Downing Street. We really did manage to make huge strides in enhancing the way the nation treats service personnel and their families. Not before time.

Efforts to cut red tape had also been high on my agenda since the early part of the 2010–15 parliament. At the start of the coalition, I had been shocked by the flood of proposals for new domestic regulation coming across my desk from all round Whitehall. Under Gordon Brown, the machine had got into the habit of responding to every newspaper story by inventing a new regulation. So Steve Hilton, Polly Mackenzie, Danny Alexander and I had put together a 'one in, one out' rule that forced departments to have the impact on business of any proposed new regulation independently verified by the economists in the Regulatory Policy Committee, and then forced them to come up with a matching deregulatory measure with the same (also independently verified) gain for business. This rule (which we later toughened to 'one in, two out') had a major effect. Within a few months, the influx of new regulation ceased and I could open my box in the evening or at weekends without coming across a pile of weird and senseless proposals to add to the regulatory burdens of our stifled economy and society.

But stemming the tide of additional regulation was clearly not enough. We were also facing incoming regulatory burdens from the EU, and we needed a large amount of positive domestic deregulation to counter-balance it. At first, I tried to interest the European Commission in organising a programme similar to ours, with independently verified impact costings and a 'one in, one out' (or 'one in, two out') rule. But, after a hilariously futile meeting with the secretary general of the Commission, I concluded that progress on this front was very unlikely to be speedy. In the event, Ed Davey's – and later Dan Korski's – efforts with 'like-minded' member states and an impressive array of businesspeople did gradually produce some recognition of the need for Brussels to contain its regulatory enthusiasms; but it was all painfully slow.

So I came to the conclusion – strongly backed by David and George, as well as by Nick Clegg, Danny Alexander, Vince Cable and David Laws – that we needed a big UK domestic deregulatory push from the centre of government, going well beyond the new rules. In conjunction with Michael Fallon and Matt Hancock, and with help from a crack team of officials brought together by Will Cavendish in the Cabinet Office as a well as a counterpart group in the Business Department, I duly pushed through a large programme of deregulation during the coalition years. Once the new, Conservative-only administration was formed, we further strengthened this process by creating a 'quad' of deregulation ministers consisting of Sajid Javid and Anna Soubry from the Business Department alongside Matt and myself at the Cabinet Office. New 'deregulation budgets' were agreed with each department round Whitehall, and we worked together from the centre to identify additional deregulatory measures that individual departments might have missed.

Throughout the six years in which I was seriously engaged in deregulating parts of our economy that had been over-burdened by often ludicrously misconceived and ineffective forms of regulation, I was struck by the extraordinary inertia in the system. We would talk to a group of businesspeople in a particular industry, discover some form of regulation that was achieving nothing whatsoever, and then spend a year or eighteen months patiently disentangling the law before we were ready to bring the appropriate deregulatory measures to Parliament. It was back-breaking work. But it was worth doing.

I was not, however, under the illusion that reducing the burden of regulation was a sufficient contribution from government to the future of manufacturing industry in Britain. Clearly, as well as reducing business taxation, improving infrastructure and training, and backing science (which were all core programmes of both the 2010 and the

2015 governments), we needed to match our deregulation with positive action to make the most of the sectors where Britain had real strengths. One of these was (and is) certainly the car industry; and I was hugely impressed with the way that Vince Cable had brought into existence the Automotive Strategy – which all the major motor manufacturers described to me in glowing terms. This led me, from 2012 onwards, to an increasing interest in the prospects for electric cars. It seemed to me that the possibility of converting both the UK car fleet and UK car production from the internal combustion engine to the electric engine offered a golden opportunity to combine an affordable way to reduce carbon emissions with a massively powerful industrial strategy.

I therefore began a systematic trawl through all of the manufacturers and also through the other industries that were most relevant – such as the producers of the batteries needed to power the cars, and the utilities who could create a proper, comprehensive system of charging points. Luckily, both George and David were huge supporters of this agenda – so I was sure I would be able to secure the necessary funding from the Treasury; and there was also support from Amber Rudd at Energy (who needed the electrification of the car fleet to make the carbon budgets add up), Liz Truss at Defra (who saw electrification as the only long-term solution to the serious problems of particulate emissions in our cities), Sajid Javid at Business (who could see the industrial logic), and Patrick McLoughlin at Transport (who recognised that the future of our road transport system was going to lie in autonomous electric vehicles). As a result of the consensus amongst the relevant ministers, as well as the work of a group of officials devoted to promoting ultra-low-emission vehicles and my own discussions with the serious experts across all of the relevant industries, we were beginning to make real progress when the referendum and the change of government intervened. I was delighted to see, in Philip Hammond's

2016 Autumn Statement, a significant slug of additional funding for the establishment of a recharging network and for research and development in electric and autonomous vehicles; I take this as a sign that the new government is carrying on where the Cameron administration left off.

But electric vehicles were not the only contribution I was trying to make to the advance of our environmental agenda beyond the energy industries. In our 2015 manifesto, as well as focusing on carbon emissions and electric vehicles, we had committed to the completion of the 'Blue Belt'. The idea – first brought to me by Zac Goldsmith, Nick Hurd and Richard Benyon – was to establish vast marine protected areas around our Overseas Territories, in which the glorious and ecologically crucial biodiversity of our oceans could be preserved and enhanced. Unsurprisingly, I found that David was massively enthusiastic about this project (and indeed helped me persuade George – when we were sitting together on a train back from one party conference – to come up with the money needed to enforce the protection of the seas in question). So I knew I had the backing I needed from the top to make this happen. I also had strong and energetic support from a group of green NGOs, including the formidably energetic Charles Clover. There followed a seemingly interminable series of meetings with officials from the Foreign Office (who at first appeared disbelieving but eventually became considerably more enthusiastic), discussions with Foreign Office ministers (who kindly cooperated with what they clearly regarded as one of Letwin's eccentricities) and some pretty difficult encounters with people representing some of our Overseas Territories.

In the end, it all proved to be worth the hassle. The UK is now in the course of establishing a truly serious set of marine protected areas. Together with the equally huge areas designated by President Obama in waters controlled by the US, this will make a major contribution to global marine ecology over the coming decades and centuries – demonstrating that, with sufficient persistence, the centre of government can bring about long-term changes that will make a difference for generations to come, even where they have almost no short-term political significance. If I had to pick one symbol of the progressive Conservative environmental agenda for which I had been pressing since 2005, it would be the Blue Belt.

As I left Downing Street for the last time in mid-July 2016, I had the satisfaction of knowing that – regardless of what the future might hold – I had made, in this respect at least, a positive contribution to the future of our planet.

CHAPTER 8

WHERE NEXT?

I t is 10 p.m., Thursday 8 June 2017. I am in our constituency home at the close of polls for the general election – eleven months, almost to the day, since my departure from Downing Street.

I turn on the television to see the results of the BBC's exit poll. Have we secured the comfortable working majority that Theresa May has been seeking from the electorate? Or more? Or less?

As Big Ben stops striking, the answer arrives. It is not a welcome arrival. In an election we didn't need to call, we have not only failed – it seems – to increase our majority; we have in fact lost it and will have to secure support from the Democratic Unionists to form a lasting government.

This cannot exactly be described as a surprise. It has been increasingly clear over the past few days that the vast Conservative lead relayed by all the polls just before the election has evaporated – that the shine has been taken off the Conservative vote, and that Jeremy Corbyn's Labour Party has been making significant advances. It has also been clear that the pollsters (who usually produce tightly grouped results, with a slight random walk around a definite mid-point) were on this occasion 'stratified', with some of them still showing big Conservative majorities on the basis that the young people who provide

Corbyn with much of his support were unlikely to turn up to the polls, while others were showing consistently narrow margins on the basis that these young voters would actually turn up on the day. Now, if the exit poll is to be believed, the latter group of pollsters have been proved right. And the effect is likely to be a hung parliament, for the second time in a decade. How can this have happened? What has gone wrong?

Elements of the analysis are obvious, and not of any real long-term interest. Our manifesto and the 'campaign' that went with it had been abysmally bad – successfully precision-bombing many of our own supporters and then losing, in a disorderly retreat, much of the credibility on which the rest of the strategy wholly depended. It was not the best way to run an election. Corbyn, meanwhile, has very cleverly used the fact that people at the start didn't give him a chance in hell – taking this as an opportunity to put forward (without attracting any serious scrutiny) a large range of attractive but clearly unaffordable goodies, which people have interpreted as totems of a generous disposition; and he has used the enthusiasm of campaigners in Momentum and elsewhere to bring over former Green and Liberal Democrat leftist voters in support of his anti-capitalist stance, thereby uniting them with core Labour voters. The result of these superficial but crucial election dynamics is that, even with a high Conservative share of the national vote, Labour has increased its share sufficiently to tip large numbers of seats on which we had relied into Corbyn's hands, often by frustratingly small margins of a few dozen or a few hundred votes.

But these are easily curable problems. A proper and emotionally effective (rather than merely polemical) dissection of 'Corbynomics', allied to a proper Conservative campaign with a few well-judged goodies on offer, can in a future election quickly make the required (small) difference in dozens of marginal seats. Indeed, serious Labour politicians, as they come to consider what must at present seem to them a deliverance from the gallows, will conclude that the electoral challenge faced by their party is a severe one – on the assumption that the Conservative Party will not be likely to run an election as badly as this one for a very long time to come.

The problem is that, underneath this, there is something much more fundamental (and hence much more long-lasting) going on. During the past fifty years of Conservative politics in our island state, of which I have given a consciously partial view in this book, we have, without warfare, though with much controversy and at the cost of much disruption in settled ways of life, reasserted free market liberalism as the dominant political force in Britain. The Conservative Party itself, having been the principal agent for that change in the 1980s and 1990s, sadly lost sight for a while of the principles of social justice and of good stewardship of our planet which are required to make the free market an acceptable social market. We paid the electoral price for that in 1997, once Tony Blair had turned Labour into another form of social market liberal party. And it took the thirteen years in opposition for us to regain a clear view of the kind of party we needed to be. Just in time, after catastrophic mismanagement of the nation's finances by Gordon Brown, we were able (at first in coalition with Orange Book Liberals and then on our own under two succeeding Prime Ministers) to give the country governments which, with more fiscal rectitude and more efficiency, have carried on the social market liberal policies that answer to the needs of our nation.

But this happy continuity of rational social market liberalism in Britain is now under threat from many quarters. Around the developed economies of the West, we see various forces of unreason gathered or gathering. A phenomenon sometimes described as 'populism' – in truth, better described as illiberal demagoguery – threatens from the right. Varieties of state socialism tinged with expansive theories of human rights threaten from the left. On the one side, we have Geert Wilders and his PVV in the Netherlands, UKIP (albeit now much reduced) in Britain, AfD in Germany, M5S as well as the Lega Nord in Italy, Marine Le Pen's Front National in France and Donald Trump in the US; on the other, we have Syriza in Greece, Corbyn's Labour in the UK, Podemos in Spain, Die Linke in Germany, and Bernie Sanders in the US. We are warned that the post-war order is fracturing; that the Western institutions that guaranteed liberalism, free trade and global capitalism (EU, WTO, NAFTA, NATO) are now discredited – and that, with them, ecology and global citizenship have been knocked off their pedestals, to be replaced by more muscular rightist and leftist concerns with nationality, community, 'positive rights' and the will of the people democratically expressed.

For those who buy into this thesis of massive fracture, there is a strong temptation to regard Theresa May's premiership in the UK as itself an example of the radicalism of the age, a rupture with the past decade of liberal Conservative politics: a new form of muscular, nationalist communitarianism that has rejected 'laissez-faire liberalism' and European free trade, seeking instead through the power of the state to tame capitalism and to ride roughshod over markets. According to this thesis, the unnecessary and ill-judged snap 2017 general election in Britain is a classic example of the global trend towards polarity of right and left – with the Conservatives reuniting the right and Corbyn reuniting the left, both on the basis of rejecting the social market liberalism espoused in different forms by Blair and Cameron.

This analysis – both in its general form as a description of what is happening in the developed Western economies, and in its specific form as a description of what is happening in domestic UK politics – is highly attractive to journalists and academics, for whom it provides that most dangerous of commodities: an interesting narrative. But it is

in fact a morass of ideological, chronological and psephological con-
fusions based on a failure to understand both what has happened and
what is happening.

To cut through the confusion, we have to disentangle discontents.
First and foremost, there are the long-dated effects of the 2008 crash.
In many ways, what is surprising is that there has been so little reaction
given the severity of what happened. In 2007/08, a cyclical downturn,
combined with massive public and private sector over-borrowing,
brought the West's financial system to its knees, producing not only the
worst recession since 1929 but also a sustained constraint on the ability
of banks to make available the credit required for recovery. A decade
later, we may not yet have seen the end of the ricochet effects on some
of the European banks – and we certainly have yet to see the real wages
of many people who were previously at or near to median income reach
the level they were at before the crash. For those who were only 'just
about managing' in 2008, the decade of reduced real income has been
extremely tough, leaving them and their children with little beyond the
bare essentials. Even in Britain, where the flexible labour market has
kept employment high and unemployment low throughout the period,
and where tax credits have made up a significant part of the income
lost by the hardest-pressed working families, there was bound to be
some political reaction. It is no surprise that, in Western economies
(or parts of Western economies) with far less well-functioning labour
markets than those in the UK – in some of which unemployment rates,
particularly for less highly qualified 18–24-year-olds, have reached as-
tronomic levels – demagogues with apparent 'quick fixes' of any kind
have become attractive to many voters.

Second, and following directly from the first, there are the fiscal effects of 2008 – causing governments throughout the West to address
significant (in Britain's case, huge) deficits through long and difficult

periods of fiscal consolidation. This has provoked some elements of taxpayer revolt. But, more powerfully, the effort to reduce real growth in public expenditure has – after ten years – produced strains in the key public services and constraints on the earnings of millions of public sector workers, which are now beyond endurance. This presents fiscally responsible governments with the need to find means of reducing the deficit further while increasing spending significantly in some key areas: inevitably, this will necessitate tax increases – politically challenging, even if cleverly targeted.

Third, there is the education and training deficit. As new information, communication and manufacturing technologies have come to dominate large parts of our lives, the productivity gains brought about by these technologies over four decades in well-managed economies such as the US, the UK and Germany have (as always before) gone hand in hand with growing workforces, in contrast to the dire prophecies made by those who predicted mass unemployment. But the gap has widened between the value of labour for those who have the skills either to manipulate the new technologies themselves or to deliver the services that they support, and that for those who do not possess any of these now-valued skills. And this secular trend has been overlaid on the cyclical effects of 2007–08. Despite the crash and its after-effects, real incomes have been rising for many people who are endowed with the right levels of education and training at just the time when real incomes for those without such skills have been falling or have failed to recover. Inevitably, the pictures of the bright young people celebrating the fruits of their highly paid and highly skilled labour in the glitzy metropolitan restaurants and wine bars have stirred a political reaction amongst those who have missed out on the skills and the pay.

Fourth, there is the demographic shift. As the population in Western countries has aged, so-called dependency ratios have increased.

More elderly people have come to depend for longer on the pensions and savings that they managed to accumulate during their working lives. In Britain at least, the poorest pensioners have been very highly protected – and have seen their real incomes rise annually in a period when incomes for many working households have been flat or declining. But this has not been true, for example, in Greece. And even in the UK, for those slightly better-off (but still by no means well-off) pensioners living on small savings or annuities, the prolonged period of vanishingly low interest rates following the crash, combined with the effects of increasing longevity on annuity rates, has produced massive impacts on real incomes, which had not been expected before 2008 and for which the pensioners in question had as a result not prepared themselves. Again, it is no surprise – given these facts – that some of the most hostile political reaction (support for insurgent parties, in particular) has come from the older section of the population. (It was, of course, some of these people who were so effectively precision-bombed by the Conservative 2017 manifesto through removal of the 'third lock' on basic state pension rises and an ostensibly rational, but wildly mistimed and ill-presented, effort to recoup the rising costs of social care from the inheritance that the elderly would otherwise hand on to their children.)

Fifth, there is globalisation, free trade and migration. At a time when incomes for the low skilled have been held down by the effects of the crash, they have been put under further pressure by the availability of even cheaper labour in emerging markets. Whether through the transfer of service sector jobs to offshore locations, or through the import of cheap, high-quality goods in an active global trading system, or through the migration of energetic workers willing to accept low wages for hard work, the WTO, NAFTA and the EU have enhanced the returns on highly skilled labour and innovative investment – and have thereby significantly raised economic growth rates across the West – but at the expense of domestic, relatively low-skilled workers. This has played into the latent xenophobia of those who seek protection from the competition of 'those bloody foreigners who are taking our jobs'. Against the background of the effects of the crash and of the widening gap between the returns on skilled and unskilled labour, it is hardly surprising that the Brexit campaign in the UK, and Trump in the US, should have been successful in turning such latent feelings into kinetic effects at the ballot box. This has been made easier in the UK because the combination of about 250,000 net immigrants per year with about the same natural increase of the indigenous population has led to a relatively rapid rate of overall population increase, with effects in many parts of the country both on the availability of housing at prices that people can afford and on infrastructure and public services. Despite the containment of the far right through most of Western Europe in recent elections, Marine Le Pen in France, Beppe Grillo in Italy, Jörg Meuthen in Germany and Geert Wilders in the Netherlands may in the next few years succeed in mobilising majorities against migration.

Sixth, there is the democratic deficit. Most of the phenomena that have afflicted those who were 'just about managing' up until the crash can, to one extent or another, be laid at the door of international entities that are described as being 'beyond our control' – the EU, which mandates free movement of workers; the WTO, EU and NAFTA, which mandate trading rules; the European Court of Human Rights, which protects the rights of migrants and asylum-seekers to safe havens and family life but not the rights of indigenous workers to higher-paid jobs; the European Central Bank, which governs the economies of the Eurozone even when, as in the case of Greece, this involves squeezing them until the pips squeak. And the demographic shift makes these non-democratic international organisations particularly electorally toxic because, to many amongst the older part of the population, they represent not a settled arrangement with which they have grown up but a constitutional outrage which they are disinclined to tolerate.

Together, these six phenomena more than adequately explain – indeed, as Louis Althusser would have said, they 'over-explain' – the rise of the demagogues of left and right across much of the Western world. However, once they are set out calmly, it also becomes evident that they are historically contingent. True, the education and training deficit is an enormously serious issue; the demographic shift creates long-term fiscal, distributional and inter-generational challenges; global trade and a globalised economy will always tend to cause problematic dislocations; and institutions (treaty organisations, courts and central banks) that are placed outside direct democratic control inevitably create tensions between the liberalism and the democracy of liberal democracies. But, like xenophobia (which is always latent), these problems and challenges and tensions were present long before 2008. And yet, they didn't generate anything like the massive wave of resentment that we are at present witnessing until the latent feelings were given real force by the long-lasting effects of the 2008 crash on lower-skilled workers and the less well-off elderly. Once that resentment was generated by the economic circumstances, it could be mobilised on a scale that had not been feasible before 2008 – bringing the underlying issues of skills, demography, industrial dislocation, xenophobia and institutional constraints on democracy into sharp relief.

This suggests, in turn, that the power of the illiberal politics of right and left that we have seen unleashed in various forms across the West is itself historically contingent – a temporary reaction to a set of economic events. There is every reason to suppose that, if and when a prolonged period of economic growth again allows real incomes across the board to rise for a long period, the demagogues will find it as difficult then as they did before 2008 to turn the ever-latent illiberal and xenophobic sentiments into a major (or at least a winning) democratic power. There is consequently no reason to believe that there has been a fundamental shift in the ideology of the West or that the post-war international order has suddenly been brought crashing down. The political reaction provoked by the events of 2008 can and very likely will dissipate once the economic effects are overcome – at least if those of us attached to social market liberal democracy hold our nerve.

But, to sustain democratic support for social market liberal policies, we need to make the case for them all over again. Nowhere is this truer than in Britain. Beneath the superficial catastrophes of the Conservative 2017 election campaign, the deep defect was the complete absence of any serious argument in favour of the social market. There was no attempt to illustrate why free markets, inward investment and the entry of skilled labour can generate (and have generated) sustained economic growth, underpinning jobs and prosperity. There was no effort to explain how, through sharing the proceeds of such growth, we can – and can alone – sustain the fine public services and the properly structured welfare system through which a social market economy delivers social justice. And, as a result of lacking these powerful positive arguments for the liberal social market, we were deprived also of the only powerful critique of Corbynomics – namely, that it fosters a cruel illusion of handouts for all while employing, in the pursuit of an egalitarian fantasy, state controls, nationalisation, deficit financing and investment-destroying levels of taxation which will inevitably undermine the ability of the free market to produce the growth and the Exchequer revenues on which the public services and welfare system of a social market in fact depend.

But the absence of a powerful argument for social market liberalism in May 2017 didn't just deprive us both of a powerful defence of

Conservative government and of a powerful critique of Corbynomics. It deprived us also of the one coherent rhetoric that could have given us any hope of maintaining the unity of the right that was the bulwark of the high Conservative vote share while, at the same time, attracting into the Conservative corner (even if not exactly the Conservative fold) a sufficient number of the younger, professional, metropolitan voters who will otherwise continue to deliver victories to Labour in high-tech cities such as London, Bristol and Cambridge. These are socially liberal and cosmopolitan voters – who can be persuaded by the arguments for the social market; but only if we make those arguments anew.

So much for analysis. What about the future? What should liberal Conservatives do next?

The answer is that we should promote policies that will actually address the underlying issues. The temptation, of course, is to seek some sudden cure-all, some 'new way' of solving the challenges facing us. But this is neither necessary nor possible. Yes, we have had a decade in which living standards for most of our population have first fallen and then been only slowly restored – with particularly painful consequences for those at or below median income, whose circumstances were in any case much more constrained than for those with larger incomes. Yes, we have seen and are still seeing electorates around the developed world responding to these prolonged effects of the financial crash by rejecting the movement of people, and by favouring anti-establishment candidates and causes. But we shouldn't either exaggerate the scale of what has happened or suppose that there is any 'quick fix'.

We continue to live in a prosperous and stable society, enjoying both liberties and a quality of life that few in the history of the world have been able to enjoy. As we struggle to deal with what are, in essence, the long-dated effects of 2008, we need to keep our eyes firmly on what will work rather than on what might sound fashionably populist. This means that we need to deliver a Brexit that includes a comprehensive free trade deal with the EU as well as frictionless customs transactions, and thereby preserves our strong industrial and commercial interests, while liberating us from the jurisdiction of the European Court of Justice. It also means that we need to maintain policies on tax, public spending, public borrowing, deregulation, infrastructure, technology transfer and inward investment that will increase domestic productivity and stimulate domestic growth. But, beyond these economic considerations, it means that we need policies on tax thresholds, public services, welfare, redistribution, social policy, international aid, environmental stewardship and corporate social responsibility that will make the free market a sufficiently social market and the basis of a sufficiently liberal state, to be justified in the eyes not only of those in the middle of their lives who are prospering but also those who are looking for security in retirement, those who are young, aspirational and liberally inclined, and those who are concerned about the fate of the least advantaged and of the planet.

None of this will be easy or straightforward. Providing good, sane government isn't ever easy or straightforward. But the fact that doing the right thing isn't easy shouldn't be taken as a reason either for pessimism or for making concessions of a kind that would lead us to do the wrong thing. As we pass through uncertain times and changing circumstances, the values of social market liberalism are permanent – because they are the truth about what works best for our people, our civilisation and our planet. There is no reason for them to be abandoned. Now, more than ever, we need to govern by them.

But, beyond governing by these values, we need to proselytise for them. We need to abandon the illusion that the reasoning behind social market liberalism is well understood, particularly amongst the young. Instead of cowering as the Corbynistas deliver their broadsides and organise their insurrections against the institutions of a liberal democracy, we have to get out there and make the arguments all over again. We need to explain why the state is far more likely to be able to protect liberal social values and the quality of public services if our economy prospers; why the poorest in our society are more likely to see progressive, sustained improvements in living standards if income is redistributed in ways that do not dampen enterprise and hard work; why free trade and the migration of skilled labour can benefit us all, rather than posing a threat to jobs and prosperity, so long as they are accompanied by world-class training for a workforce of the future; why, in an open, liberal society, a proportionately shrinking working population can generate sufficient innovation and productivity to provide a proportionately growing elderly population with security in retirement; why all of these things are compatible with – are indeed ultimately the only sustainable basis for – the protection of our ecology, the flourishing of our culture and the enhancement of the beauty of our surroundings. These are the arguments that, because they are true, will ultimately carry conviction; and they are the arguments that will position the Conservative Party as the party of the future, of aspiration and of hope, capable of attracting not just the old and the middle aged but also the young; not only the rich and the comfortable, but also the struggling and those who are barely managing; people from every background and of every type.

We have learned much from our successes and our failures over the last half-century. But, above all, we have learned that the Conservative Party will move forward when it leads the nation towards the optimism of the liberal social market, rather than indulging in the pessimism of chauvinism and reaction. The task now is to recapture that optimism, and to help the nation recapture it. That way lies victory, prosperity and social justice.

INDEX